Digital Rights Management

Chandos
Information Professional Series

Series Editor: Ruth Rikowski
(email: Rikowskigr@aol.com)

Chandos' new series of books are aimed at the busy information professional. They have been specially commissioned to provide the reader with an authoritative view of current thinking. They are designed to provide easy-to-read and (most importantly) practical coverage of topics that are of interest to librarians and other information professionals. If you would like a full listing of current and forthcoming titles, please visit our web site **www.chandospublishing.com** or contact Hannah Grace-Williams on email info@chandospublishing.com or telephone number +44 (0) 1993 848726.

New authors: we are always pleased to receive ideas for new titles; if you would like to write a book for Chandos, please contact Dr Glyn Jones on email gjones@chandospublishing.com or telephone number +44 (0) 1993 848726.

Bulk orders: some organisations buy a number of copies of our books. If you are interested in doing this, we would be pleased to discuss a discount. Please contact Hannah Grace-Williams on email info@chandospublishing.com or telephone number +44 (0) 1993 848726.

Digital Rights Management

A Librarian's Guide to Technology and Practise

GRACE AGNEW

Chandos Publishing
Oxford · England

Chandos Publishing (Oxford) Limited
TBAC Business Centre
Avenue 4
Station Lane
Witney
Oxford OX28 4BN
UK
Tel: +44 (0) 1993 848726 Fax: +44 (0) 1865 884448
Email: info@chandospublishing.com
www.chandospublishing.com

First published in Great Britain in 2008

ISBN:
978 1 84334 125 3 (paperback)
978 1 84334 182 6 (hardback)
1 84334 125 5 (paperback)
1 84334 182 4 (hardback)

British Library Cataloguing-in-Publication Data.
A catalogue record for this book is available from the British Library.

Typeset by Domex e-Data Pvt. Ltd.
Printed in the UK and USA.

Printed in the UK by 4edge Limited - www.4edge.co.uk

Contents

List of figures

About the author

Grace Bousfield Agnew is Associate University Librarian for Digital Library Systems at the Rutgers University Libraries, New Brunswick, New Jersey. She is a lead designer and co-P.I. for NJVid, the digital video portal for the state of New Jersey, funded by the Institute of Museum and Library Services, and the architect of Moving Image Collections (MIC), an international portal to moving image collections co-sponsored by the Library of Congress and the Association of Moving Image Archivists and funded by the National Science Foundation. She lectures, consults and publishes in digital rights management, metadata, digital repositories and digital video. She is the co-author, with Jean Hudgins, of the book *Getting Mileage out of Metadata: Practical Applications for the Library* (ALA, 1999).

The author may be contacted at:
gagnew@rci.rutgers.edu

Acknowledgments

The author gratefully acknowledges her colleagues who contributed their expertise in law, library standards, authentication and authorisation strategies, and digital rights management technologies in the review and revision of this book. Much that is valuable in this work is a credit to their efforts. All errors are the sole responsibility of the author.

Karen Coyle, Digital Library Consultant

Jeremy Frumkin, Head, Emerging Technologies and Services, Oregon State University Libraries

Michael J. Giarlo, Information Technology Specialist, Library of Congress

Chris Hodge, University of Tennessee

Ronald C. Jantz, Digital Library Architect, Rutgers University Libraries

Andrea Leigh, Metadata Librarian, UCLA Film & Television Archive

Lisa A. Macklin, Coordinator, Intellectual Property Rights of the Emory University Libraries

Mary Minow, LibraryLaw.com

Glenn Patton, Director, WorldCat Quality Management, OCLC

Renee Shuey, Senior Systems Engineer, The Pennsylvania State University

Dr Sherry Vellucci, Professor and Dean of the University Library, University of New Hampshire

Mary Beth Weber, Head of Technical Services, Rutgers University Libraries

Figure 1.1, DRM model, designed by Chad M. Mills, Rutgers University Libraries

1

Introduction

Digital rights management (DRM) is a commonly used term in a number of professional arenas: libraries and archives, publishing, media creation and production, and information technology, to name just a few. DRM is one of those ubiquitous terms that is often used imprecisely. Some define it as a framework of systems and services intended to manage the access and use of rights-protected *digital* resources. With this definition, DRM could include physically checking a user's identification before supplying a DVD containing a digital resource for the user or providing a password to use a library computer workstation. Others define DRM as *digital* systems and services to manage the access and use of rights-protected resources. Under this latter definition, a digital swipe card authentication and authorisation system to enable physical access to a closed library would be a DRM technology. This book will use, as a practical definition, the *digital* management of rights pertaining to the access and use of *digital* materials. There is some discussion of analog resources, particularly where DRM technologies are designed to manage any type or resource or to close the 'analog hole' where digital resources are visible or audible and can thus be captured, but the focus of this book is the interaction of resource rights owners and resource users in the digital space.

DRM is often discussed in the context of each stage in the life cycle of an information resource: creation, packaging, distribution, trading and use. This approach does not give due respect to the other critical entities in a rights model: the owner/creator and the user. This book is primarily organized around a core DRM model. In this model, the **resource**, the **rights owner** and the **user** are all entities of equal importance, and all three entities engage with the usage **rights** in a **use event** – the managed, appropriate use of a rights-protected resource within a DRM framework.

At heart, effective DRM involves establishing a framework of policy and practice that supports the rights of the creator/rights owner, the user and the resource. Libraries can address each entity in turn to develop a comprehensive yet manageable digital rights strategy. In addition, it is hoped that readers will come away with a strong understanding of the current DRM landscape, the technologies employed, and the issues and concerns that remain to be addressed.

This book discusses each of the model components in turn, and examines current issues, strategies and technologies for

Figure 1.1 DRM model

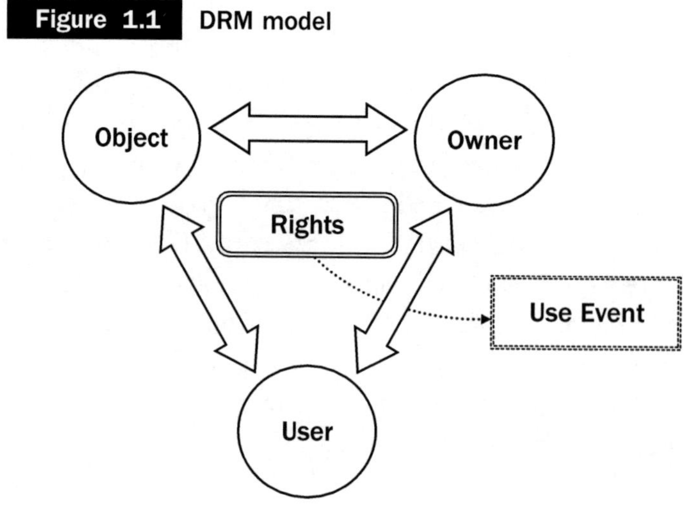

each component that can be utilized within a library environment to support the use of rights-protected resources in ways that are legal, principled and consistent.

Rights provide the legal and moral context for providing managed access to copyright-protected resources in ways that protect the creator's exploitation of his/her work and the privacy of the resource user. Chapter 2 examines the international copyright framework for protecting works of original creation, as well as the copyright environments for selected English-speaking countries. The focus on English-speaking countries represents my linguistic limitations rather than any belief that copyright laws are less complex or less important in other countries. It is hoped that the brief review of copyright laws across selected English-speaking countries will highlight the different ways that countries interpret international treaty within national legislation. Chapter 3 provides an overview of other important rights, such as related rights, moral rights and privacy, as well as strategies for supporting these rights, as part of a library's DRM strategy.

A critical issue for effective DRM, particularly in a digital environment where resources can be readily duplicated and altered, is to identify and support the authentic **resource.** Chapter 4 examines the issue of resource identification and authenticity in the digital world and identifies strategies libraries can employ to manage resources for authenticity and attribution in the digital space.

Perhaps the greatest barrier to the use of rights-protected resources is the inability to identify and locate rights **owners.** Chapter 5 examines issues and strategies for identifying creators/rights owners to support attribution, and to enable future communications between rights owners and potential users. The core of a DRM implementation is enabling **users** to make appropriate use of rights-protected resources. Chapter 5 also examines authentication (*who you are*) and authorization (*what you are permitted to do*) standards, strategies, and technologies. Authentication and authorization – when implemented well – safeguard the rights of the user while ensuring authorised access to a resource and thus are the core of any DRM framework.

Chapter 6 examines a key enabling technology for DRM, namely rights metadata, providing both documentation of the rights status of the resource and expression of rights policies, agreements and transactions. Effective expression of rights status and policy is critical for enabling legal and effective access to resources in the digital environment.

Chapter 7 explores the DRM technologies that are increasingly becoming a ubiquitous prerequisite for access to digital resources in many settings, but particularly as employed by commercial content owners and publishers. In the increasingly protected digital information space, libraries may be supplying digital content that is controlled by DRM technologies that the library may not manage. It is critical for libraries to be aware of commercial DRM applications and to understand the technologies and their implications for the digital information commons.

Libraries are often administrative divisions within a larger entity such as a university or local government. Libraries are also complex organisations that frequently utilise many different information management systems to organise and preserve resources. Chapter 8, *Putting the Pieces Together*, discusses the major issues for DRM within the larger information context and establishes an agenda and roadmap for library activism in the DRM space.

This book invites you to explore one of the most interesting and challenging areas emerging in librarianship today: DRM. If this book does its job correctly, you should not only understand the basic principles and practices of DRM, but you should also be able to develop a digital rights policy and practice framework for your organisation. DRM is very much an attempt to 'nail water to the wall' – to take the complex, imprecise and context-dependent world of legal rights and distill it into practical and concrete practice. Can this be done? After finishing the book, readers will, I hope, be able to answer this question to their satisfaction. ... And every answer will probably be different.

Copyright

This and the following chapter examine the predominant legal rights that are associated with the resource, the copyright owner and the resource user. An effective DRM strategy will clearly identify and safeguard any rights that the organisation has decided to manage, including, of course, those rights that are mandated by law.

Rights may appear at first glance to be straightforward. They are often expressly documented in laws and treaties. However, in some cases, rights were expressed so concretely with respect to the tangible form of a protected work that older laws cannot cover newer modes of expression, publication or transmission, thus requiring new or amended laws and treaties. Many countries also recognise exceptions to legally mandated rights in order to support the public good. As stewards of public culture, libraries particularly want to develop DRM strategies that safeguard rights exceptions to support the public's access to information.

Supporting rights to use resources requires considerable groundwork on the part of the library. The library must first ensure that it thoroughly understands the rights that pertain to the resources, the rights owners and the users that the library supports. In the web-based environment, digital resources that the library makes available may have an international audience. It is important to understand intellectual property rights in both the national and the international context in order to ensure appropriate use of digital resources.

The library's context for providing access to rights-protected resources is critical for identifying the rights to be supported and safeguarded through a DRM strategy. Is the library developing an institutional repository that is able to closely associate the creators with their creative works? Does the library want to digitally reproduce and make available published or unpublished works, where the creators are not readily identifiable or available to authorise permissions for use of the works?

The subject matter of the digital resources that the library makes available can also be important. There may be legal or ethical rights involved with exposing information about living individuals or sharing culturally sensitive materials, such as digital reproductions of aboriginal artifacts. In addition, the library should be clear about permitted use of resources, any restrictions to those permitted uses that the library must enforce and what actions, if any, the library will take if its policies on permitted use are violated. Finally, the library must address the rights to privacy of identity and confidentiality of resource use that it will afford the users of its digital resources.

Understanding and documenting the rights to be safeguarded and managed through DRM is a critical and necessary first step for any DRM implementation. The library should develop and publish the policies that underlie its DRM strategy. A good DRM implementation will effectively realise the library's published policies. There should be no surprises for rights holders or for resource users. In addition to published policies concerning copyright and appropriate use, adherence to a published statement of ethics concerning the right of users to have their identity and their information use safeguarded is critical to establish and maintain the trust of the copyright owner and the resource user – two key players in the core DRM model.

I will begin with an overview of copyright – perhaps the principal right that a DRM implementation is designed to safeguard.

The rights of creators to control the disposition and use of their creative works are recognised by international treaty, as well as within the laws of many countries. These rights are known collectively as 'copyright'. Copyright grants the author or creator many exclusive rights with regard to further use of a copyright-protected work. Copyright is an intellectual property right that may be transferred or inherited, similar to the rights of ownership for tangible, physical property, which may also be transferred. However, copyright differs from standard property rights in one crucial aspect. The term of copyright ownership is limited by law – within the national law of countries with copyright protection and by international treaty.

The term of copyright is limited in recognition of the inherent social value of creative expression to promote discovery, culture and learning. It is understood that creators will feel encouraged to create and make available works of literary, artistic and creative expression that are valuable for others if they are able to exploit these works economically. However, it is also understood that new knowledge and new creative expressions are often built upon previously created works. These tangible works of expression – which include written works, musical works, graphic and artistic works, films, audio recordings, choreographed and performed works – collectively form the culture of countries, regions and the world. Access to the artifacts of their culture is critical to promote an educated and progressive citizenry. The term of copyright is crafted in each country to balance the economic, legal and moral benefits that obtain to the author of a creative work against the needs of the citizenry for broad and equitable access to culture and information.

Copyright, which protects the right of the creator to control the reproduction, distribution, public display or public performance of the creator's copyright-protected work, is the primary impetus for the development of DRM strategies. Copyright is legally enforceable, with remedies for legal redress prescribed in law and treaty. It would be nice to say that DRM technologies have evolved organically to support appropriate use of protected resources, in order to protect against unwitting infringement by users. In reality, DRM technologies emerged for many reasons, including an intent on the part of copyright owners to pre-empt infringing uses by managing all use of digital resources, whether infringing or not.

A thorough understanding of copyright, in both the international and the national arena, and a published copyright policy that applies to the library and any larger organisation that the library serves, are important tools for designing a DRM strategy that supports legal and appropriate use of copyright-protected resources. Otherwise, the library may find itself supporting DRM strategies that limit all uses of a resource, whether or not the uses are infringing, simply due to the inherent purpose and design of many DRM technologies.

The following section looks at the copyright legal landscape. Copyright is an international right, with core principles documented and enforced by treaty for all member states. Member states then enact state-specific laws to implement, and in some cases go beyond, their treaty obligations.

International copyright

This section looks at the key treaties that form the legal framework of international copyright.

Berne Convention (Paris, 1971)

The primary international copyright treaty, serving as the basis for most subsequent treaties, is the *Berne Convention for the Protection of Literary and Artistic Works.*[1] It was first adopted at Berne, Switzerland, in 1886 and has been revised several times. The Paris 1971 revision, which was further amended in September 1979, serves as the foundation for international copyright treaty law today. This treaty is designed to 'protect, in as effective and uniform a manner as possible, the rights of authors in their literary and artistic works' (Preamble). The *Berne Convention* provides minimum enforceable standards that are intended to provide harmony across the laws and standards of its signatory countries. The most significant minimum standard is the term of protection granted to a work: life of the author plus 50 years. Terms of protection vary under the *Berne Convention* depending on the nature of the work (e.g. photographic works and works of applied art are protected for a period of 'twenty-five years from the making of such a work' (art. 7).

The *Berne Convention* protects published and unpublished works. Authors are not required to register a work with a copyright registration authority or to affix a standardized copyright statement to a work to enjoy protection for that work. One of the key provisions of the *Berne Convention* states, with regard to the author of a protected work, 'it shall be sufficient for his name to appear on the work, in the usual manner' (art. 15) or, in the case of anonymous and pseudonymous works, 'the publisher whose name appears on the work shall, in the absence of proof to the contrary, be deemed to represent the author, and in this capacity he shall be entitled to protect and enforce the author's rights.' (art. 15).

Prior to signing the *Berne Convention* some countries, notably the United States, placed the burden of proof for copyright protection on the author, with requirements for registration and standardised copyright notification on the published work. The *Berne Convention* played an important role in pushing the burden of proof for authorship to those contesting authorship or contesting the copyright-protected status of a work. The author or publisher is merely required to assert authorship at time of first issuance for a work, whether in published or in unpublished form. No formal certification, through registration or symbol, is required to assert authorship and enjoy the copyright protections afforded by this authorship.

Exclusive rights granted to authors under the *Berne Convention* are the making and authorising of translations, adaptations, arrangements and other alterations (art. 8, 12) and reproductions of works in 'any manner or form' (art. 9). Authors also enjoy exclusive rights to authorise any public performance or public communication of dramatic, dramatico-musical and musical works. Authors of literary and artistic works enjoy exclusive rights to authorise broadcasts, public recitation and other public communication of literary and artistic works, as well as cinematographic adaptations of such works (art. 11*bis*, 11*ter*, 14).

An important provision of the *Berne Convention* is the assignment of governance for copyright protection to the country of origin rather than to an international governing body. Authors are given the protections of the country of origin, in addition to the minimum protections specified in the *Berne Convention*, regardless of whether or not the author is a national in the country of origin for the work. 'Country of origin' is an important concept in the *Berne Convention* and is defined primarily as the country of first publication, provided that country is a party to the *Berne Convention* and thus a member of the Union, formed by all the signatory states 'for the protection of the rights of authors in their literary and artistic works.' (art. 1). If a work is published simultaneously in several countries that are parties to the convention, the country of origin is deemed to be the country granting the shortest term of protection. For unpublished works, or works first published in a country that is not a member of the Union, the country of origin is deemed to be the country of which the author is a citizen, provided that country is a member of the Union (art. 5).

Other important provisions of the *Berne Convention* include moral rights, as specified in Article 6*bis*: 'the author shall have the right to claim authorship of the work and to object to any distortion, mutilation or other modification of, or other derogatory action in relation to, the said work, which would be prejudicial to his honor or reputation.' This right is maintained after the author's death at least until the expiry of economic rights, except in those countries that do not provide for the protection of all rights after the death of the author (art. 6*bis*). Not every member state fully implements Article 6*bis*. In the United States, moral rights pertain only to creators of works of visual art, for example (17 U.S.C. § 106A).[2]

Berne also recognises and acknowledges standards and requirements that are not required by the Convention but may apply within the laws of signatory countries, such as the requirement that a work must be fixed in a tangible medium of expression to be protected by copyright. Another provision that is left to national determination is whether or not copyright law protects official texts and political speeches (art. 2, 2*bis*). The *Berne Convention* acknowledges the right of member nations to decide on standards for protection beyond the provisions of the *Berne Convention* (art. 19). These country-specific standards are acknowledged within the *Berne Convention* as enforceable protections afforded within the laws of the country of origin.

The *Berne Convention* is currently administered by WIPO, the World Intellectual Property Organization. The United States was slow to ratify the *Berne Convention*, finally entering into compliance through the *Berne Convention Implementation Act of 1988*. The United States was particularly concerned with the provision that registration was not required for copyright to take effect and also with the moral rights requirements of the *Berne Convention* Article *6bis*. As of 1 March 1989, the United States no longer required registration for copyright and determined that sufficient legal support in US copyright and other statues already existed to support the moral rights requirement.[3]

Universal Copyright Convention (Geneva, 1952 and Paris, 1971)

The Universal Copyright Convention (UCC), developed by the United Nations Educational, Scientific and Cultural Organization (UNESCO), differs from other treaties, such as the *Berne Convention*, by supporting the rights of member states to require registration and copyright notice and by establishing the use of the copyright symbol as the universal symbol that a published work is copyright protected (Universal Copyright Convention, art. III (1)).[4] Each member state is also required to extend copyright protection to unpublished works of nationals of other member states [art. III (4)].

The UCC addressed the need to harmonise copyright for countries that were not prepared to support the provisions of the *Berne Convention*, particularly the fact that copyright registration and notice were not required. The US, in particular, required registration and notice such that compliance with Berne would require significant legislation as well as major changes to policy and practice. The then USSR objected to the provisions of Berne as having a Western bias. The UCC established 'national treatment', for copyright-protected works, which required member states to provide the same protections to authors from other member states that they accorded their own authors. Over time, the *Berne Convention* has supplanted the UCC as the treaty underpinning most national copyright law and practice.

WIPO Copyright Treaty (Geneva, 1996)

Article 20 of the *Berne Convention* provides for the ability of governments of signing countries to enter into subsequent agreements, 'in so far as such agreements grant to authors more extensive rights than those granted by the Convention, or contain other provisions not contrary to this Convention' (*Berne Convention*, art. 20). The *WIPO Copyright Treaty* (WCT),[5] administered by WIPO and signed in Geneva on 20 December 1996, added a number of important additions to the copyright laws enforced within the *Berne Convention.*

Perhaps one of the most important provisions of the WCT was the reinstatement of the 'Berne three-step test'. The *Berne Convention* recognises the ability of member countries to allow exceptions to copyright. However, the *Berne Convention* of 1967 imposed a three-step test that member countries must apply to exceptions to the exclusive right of reproduction that is given to the author of a creative work. This three-step test disappeared from the text of the *Berne Convention* of 1971. The WCT reinstated the Berne three-step test in *Article 10, Limits and Exceptions*, which limits contracting parties from creating national legislation that provides exceptions to copyright protections, according to the following circumstantial test: 'certain special cases that do not conflict with a normal exploitation of the work and do not unreasonably prejudice the legitimate interests of the author.' Exceptions to copyright (1) must therefore be for *special cases* rather than the normal use of resources, (2) must not conflict with '*normal exploitation of the work*' and (3) must not '*unreasonably prejudice the legitimate interests of the author*' (WCT, art. 10). While the Berne three-step test does acknowledge that exceptions to copyright are legitimate, it also asserts the primacy of the author's right to exploit the value of his/her creative work over the benefits to society resulting from broader access to the work.

Other key provisions of the WCT include protection for computer programs as literary works (art. 4); acknowledgment of copyright status for 'compilations of data or other material', based on the creativity involved in selection or arrangement within the compilation (art. 5); and additional exclusive rights, beyond the *Berne Convention*, for authors, including the right for authors of computer programs, cinematographic works or 'works embodied in phonograms' to authorise 'commercial rental to the public of the originals or copies of their works' (art. 7). The WCT also explicitly eliminated the 25-year protection period for photographic works specified in Article 7(4) of the *Berne Convention*, thus bringing the term of protection for photographic works in line with other artistic, literary and creative works (art. 9).

Perhaps the most controversial requirements in the WCT are the DRM provisions of the treaty. The treaty requires signatory countries to 'provide adequate legal protection and effective legal remedies' against the circumvention of technological measures 'that are used by authors in connection with the exercise of their rights under this Treaty or the Berne Convention and that restrict acts, in respect of their works, which are not authorized by the authors concerned or permitted by law' (art. 11). This provision represents a critical change in the treatment of infringement by providing for the *prevention* of infringing uses of a work. Previously, the *Berne Convention* provided for legal remedies against infringing use after the fact, within the country of origin for the work. For the first time, the WCT provided authors with the legal ability to technically prohibit or restrict infringing uses of a work in advance of such use, and legally binds the signatory countries to protect against the circumvention of these technological measures. In addition, the WCT may be interpreted as extending the ability of authors to restrict use of their works beyond copyright, in the controversial phrasing '... restrict acts of use that *are not authorized by the authors concerned* or permitted by law.'

The WCT also requires that signatory countries provide legal remedies against any party that knowingly removes or alters rights management information, where this information is defined as 'information which identifies the work, the author of the work, the owner of any right in the work, or information about the terms and conditions of use of the work, and any numbers or codes that represent such information, when any of these items of information is attached to a copy of a work or appears in connection with the communication of a work to the public.' (art. 12).

Rome Convention for the Protection of Performers, Producers of Phonograms and Broadcasting Organisations (1961)

The Rome Convention, administered jointly by WIPO, the ILO (International Labour Organization) and UNESCO, protects the intellectual property rights of performers and producers of phonograms in creative works fixed as phonograms and broadcasts, including protecting performers' rights to authorise live performances to be fixed as a phonogram, broadcast or shared by any other public communication. Producers of phonograms have the exclusive right to authorise or prohibit the direct or indirect reproduction of their phonograms, which are defined as 'any exclusively aural fixation of sounds of a performance or of other sounds.' (International Convention for the Protection of Performers, Producers of Phonograms, and Broadcasting Organizations, art. 3).[6] The Rome treaty addressed the rights of performers and producers as distinct from broadcasters. The Convention requires 'a single equitable remuneration' to producers, performers or both for broadcasting or other communication to the public (art. 12). Minimum rights for broadcasting companies, as prescribed by the Convention, are rebroadcasting of broadcasts, fixation of broadcasts and reproduction of fixations (art. 13). The Rome Convention supports exceptions to these rights, as prescribed by national law within member countries. These exceptions, intended to benefit the public interest, are aligned with the exceptions provided to exclusive rights for literary or artistic works. Protection for the performances, phonograms and broadcasts addressed by this treaty was mandated at least until the end of a 20-year period, defined as the period from the end of the year when the fixation was made or the performance or broadcast took place (art. 14).

The WIPO Performances and Phonograms Treaty (WPPT) (Geneva 1996)

WPPT updates and extends the Rome Convention to support performances and phonograms in the digital environment.[7] Article 1 notes that the WPPT will not derogate from the existing obligations incurred by member contracting nations of the Rome Convention (WIPO Performances and Phonograms Treaty, art. 1). WPPT defines a phonogram as 'the fixation of the sounds of a performance, or of other sounds, or of a representation of sounds, other than in the form of a fixation incorporated in a cinematographic or other audiovisual work' (art. 2). A phonogram that is ultimately incorporated in a cinematographic or other audiovisual work is a copyright-protected resource in its own right prior to its incorporation into the larger work. Incorporation of the fixed performance in the larger work represents a reproduction of a copyright-protected work that must be authorised by the performer or phonograph producer or both.

Fixation is defined as the 'embodiment of sounds, or the representations thereof, from which they can be perceived, reproduced, or communicated through a device' (art. 2). The WPPT extends the rights of performers and phonogram producers for the exclusive disposition of their creative works. Performers have the exclusive right to authorise broadcasting, public communication and fixation of their unfixed performances (art. 6). Performers enjoy the exclusive right to authorise direct or indirect reproduction of performances 'fixed in phonograms, in any manner or form' (art. 7). Other rights include the rights of distribution of performances fixed in phonograms, commercial rental of originals or copies of performances fixed in phonograms, and to make their performances fixed in phonograms available to the public on demand 'by wire or wireless means' (art. 8, 9, 10).

Producers of have similar exclusive rights to authorise 'direct or indirect reproduction' of phonograms, to distribute the original or copies of phonograms, to authorise commercial rental of their phonograms, distribute the original and any copies of their performances, and to make their phonograms available to the public on demand by wire or wireless means, 'in such a way that members of the public may access them from a place and time individually chosen by them' (art. 11, 12, 13, 14).

The rights of both performers and producers may, under conditions determined by the contracting countries, be exhausted after the 'authorized first sale or transfer of ownership of an original or copy' of a fixed performance or phonogram (art. 8, 12). The exclusive right to producers and publishers for commercial rental of originals or copies may be limited by any system of equitable remuneration in effect as of 15 April 1994, 'provided that the commercial rental of phonograms is not giving rise to the material impairment of the exclusive right of reproduction' belonging to performers and producers of phonograms (art. 9, 13).

WPPT establishes the right of performers and producers of phonograms to a 'single equitable remuneration for the direct or indirect use of phonograms published for commercial purposes for broadcasting or for any communication to the public.' Whether this remuneration is provided by the user to the performer, to the producer of the phonogram or to both may be established by national legislation by any member of the WPPT. In particular, countries may establish the terms by which this single equitable remuneration is shared between producers and performers, in the absence of an explicit agreement between the two parties (art. 15).

WPPT extends the protections afforded for the works covered by this treaty to a minimum of 50 years from the end of the calendar year in which the performance was fixed in a phonogram (art. 17). WPPT continues the exceptions to the exclusive rights of performers and phonogram producers commensurate with the exceptions afforded to literary and artistic works in the *Berne Convention*, except that the 'Berne three-step test', as also defined in the WCT, must be applied to any exceptions (WIPO Performances and Phonograms Treaty, art. 16). The WPPT also mandates the same obligations as the WCT to provide legal protection and remedies against the circumvention of technological methods to prevent infringing use of works and to prevent the removing or altering of electronic rights management information (art. 18).

WTO Agreement on Trade-Related Aspects of Intellectual Property Rights (TRIPS)[8] (1995)

TRIPS 'introduced intellectual property rules into the multilateral trading system for the first time'.[9] It was negotiated in the Uruguay Round of the General Agreement on Tariffs and Trade (GATT) (1986–1994). TRIPS is a comprehensive treaty mandating minimum standards for the protection of intellectual property among all World Trade Organization (WTO) member states. It covers copyright-protected intellectual property as well as protecting the related rights of performers, phonogram producers and broadcasters. TRIPS also mandates minimum standards for the protection of trademarks, industrial designs, patents, integrated circuits and undisclosed information, such as trade secrets.

TRIPS incorporates other treaties by reference, most notably the *Berne Convention for the Protection of Literary and Artistic Works* (Paris, 1971), the Rome Convention, and the *Paris Convention for the Protection of Industrial Property* (TRIPS, pt. I, art. 1, 3). TRIPS supports the copyright provisions of the *Berne Convention*, with the exception of the moral rights for authors in Article 6*bis* to claim authorship in a work and object to any alteration of a work that is deemed prejudicial to the author's honor or reputation (TRIPS, pt. II, s. 1, art. 9, 1). TRIPS standardises the general term of protection for a work to 50 years from the end of the calendar year in which the author dies, or the work is published or created. Photographic works and works of applied art are exempted from the 50-year term of protection (pt. II, s. 1, art. 12).

TRIPS also extends the subject matter of protected works to include computer programs, databases or other compilations of data and defines protected works generally as expressions, and not ideas, procedures, methods of operation or mathematical concepts (pt. II, s. 1, art. 9, 10). By contrast, the *Berne Convention* allowed member states to enact national legislation limiting copyright to expressions not ideas rather than inherently defining this limitation (*Berne Convention,* art. 2 (2)). TRIPS mirrors the WIPO treaties (WCT and WPPT) in applying the Berne three-step rule to exceptions to the treaty (pt. II, s. 1, art. 13).

There are several significant provisions in the TRIPS treaty. First, compliance with TRIPS is required for membership in the WTO, although staggered terms for enforcing the provisions were provided to developing countries, transition economies and least-developed countries (pt. VI, art. 65). TRIPS is also notable for being the first treaty to integrate intellectual property into a multilateral trade agreement. Several key provisions of TRIPS specifically support international trade, including:

- National treatment and most favored nation treatment, which require the same treatment for nationals of member states that is accorded to the member's own citizens and also requires that any most favored nation treatment that a member accords to another country must be accorded equally to all WTO member states (pt. I, art. 3, 4).

- Geographic indications that identify the locality of origin of a good, to prevent counterfeiting practices that mislead consumers with respect to the origin of a good (pt. II, s. 3, art. 22, 23).
- Enforcement standards that provide explicit remedies for infringing uses of intellectual property (pt. III). As Wikipedia notes, 'States can be disciplined through the WTO's dispute settlement mechanism.'[10]
- Control of anti-competitive licensing practices (pt. II, s. 8).

TRIPS has sparked considerable controversy, particularly with regard to requirements for implementation and patents. Concerns have particularly been articulated by developing countries and non-governmental organisations (NGOs), including the concern that patents for essential medicines limit their availability in developing countries.[10] The Doha Development Agenda contains negotiations on patents for agriculture, implementation of TRIPS provisions, and other areas of concern for developing nations and NGOs, based on negotiation mandates and decisions derived in Doha in 2001 and refined in subsequent meetings through 2005.[11] In the *TRIPS and Public Health* declaration, 'the ministers stress that it is important to implement and interpret the TRIPS Agreement in a way that supports public health – by promoting both access to existing medicines and the creation of new medicines.'[12]

The TRIPS Council, which is open to all 152 WTO members, administers the TRIPS Agreement. In addition, WIPO plays a role in helping to support and administer the provisions of the TRIPS Agreement, particularly with regard to enabling developing countries to bring TRIPS provisions into force.

WIPO Treaty on the Protection of Broadcasting Organisations

Beginning in 2003, the WIPO Standing Committee on Copyright and Related Rights (SCCR) initiated work on a treaty intended to 'develop and maintain the protection of the rights of broadcasting organisations in a manner as effective as possible' (p. 3).[13] The WIPO Broadcasting Treaty, as it is generally known, has been a subject of intense debate and controversy. Proposed provisions such as the proposed 50-year term of protection have been deemed to have a chilling and unpredictable effect on the flow of information, particularly as the technologies defined as 'broadcasting' may not exist in 50 years. The treaty proposes legal protections to prevent circumventing of technological protection measures that safeguard the broadcast content from unauthorised use. Much concern was expressed about broadcasts that include content that is copyrighted to the creator rather than the broadcaster or that is freely available in the public domain, where this content that might otherwise be available could be restricted based on the method of transmission rather than the rights inherent to the content. In an effort to pull together a basic proposal that takes a 'signal based approach' the *Non-paper on the WIPO Treaty on the Protection of Broadcasting Organizations* was issued by the WIPO SCCR on 20 April 2007. The provisions in the non-paper include an explicit focus on the 'object of protection' – the 'program-carrying signal' rather than the content, which is acknowledged to be separately protected through the existing copyright treaty framework (p. 3).

Specific related-rights protections afforded to the broadcast signal are retransmission and deferred transmission. A term of protection for the broadcast signal is not addressed in the non-paper. The right to legal redress if technological protection measures are circumvented is maintained. Also maintained is the right of member countries to enact national legislation to provide exceptions to copyright protection consistent with the exceptions provided for creative works, such as fair dealing exceptions. National treatment must be accorded by any member state to the broadcasts of other member states. The non-paper will provide the basis for developing a final draft for discussion and ratification by member states. The non-paper does not explicitly address individual use of broadcasts through time shifting (i.e. recording a broadcast to view at a later time); format shifting (transferring a broadcast to another medium, such as a DVD or MP3 file); or space shifting (experiencing a broadcast via a separate device, such as a computer instead of a television) although these exceptions could presumably be enacted at the national level as part of the exception provision addressed in the non-paper.

The Library Copyright Alliance, a group of library organisations and consortia in the United States, including the American Library Association and the American Association of Law Libraries, issued a position paper, *Library Concerns with the WIPO Broadcast Treaty* in May 2007, which stated that 'The U.S. libraries' position is that there is no compelling public policy reason for the broadcast treaty, given the existence of the Rome Convention and the absence of any evidence of harm suffered by broadcasters.'[14]

Despite the controversy surrounding the WIPO broadcasting treaty, at a March 2008 meeting of the WIPO member states, the SCCR 'decided to continue discussions on the protection of broadcasting organisations with a view to concluding an international instrument.'[15]

European Union Directive 2001/29/EC (EUCD)

EUCD is the commonly known acronym for the *European Union Directive 2001/29/EC of the European Parliament and of the Council of 22 May 2001 on the harmonisation of certain aspects of copyright and related rights in the information society.*[16] The EUCD is intended to implement the WCT and provide minimum standards and guidance to member states. Provisions of the treaty include anti-circumvention of technological measures to prevent copying, as specified in the WCT. The EUCD maintains fair use or fair dealing exceptions but also allows for fair compensation to rights holders for use of copyright-protected resources, even in 'certain cases of exceptions or limitations' to a copyright owner's exclusive reproduction right. The provisions of the EUCD for fair use exceptions are broadly but cautiously worded, with an emphasis on the non-commercial nature of fair use and the importance of not interfering with the rights holder's legitimate commercial exploitation of his or her copyright-protected works, particularly in the digital environment (Council Directive 2001/29/EC, (35), (36)).[16]

Adoption of the EUCD was slow, as member states struggled with issues such as enforceability of anti-circumvention measures and public controversy over the provisions. The UK enacted laws to implement the EUCD on 31 October 2003.

Other recent directives of the European Commission have addressed specific areas of copyright: *2001/84/EC* (resale rights of original works of art); *96/9/EC* (protection of databases); *2006/116/EC* (term of protection); *93/83/EEC* (satellite broadcasting and cable retransmission); *2006/115/EC* (rental and lending rights); and *91/250/EEC* (protection of computer programs).[17]

In 2005, the European Commission launched an initiative to simplify and harmonise legislation, including an examination and 'recasting' of the body of law governing European copyright, the copyright acquis. According to the UK Intellectual Property Office, ' "recasting" is defined as simultaneously amending and codifying the legal acts in question.'[18] As an initial step, Professor Bernt Hugenholtz, Institute for Information Law, University of Amsterdam, was commissioned to conduct two studies, on the recasting of the copyright acquis and the implementation of *Directive 2001/29/EC* on Copyright in the Information Society. Several studies have been released in 2007 that discuss the impact of *Directive 2001/29/EC* on member states and the harmonisation of national copyright laws, the recasting of copyright and related rights, and the contributions to the European economy of copyright and related rights.[19] The recommendations in these reports, as well as reactions by member states, will inform the working program of the European Commission.

An important recent development within the European Commission is the proposal by Internal Market Commissioner Charles McCreevy to extend the term of copyright protection for European performers within sound recordings from 50 to 95 years, which would be longer than the term of protection for composers – currently the lifespan of the composer plus 70 years. This recommendation is scheduled for consideration in mid 2008.[20]

National copyright legislation

Many countries have enacted national copyright legislation to support or extend the provisions of international copyright treaties or other multinational agreements or to localise copyright law to the unique needs of the country and its intellectual property. National copyright legislation has a venerable history, significantly pre-dating international copyright law. This section looks briefly at copyright law in representative English-speaking countries (dictated by my modest linguistic skills in other languages): the United Kingdom, Australia, Canada, New Zealand and the United States. It is recommended that this information serve only as a starting point that demonstrates how copyright law among countries differs in critical areas, such as copyright term and exceptions to copyright, and also how frequently copyright is reviewed and revised. As noted earlier in this chapter, a thorough understanding of the relevant national copyright legislation, so that the library can embody national copyright legislation in its copyright policy, is a recommended first step for a DRM implementation.

Copyright in the UK

Copyright, as a term and a concept, had its beginnings in England, coincident with the development and availability of the printing press, and thus the ability to make and disseminate copies of works to a broad audience. In 1537, Queen Mary granted a charter to the Stationers' Guild, granting them the sole privilege or right to print copies of works. This powerful, monopolistic copyright was further codified in the *Licensing Act of 1662*, in which a register of books was established, to be administered by the Stationers' Company. The Company was given the authority to search out and destroy unregistered books (Mitchell, p. 48).[21] The Company was the sole arbiter of book registration and the right to print and distribute books. There was no legal redress from the decisions of the Stationers' Company until 1710, when An *Act for the Encouragement of Learning by vesting the Copies of Printed Books in the Authors or Purchasers of such Copies, during the Times therein Mentioned*, more commonly known as the Statute of Queen Anne, was passed. This was a significant event in the history of copyright, introducing the twin concepts that have been the foundation of modern copyright law: the primacy of the author as the owner of copyright as well as the concept that copyright is a fixed term of ownership rather than a right in perpetuity. The Statute of Queen Anne also moved the venue for copyright dispute to the courts, rather than the Stationers' Company. Although the Stationers' Company retained its role to register works for copyright, it could be fined for refusing to register a work. Authors could sell their copyright, but anyone could purchase the copyright and not just the Stationers' Company (Mitchell, pp. 33–34).[21]

British copyright has evolved over time to enact changes to copyright duration, with the passage of the *Copyright Act 1911* and, beginning with the passage of the *Copyright Act 1956*, to harmonise with international treaties, such as the *Berne Convention*, WIPO treaties and EU directives and to accommodate new formats and the needs of the digital information era.

The current UK copyright law is the *Copyright, Designs and Patents Act 1988*. The law has been frequently amended by Statutory Instruments, particularly to harmonise with EU Directives. The most significant amendment to copyright law, the *Copyright and Related Rights Regulations 2003*, went into effect on 31 October 2003, in response to an EU Directive passed in 2002.[22] Highlights of the 2003 copyright law changes are discussed below.

As in other counties, copyright is automatic and goes into force as soon as a work is created. No formal system of registration exists, although creators may register their work with the UK Copyright Service, an independent, fee-based service that provides an evidentiary trail to support the creator in copyright disputes.[23] Duration of copyright in the UK varies by format.. Literary, dramatic, musical, filmed and artistic works are protected for 70 years beyond the death of the creator; sound, computer-generated works and performances, and public communications (including websites and broadcasts) are protected for 50 years; typographical arrangements of published editions are protected for 25 years.[24] In addition to copyright, there are two noteworthy additional rights for created works (Copyright and Related Rights Regulations 2003 no. 2498, s. 28A). A database may be protected under copyright for 70 years, particularly if the database entries or selection and organisation demonstrate creativity as a literary work. However, a specific database right also exists, introduced on 1 January 1998 via the *Copyright and Rights in Databases Regulations 1997 no. 3032*, particularly for databases that represent a substantial investment by the organisation, which protects against re-use of the database and its contents for 15 years past the date of creation or publication.[25]

Another significant additional right is publications right, which emerged after the EU Directive of 1993 and provides 25 years of rights to anyone publishing unpublished material that is no longer copyright protected. It can be difficult to determine that an unpublished work, particularly if anonymous, is actually out of copyright, but the intent of publications right is to reward individuals for contributing to the public good through the dissemination of previously unavailable material.[26]

In addition to exclusive rights under copyright, UK copyright law also provides performers' rights with a term of 50 years, which governs performers' rights to authorise broadcasting, recording, copying, distribution, renting, lending, broadcasting, public performance and communication to the public by electronic transmission for their performances.[27] As noted in the previous section, this term has been proposed for extension to 95 years across Europe for all European Commission member states.

The UK does allow uses of materials under 'fair dealing' conditions that do not require the approval of the copyright holder. Fair dealing in UK copyright law includes news reporting and research and private study, provided 'sufficient acknowledgement' is provided whenever practicable. Criticism and review are also fair dealing exceptions, provided the work has been made publicly available and 'sufficient acknowledgement' is provided. Incidental inclusion, in which a part of a copyright work is unintentionally included, such as a copyright-protected movie displayed on a television in a video interview in someone's home, is also a fair dealing exception. However, 'a musical work, words spoken or sung with music, or so much of a sound recording or broadcast as includes a musical work or such words, shall not be regarded as incidentally included in another work if it is deliberately included.' (pp. 39–41).[28] Fair dealing only pertains to 'literary, dramatic, musical, artistic and the typographical arrangement of published editions.'[29] UK copyright law also allows 'time shifting' – the copying of a broadcast for listening or viewing at a later time (Copyright and Related Rights Regulations 2003 no. 2498, s. 17A(1)).[22]

The UK does not specify the amount of a copyright-protected work that can be copied for research and study under fair dealing. 'The librarian of a prescribed library' may supply a copy of a 'reasonable proportion' of the work for the cost of reproduction (*Copyright Designs and Patents Act 1988, c. 48, Part I, s.38, 39*).[24]

A notable change to fair dealing in the *Copyright and Related Rights Regulations 2003* is the requirement that the researcher must satisfy the librarian that the requested copying is research for a non-commercial purpose or for private study. UK libraries generally require the user to sign a form affirming that the use of copied materials is for private, non-commercial purposes (Copyright and Related Rights Regulations 2003 no. 2498, s. 38, 39). Other changes to copyright law occurring in the 2003 law include the new exclusive right obtaining to copyright holders of communicating a work to the public through electronic transmission; affirming the illegality of tampering with access control mechanisms and digital rights information, as required in WCT and WPPT; and the right for users to make temporary copies of electronic resources, as needed to run or display the information (Cornish, 3).[30]

An interesting change occurring with the 2003 law is the provision of copying rights for the visually impaired that allow them to make copies of resources in usable forms. Resources that can be copied into other formats are limited to those materials that the visually impaired user has a legal right to view (Cornish, 15).[30] A change with far-reaching implications, particularly for libraries engaged in digitisation, is that the duration of copyright for sound recordings is now defined as 50 years from the end of the year in which it was recorded, published or, if not published, 50 years from the point at which it was publicly played or communicated. As noted by Graham Cornish, if your library or archive owns unpublished sound recordings that may be copyright protected that you then expose to the public – perhaps through digital communication over the web – copyright will be automatically extended for 50 years (Cornish, 6).[30] This has implications for 'orphan works', where the copyright status may not be known or the creator may be difficult to identify or locate, yet the archive may unintentionally extend the period of copyright protection through public communication or broadcast.

Collective licensing agencies or collecting societies have emerged in the UK as a way to make copyright-protected materials readily available for users, particularly those in libraries or academic settings. The Copyright Licensing Agency (CLA) is the most prevalent licensing agency, particularly for print resources. The CLA offers licenses for every type of educational institution, public body, government agency or other entity.[31] The CLA has also established a 'Sticker Scheme' project in which stickers may be purchased and attached to copies, for uses that are not deemed fair use, such as individual copying for commercial purposes.[32] The Copyright Tribunal and the Performing Right Tribunal exist to adjudicate when a user feels that he/she has been unfairly denied a license to use copyright-protected resources or charged unfairly for a license.[33]

One final law to discuss is the Legal Deposit Libraries Act 2003. Six libraries: the Bodleian Library (Oxford), the Cambridge University Library, the National Library of Scotland, the Library of Trinity College Dublin, the National Library of Wales and the British Library, have all been designated legal deposit libraries. The Agency for the Legal Deposit Libraries requests and accepts copies of publications on behalf of the five deposit libraries, with the exception of the British Library, which has its own internal agency, within 12 months of publication. Each publisher must supply copies for each deposit library upon request.[34]

Andrew Gowers, a British journalist and former Editor of the *Financial Times*, was appointed by the Chancellor of the Exchequer in December 2005 to review intellectual property rights and management in the UK. His report, *The Gowers*

Review of Intellectual Property, released in December 2006, examined the law and prevailing practices and made recommendations for improvements to the legal and economic management of intellectual property rights in the UK in four areas: patents, copyright, trademarks and designs. Gowers stated, 'I do not think the system is in need of radical overhaul.' (Gowers, 1).[35] The report nonetheless made significant recommendations, many of which are important for libraries. These recommendations include:

- proposing an 'orphan works' provision to the European Commission, which would enable the re-use of works with no identifiable or locatable creator;
- clarifying the research exception to support private research utilising copyright-protected resources within universities and businesses;
- enabling libraries to copy resources and shift formats for master copies of archival works;
- enabling format shifting of copyright-protected materials for private use, such as copying music from an MP3 file to a CD;
- retaining the copyright term of 50 years for sound recordings and performers' rights;
- establishing the policy that changes to the terms and conditions of copyright should not be applied retroactively to resources already governed by copyright before the changes came into legal force and effect.[35]

Some of the recommendations in the *Gowers Review* echo recommendations in the British Library's *IP Manifesto* issued on 25 September 2006. Key recommendations of the *Manifesto* addressed the need for an orphan works copyright exception, support for existing exceptions, including fair dealing, in the digital environment, and a life plus 70 years term of copyright protection for unpublished works, to correspond with published works.[36]

On 8 January 2008, the UK Intellectual Property Office made a number of recommendations for changes to copyright law based on the *Gowers Review*. Key recommendations are intended to support distance education and enable educational institutions to leverage digital technologies as well as to enable libraries to preserve resources that are deteriorating or in obsolete formats. Other provisions enable individuals to copy legally obtained resources to other formats ('format shifting') and adds a new exception for parody. Educational provisions would allow distance-learning students to receive and view broadcasts remotely and to receive copies of passages from published materials via electronic whiteboards. Another important recommendation is to expand the fair dealing exception for private research and study beyond literary, artistic, dramatic and musical works to content of all types and formats. Of particular interest to libraries is the recommendation to expand copying for preservation and replacement to films, broadcasts and sound recordings, in addition to the existing provision for copies of literary, dramatic and musical works. The new library copying provision also allows format shifting and multiple copies as needed.[37] The proposed changes are open for comments until 8 April 2008.[38]

Copyright in Australia

Copyright is legislated in Australia through the *Copyright Act 1968 (Cth)*, which is also entitled *An Act relating to copyright and the protection of certain performances, and for other purposes* and specifies copyright regulations for materials created before and after 1968. Copyright protection is automatically applied to protected materials upon creation.

There is no copyright registration in Australia. As with other countries, Australian copyright law has been regularly amended since 1968, and the provisions of copyright law have been interpreted over time through adjudication of copyright cases in Australian courts. The term of duration for copyright protection was originally 50 years from the end of the year in which the creator died, or, in the absence of a discoverable creator, the end of the year in which the protected material was created. As a result of the Australia/US Free Trade Agreement, the term of protection has been extended, as of 1 January 2005, to 70 years from the end of the year in which the creator died or the protected material was created.[39] This extended term of duration does not extend the term of protection for materials that are out of copyright as of 1 January 2005. The Australian Copyright Council has published an information sheet, Duration of Copyright, which provides a table to help determine if an Australian work is still under copyright protection.[40]

Australian copyright covers creative expression fixed in tangible form, such as text, computer programs, artistic works, compilations, dramatic works, musical works, cinematograph films, broadcasts and published editions. Standard exclusive rights, as already described above in international treaties, are granted to the copyright owner, who may assign or transfer one or more rights to others.[41]

Australian copyright includes a 'fair dealing' provision to identify non-infringing uses of copyright-protected materials that do not require the prior permission of the copyright holder. The following purposes are identified: research or study, criticism or review, reporting news, parody or satire, professional advice by an attorney, including a patent or trademark attorney. Parody or satire is a recent addition to the fair dealing use exceptions, from the *Copyright Amendment Act 2006 (Cth)*. The amount of material that may be reproduced for fair dealing is limited and cannot include a 'substantial part' of the work.[42]

The reproduction of a work for research or study within the provisions of fair use depends on five factors: the purpose or character of the use; nature of the work; availability of the work for reasonable purchase; effect of the use on the market value for the work; and the amount of the work copied in relation to the whole. Unlike fair dealing generally, the amount of material that can be copied from a textual work for research or study is explicitly defined as 10% of the text (number of pages or number of words, for electronic texts) or one chapter, and exceptions to this limit for reproduction of a work may only be identified by considering the five factors affecting the fair reproduction of a work.[43]

Australian libraries are able to use copyright materials without the prior permission of the copyright holder to supply to users for their research or study; to supply to other libraries for their collections or to supply to other libraries' users; for preservation; for on-premises research; and for replacement, if a replacement copy cannot be reasonably purchased. Exceptions for libraries were expanded in the *Copyright Amendment Act 2006 (Cth)*. One key provision is that libraries are no longer required to be non-profit as long as the library's collection (or part of the collection) is available to the public for on-premises use or through interlibrary loan. Libraries can also use copyright materials to maintain or operate a library; can make replacement copies; and, if defined as a 'key cultural institution', can make three preservation copies of certain original materials. There are many conditions and ambiguities in the *Copyright Amendment Act 2006 (Cth)*, which require careful reading by libraries and, in some cases, legal advice, before the library applies the exceptions.[44] The *Copyright Amendment Act 2006 (Cth)* is discussed further below.

In August 2000, a comprehensive amendment to the Copyright Act 1968 was enacted, the *Copyright Amendment (Digital Agenda) Act 2000 (Cth)*. Key provisions of this Act include the right to approve electronic communication of copyrighted works. This Act also supports provisions of the WCT and WPPT through anti-circumvention provisions for DRM technologies and the provision against the trade of devices that exist to circumvent DRM protections. The Act continued support for 'fair dealing' exceptions and exemptions for libraries and archives for digital information.[45]

A further amendment, the *Copyright Amendment Act 2006 (Cth)*, was enacted in 2006, with some provisions delayed until January 2007. The Act addressed time-shifting, space-shifting and format-shifting; exceptions for libraries, educational institutions and cultural institutions; the extension of fair dealing to cover parody and satire; technological protection measures; and criminal penalties for infringement.[46]

Time-shifting, format-shifting and space-shifting are permitted under the amendment for private, personal use only, although the Act specifically states that time-shifting from TV and radio should not be used to build up a private collection of copyright-protected broadcasts, to play back repeatedly for an indefinite period of use. The Act does not allow the further distribution of copies made for private use, such as giving away or selling a private copy of a legally acquired resource to another. The Act does allow circumventing a copy control technological protection measure in order to make a lawful copy of a resource but not circumventing an access control technological protection measure.[47] Copying exceptions are provided to libraries, archives and educational institutions for the following purposes: maintaining or operating a library or archive; giving educational instruction; or assisting a person with a disability to use a copyright-protected resource. There remains some ambiguity for these exceptions that may require legal counsel to resolve. A 'key cultural institution', which is not explicitly defined in the Act, is allowed to make three preservation copies of resources in its collection, if the organisation has a national or state legal function to maintain a cultural collection and the material in question is of 'historical or cultural significance to Australia.'[46]

Copyright in Canada

Canadian copyright is legislated through the country's *Copyright Act R.S., 1985 c. C-42.*[48] As in other countries, Canadian copyright covers literary, dramatic, musical and artistic works, as well as distinct copyright rights and duration of rights for different copyright holders: creators, performers, broadcasters of communication signals and makers of sound recordings. Registration is not required but is encouraged to provide an audit trail in the event that copyright is contested. As in other countries, copyright applies at the time of creation for the work. The general duration for copyright in Canada is 50 years following the end of the calendar year in which the author dies (*Copyright Act R.S., 1985 c. C-42, s. 6*). While copyright duration is generally based on the lifetime of the author, for works for which a personal author cannot be identified, for example a photograph produced by a corporation, copyright is based upon the lifetime of the person who is the principal shareholder. If no principal shareholder exists, duration is 50 years beyond the calendar year in which the negative or plate was created.[49] Cinematographic works, sound recordings and performances are similar, in that copyright protection lasts for 50 years after the calendar year in which the work is first published, or if unpublished, first fixed or performed. A work by an unknown author has a slightly different period of duration: 50 years after the calendar year of publication, or 75 years after the calendar year of the making of the work, for an unpublished work.

Canada's fair dealing provisions allow non-infringing use of copyright-protected resources for private study or research, criticism or review, or news reporting, although attribution is required for criticism, review and news reporting. No guidance is provided concerning the amount of a work that can be used or reproduced without permission (*Copyright Act R.S., 1985, c. C-42 s. 29*). Canada also allows non-profit educational institutions to make copies and perform copyright-protected works within the classroom. Reproduction for classroom use is fairly restricted, including specifications for the method of reproduction for classroom use and the requirement that the educational institution must be non-profit. The exemption does not apply if the work is commercially available in a medium suited to the educational purpose (*c. C-42 s. 29*).

As in the UK, there are many collective societies that represent authors to provide fee-based licenses for copyright-protected works, such as Access Copyright.[50] The AUCC (Association of University Colleges of Canada) has developed model licenses with collective licensing agencies, such as Access Copyright (previously CANCOPY).[51]

Canada permits non-profit libraries, archives and museums to make copies of copyright-protected works for the purposes of maintenance and management of collections, such as the making of a copy in the following circumstances: when a rare or unpublished original is damaged or in danger of damage; for preservation or onsite use; to create an alternative format to replace an obsolete format; for internal record keeping or cataloging; or for insurance purposes and police investigation. These exceptions do not apply if 'an appropriate copy is commercially available in a medium and of a quality that is appropriate for the purposes' (*Copyright Act R.S., 1985, c. C-42 s. 30.1(2)*).

Canada requires the deposit of two copies of each book, pamphlet, serial, microform, spoken word sound recording, video recording and electronic publication in physical form (e.g. CD-ROM) published in Canada and one copy of each musical sound recording and multimedia kit, in the Library and Archives Canada collection, as mandated in the *Library and Archives of Canada Act*.[52]

One interesting provision of Canadian copyright law is the ability to petition the Copyright Board of Canada for a license to use a copyright-protected resource if the copyright owner cannot be located. The bar for attempting to locate the copyright owner is high, but if the copyright owner cannot be found, the Copyright Board of Canada, a regulatory body that establishes royalty fees to be charged by licensing collectives and adjudicates agreements between licensing collectives and users, will establish a license and royalty for use of the work. The license application must fully describe the work, everything that is known about the copyright owner, the explicit uses for which the license is sought and similar royalties the user has paid for equivalent resources. If the Board is satisfied that a thorough search has been undertaken for the copyright owner, and that the work, the copyright owner and the use are sufficiently described, a license will be issued.[53]

At the time of writing, Canada has signed both the WCT and the WPPT but has brought neither treaty into force via copyright legislation. A bill addressing provisions of the two treaties, *Bill C-60, An Act to Amend the Copyright Act*, sparked considerable opposition and died with the calling of the 29 November 2005 federal election. New copyright legislation to address the requirements of both treaties is apparently under development.[54]

Copyright in New Zealand

The primary legislation governing copyright in New Zealand is the *Copyright Act 1994*.[55] The term of copyright in New Zealand is 50 years. For literary, musical, dramatic and artistic works, the term of coverage extends 50 years beyond the end of the year in which the creator dies. For sound recordings, films and broadcasts, coverage continues for 50 years after the end of the year in which it is made. Or, for films and sound recordings, if the resource is made publicly available within 50 years of creation, copyright will extend to 50 years after the year in which it is first publicly made available. The typographic right of publishers in their editions lasts 25 years after the year in which the edition is first published. As with other countries, copyright is automatic when a creative work is first fixed into tangible form (*Copyright Act 1994, s 22, 23, 24, 25*).

A number of collecting agencies administer access to many copyright-protected materials in New Zealand. A copyright tribunal exists to adjudicate licensing disputes with collecting agencies, such as claims that a collecting agency has unfairly withheld a license to use a copyright-protected resource or assessed license fees that were unfair.[56] The *Copyright (New Technologies and Performers' Rights) Amendment Bill* amends the *Copyright Act 1994*. The Commerce Committee of the New Zealand Parliament recommends in its reporting of the bill that the name be changed to the *Copyright (New Technologies) Amendment*, noting that the provisions to performers' rights are only intended to make these provisions 'technologically neutral' (*Copyright (New Technologies and Performers' Rights) Amendment, Commentary*, 2).[57] This law harmonises with many provisions in the WCT, including anti-circumvention measures for technologies that prevent copying and protection for electronic rights information. The new law extends 'fair dealing' to digital resources, particularly for libraries and educational institutions, providing for the ability to preserve collections digitally, to provide both onsite and remote access to digital materials, and to share materials digitally with patrons and other libraries. Educational institutions can also cache websites for teaching and digitally share materials that may legally be copied. The bill applies significant criminal penalties for large-scale copyright infringement practices, particularly with regard to resources that have had electronic rights information removed or altered and for dealing in circumvention technologies to remove or bypass technological protection measures. The bill also provides rights to performers to control the recording and distribution of recordings of their performances. The Amendment provides for time-shifting of digital materials for personal use (except 'on-demand' services) and format-shifting for legally acquired sound recordings, which may be re-recorded to another format for personal listening. The Commerce Committee in its report recommends that the purchaser creating the copy be required to retain both the original and the copy made for personal use (*Copyright (New Technologies and Performers' Rights) Amendment, Commentary*, 4).

The bill was introduced and received a first reading in December 2006 and was remanded to the Commerce Committee for further consideration. The Commerce Committee reported the bill on 27 July 2007.[57] The bill has not yet become law.

Copyright in the United States

Article one, section eight of the US Constitution states, 'The Congress shall have Power ... To promote the Progress of Science and Useful Arts, by securing for limited Times to

Authors and Inventors the exclusive Right to their respective Writings and Discoveries.' (US Const. *art. 1*, § 8).[58] The concept of copyright is thus part of the foundation of US Government. Congress enacted the first copyright law in the US in 1790. Copyright law has undergone numerous revisions since that date, to accommodate the needs of specific formats, and the authors of those formats, such as photographs, phonograms and digital materials; to harmonise with international treaties; and to respond to the requirements of the digital information era. The emphasis in article 1, section 8 of the Constitution is clearly on the promotion of knowledge and secondarily on the rights of authors. Over time, through legislation, this balance has shifted to a greater emphasis on the economic rights of creators to exploit their works.

US copyright is established as Title 17 in the United States Code and protects literary, dramatic, musical, pictorial, graphic and sculptural works, as well as pantomimes and choreographic works, motion pictures and audiovisual works, sound recordings, architectural works and computer software. Databases are protected as compilations based on the original arrangement of the information contained therein (*17 USC.* § 103). Works created by the federal government are exempted from copyright protection, although exceptions may occur for works created by contractors to the federal government, depending on the contractual terms of agreement (*17 USC.* § 105).

Copyright law in the United States has undergone extensive revision with regard to requirements for registering and documenting copyright. A major revision to copyright law occurred in 1976 but took effect on 1 January 1978. Prior to 1978, copyright registration, and renewal upon the expiration of copyright, was required to continue copyright protection for the work. Duration of renewal changed over time, from 28 years to 47 years in the 1960s, and then to life of the author plus 50 years, or 75 years for corporate authorship, with the Copyright Act of 1976. The rules governing the copyright notice to be affixed to the copyrighted work were precise and rigid. Failure to adhere to notice requirements resulted in loss of copyright protection.

As of 1 January 1978, copyright renewal was not required. Copyright notice was required until 1989, but for works published on or after 1 January 1978, a copyright owner could remedy a missing or incorrect copyright notice, thus fully restoring copyright protection. In 1998, Congress added 20 years to the term of protection in the *Sonny Bono Copyright Term Extension Act* (P.L. 105–298), so that copyright extends from life of the creator plus 70 years, and, for works of corporate authorship, 120 years from year of creation or 95 years from date of first publication (*17 USC.* § 302). Practically, works published before 1978 will generally enjoy 95 years of copyright protection. Copyright duration for works published on or after 1 January 1978 is 70 years beyond the end of the year in which the creator dies.

To comply with the *Berne Convention*, copyright in the United States vests immediately and automatically when a work is first fixed in tangible form. No registration or renewal is required, although registration can provide proof of copyright in the event of copyright dispute or infringement. Voluntary online registration of copyright will soon be available from the US Copyright Office. The Electronic Copyright Office (eCO) is in beta test as of July 2007.[59]

Changes in copyright law are generally not retroactive, making it challenging to determine the copyright status of works that became available before 1 January 1978.

Numerous charts are available providing guidance for determining the copyright status of a work. June Besek provides a useful 'rule of thumb' guideline for works created and published before 1 January 1978: works published before 1923 with a copyright notice are in the public domain, and works published between 1923 and 1963 with a copyright notice are protected for a total of 95 years from publication if copyright was renewed in the 28th year. If copyright was not renewed, the work is in the public domain. Works published from 1964 to 1977 are protected for 95 years from publication.[60] Copyright registration and renewal are difficult to research, since the US Copyright office has both online and paper records. In particular, works that were copyrighted or renewed before 1978 are documented in manual records that must be searched onsite. The US Copyright Office will conduct registration searches of its manual records for a fee. Online records can be searched over the Web.[61]

Important sections of Title 17 include Section 107, which governs fair use limitations to copyright, and Section 108, which governs reproduction by libraries and archives to support replacement of lost, damaged or obsolete works, as well as the ability of libraries to fulfill patron requests for copies of works and to fulfill interlibrary loans to other libraries and their patrons. Section 108(h) allows libraries and archives to reproduce, distribute, perform, or display works, facsimiles of copyright-protected works or digital transcripts of works, in analog and digital form, beyond the confines of the library in the last 20 years of the copyright term, if (a) the work is no longer subject to normal commercial exploitation, (b) no copy of the work can be obtained at a reasonable price and (c) the copyright holder does not provide formal notice to the Copyright Office that conditions (a) and (b) apply (*17 USC.* § 108(h)). Other important copyright provisions are contained in Section 109, also known as the 'first sale doctrine', which grants the owner of a lawfully obtained copy the right to dispose of the copy through sale, loan or gift, and Section 110, which supports performance and display of copyright-protected resources in the classroom and through distance education, when explicit requirements are met (*17 USC.* § 109).

A recent amendment to US copyright law is the *Digital Millennium Copyright Act (1998)* (DMCA), which implements provisions of the WIPO copyright treaties, WCT and WPPT. DMCA has several key provisions, including limitations on the liability of online service providers for copyright infringement, provisions against removing or tampering with copyright information, and anti-circumvention legislation, making it illegal to circumvent technological copy protection measures, except for specified exemptions, and prohibiting the manufacture of devices or offering of services to circumvent technological protection measures. DMCA recognised the controversial nature of its anti-circumvention measures and the potential chilling effect upon fair use. Several safeguards were introduced: a 2-year deferral before the anti-circumvention measure took effect and a mandated study of possible exceptions by the Librarian of Congress and authorisation for the Librarian of Congress to authorise a 3-year waiver from the anti-circumvention provision if there is evidence that the new law is having an adverse affect on fair use or other non-infringing uses of information. DMCA also provides for digital preservation copying by non-commercial libraries and archives, which may make up to three digital copies of an eligible copyright-protected work; the ability to digitally loan protected works to other qualifying institutions; and to allow digital preservation of a work to overcome format obsolescence of the original.[62]

The Librarian of Congress has exempted classes of works from DMCA three times in a process known as Section 1201 Rulemaking. Each exemption class expires with the next 3-year rule making. The most recent Section 1201 Rulemaking occurred in November 2006, when exemptions included allowing circumvention of technological protection measures for audiovisual works held in libraries of educational institutions or film studies departments in order to make compilations for educational use in the classroom; preservation or archival reproduction of published digital works in obsolete formats; literary works in e-book formats to enable read-aloud functionality or screen readers that render the text in specialised formats; and sound recordings and audiovisual works in CD format that contain technological protection measures that exploit security flaws or vulnerabilities that can compromise the security of a computer system, where circumvention is intended to test and repair these security vulnerabilities.[63]

Another significant amendment to US copyright statute is the Technology, Education and Copyright Harmonization, or TEACH, Act. The TEACH Act, which became law in 2002, provides conditional exemptions for accredited non-profit educational institutions to utilise copyright-protected resources in the classroom and for distance education, including digital transmission, without requiring the approval of the copyright holder or the payment of royalties. The TEACH Act requires institutional policies and technologies to ensure that use of copyright-protected resources is limited to specific classroom or course use and that information about copyright is provided to participants.[64]

In March 2006, the US Copyright Office published a report on orphan works. The report defines orphan works as 'a term used to describe the situation where the owner of a copyrighted work cannot be identified and located by someone who wishes to make use of the work in a manner that requires permission of the copyright owner.' (Register of Copyrights, p. 1).[65] The report investigates the practical and legal issues surrounding orphan works and concludes by recommending an amendment to the remedies section of the Copyright Act. The report recommends that if a 'reasonably diligent' search has been conducted, the remedies available to the copyright owner based on a subsequent unauthorised use by the searcher should be limited. The report also recommends attribution to the creator, assuming that the identity of the creator can be discovered (pp. 7–11).[65] Legislation to implement these recommendations was proposed in the US House of Representatives in 2006 but withdrawn from consideration. On 24 April 2008, legislation was introduced in the US Senate as the *Shawn Bentley Orphan Works Act of 2008* (S.2913)[66] and in the House (H.R.5889) to enable users to exhibit orphan works if the copyright owner cannot be located after a 'good faith' documented search to locate the copyright owner. The bill requires reasonable compensation to the rights holder, after the fact, if the rights holder is subsequently identified. The bill also specifies requirements for the good faith searches and requires that 'the Register of Copyrights shall undertake a certification process for the establishment of an electronic database that facilitates the search for pictorial, graphic, and sculptural works that are subject to copyright protection under title 17, United States Code.' (S.2913, sec. 3) The Senate bill has been remanded to the Judiciary Committee for review.

US copyright law probably has the most expansive application of fair use among the countries acknowledging fair use or fair dealing exceptions to copyright. Fair use supports the non-infringing use of copyright-protected resources without requiring either the permission of the copyright holder or the payment of royalties. Non-infringing uses are determined by the application of four factors intended to determine whether or not a use may be reasonably considered to be non-infringing. These four factors are considered together, in a balancing test, although all four factors do not need to apply, or apply equally, for a use to be non-infringing. The four factors are also non-exclusive but are identified in the preamble of Section 107 as being factors to include when determining whether use of a work is fair use. The four factors are broadly rather than comprehensively described, with examples that are illustrative rather than conclusive. The limits of fair use are thus tested and defined via case law, with the onus upon the copyright holder to prove infringement.

The four factors to be included in determining fair use are:

1. 'the purpose and character of the use, including whether such use is of a commercial nature or is for non-profit educational purposes;
2. the nature of the copyrighted work;
3. the amount and substantiality of the portion used in relation to the copyrighted work as a whole and;
4. the effect of the use upon the potential market for or value of the copyrighted work.' (*17 USC.* § 107)

Fair use in US copyright has been adjudicated after the fact in judicial decisions. The Digital Millennium Copyright Act's curtailing of fair use for digital resources protected by technological control measures, which pre-empts the judgment of the user to determine whether or not use is infringing, has been of considerable concern to librarians, educators and legal activists. A 2007 bill, H.R.1201, *The Freedom and Innovation Revitalizing US Entrepreneurship*

Act of 2007, would allow the circumvention of technological protection measures for non-infringing resource use, including fair use. The bill has been remanded to the US House of Representatives Committee on the Judiciary. Subcommittee on Courts, the Internet and Intellectual Property for review.[67]

Other recent copyright legislation in the US includes a bill introduced in the Senate in 2007, S.522, the *Intellectual Property Rights Enforcement Act*, which would establish policies and coordinate the enforcement of intellectual property rights among government agencies and protect US property rights overseas through an international task force. The bill has been remanded to committee for review.[68] In late 2007, the *Prioritizing Resources and Organization for Intellectual Property (PRO-IP) Act of 2007* (H.R.4279) bill was forwarded to the House Committee on the Judiciary by the Subcommittee on Courts, the Internet, and Intellectual Property. The bill is intended to substantially strengthen enforcement of copyright, patent and trademark laws and increase the penalties for infringement of these laws. Among other things, the bill proposes the creation of an Office of the US Intellectual Property Enforcement Representative in the executive branch, to coordinate activities by government and international entities to enforce intellectual property protection laws and prosecute infringement.[69]

A recent law of considerable interest to the open access movement is the *Consolidated Appropriations Act of 2007* (P.L. 110–161), which includes a provision directing the National Institutes of Health (NIH) to make available to the public online access to findings from its public research. In its *Revised Policy on Enhancing Public Access to Archived Publications Resulting from NIH-Funded Research* 'all peer-reviewed articles that arise, in whole or in part, from direct costs funded by NIH, or from NIH staff, that are accepted for publication on or after April 7, 2008' must be deposited in *PubMedCentral*, providing open access to all US citizens and any other interested party, 'no later than 12 months after the official date of publication.'[70]

Copyright and libraries: practical steps

Every country has different laws, and every type of library has different needs for providing users with access to resources that may be copyright protected. The remainder of this chapter provides basic guidance for librarians to develop a framework of copyright support for library services.

Develop and publish a copyright policy

Every organisation that creates or makes use of copyright-protected information should develop and publish a copyright policy. This policy should ideally encompass the entire organisation, given that the library is generally part of a larger unit that often creates and consumes copyrighted resources. It is important to have the active collaboration as well as the subsequent buy-in from the administrators, legal counsel and members of the organisation served by the library, whether a university, municipal government or other entity.

A copyright policy may be part of a larger information policy, which governs areas such as network security, acceptable use of networked equipment and resources, privacy, retention and archiving of organisational records, and other non-copyright areas of information use. In this case, the copyright policy may be contained within the larger policy, or separate but referenced by the larger policy.

It is important that the copyright policy integrates with other information use policies within the organisation, and also that other policies do not violate copyright provisions, so the first step is to search for existing policies and documents within your organisation, by searching policy manuals and websites and contacting relevant departments. These departments include the IT department, which generally sets policies for network security and use but may also manage significant intellectual property, such as the organisation's data warehouse, and the public information department, which may manage any organisational trademarks and often has policies for public information, such as guidance on developing and presenting official websites, reports, etc. The organisation's legal counsel will always play a prominent role in developing and approving the copyright policy. If your organisation does not have legal counsel, it is a good idea to solicit legal advice from an intellectual property attorney in the review of your copyright policy.

A copyright policy should address, at a minimum, the following areas:

- *Purpose and goals of the copyright policy.*

Policies are more likely to have organisational acceptance if everyone understands the purpose and value of the policy in the context of the organisation's mission and business model.

- *Ownership of resources created by employees or members of the organisation.*

Universities, in particular, consist of faculty who publish creative and original works through many avenues, including published books and articles, faculty or departmental websites, and web-based lectures and presentations. Every university must decide ownership of rights for the resources created by faculty. Common practice is to cede ownership of rights for published and unpublished works to faculty or to retain ownership but provide a non-exclusive license to faculty to enable them to exploit their own creative works fully. A distinction is often made for works that involve significant use of university resources or that would directly compete with the university's business interests, such as lecture or course material that can be marketed institutionally for reuse, for example in online courses.

Universities will usually retain or share the rights, and thus the exploitation, of course materials, patentable inventions and other commercially exploitable intellectual property created while in the employ of the university and using significant university resources in the creation. Municipal governments and other organisations also create intellectual property, such as reports, courses, websites and other materials. Reports, minutes and other documents produced in the course of organisational business will often be deemed to be works made for hire. The copyright policy will indicate whether the employee can further exploit such works through a license granted by the organisation. A copyright policy should also provide guidance on works created by consultants or contractors, so that departments within the organisation, when engaging a contractor, can successfully address the issue of intellectual property ownership for the reports and other products of the contractor, in any contract or agreement with the contractor.

- *A process for resolving conflicts over ownership.*

No policy can address every circumstance that will arise when individuals within an organisation are creating works of intellect. A procedure needs to be established and documented within the policy to adjudicate any conflicts over ownership of intellectual property. The policy should enable a legally binding way for all parties to air their concerns and to participate equally in a process for resolving conflicts arising from ownership disputes.

- *Use of copyright-protected resources by members of the organisation.*

The copyright policy should provide guidance to members on using copyright-protected resources within the context of the organisation's business model and practises. In a university setting, for example, the copyright policy will address the use of copyright-protected resources in instruction, study and research. The copyright policy should also address the use of organisational resources to use (or misuse) copyright-protected resources, such as the use of the organisation's network to illegally obtain copyright protected resources.

- *Acceptable use of the organisation's intellectual property.*

A copyright policy may address the use by others of the intellectual property created at the organisation. Universities and other complex organisations create a wide range of copyright-protected resources, so an organisation may be hesitant about including 'blanket' provisions concerning the appropriate use of the organisation's intellectual property, except in very broad terms. However, the copyright policy may mandate or strongly recommend that each department or project provide a statement or policy on acceptable use for the intellectual property created within the project or department. It is standard practise to include an acceptable use policy on a website, for example, or to employ a web-accessible license, such as a Creative Commons license, which is discussed elsewhere in this book.

Acceptable use can require attribution, in which case the acceptable use policy may provide guidance on citing works contained within the website or project. The acceptable use policy may limit reuse without additional permissions to members of the organisation or to non-commercial or educational use. The acceptable use policy should always provide contact information and guidance on obtaining permission for further uses of copyright-protected resources beyond those uses specified as being acceptable in the published acceptable use policy. The organisation's copyright policy should provide guidance and cite examples of acceptable use policies for its members who create the intellectual property addressed by the overarching copyright policy.

- *Further guidance on copyright.*

A copyright policy can only address the business model of the organisation as it references copyright in fairly broad brushstrokes. Members of the organisation will need more specific guidance on their unique circumstances, such as 'can I place a photograph of a recently purchased outdoor sculpture on my newsletter?' The policy should reference the relevant national law, authoritative explanatory sources on copyright, and also identify person(s) who can provide further copyright guidance within the organisation.

- *Specific guidance for library services and collections.*

The library will want to provide specific guidance for library services, particularly interlibrary loan; reserves; use of primary resources in the library's special collections or archives; photocopying or scanning of copyright-protected resources; and use of member resources deposited in the library, such as faculty documents or papers deposited in the library's archive or electronic repository. This guidance may be incorporated into the organisation's copyright policy or may reference it. Library-specific policies must not contradict the larger organisation's policy, so it is important that the library plays a significant role in developing the organisation's copyright policy.

- *Identification of the individuals and agencies responsible for creating the copyright policy.*

Acknowledging the creators of the policy serves several objectives: demonstrating appreciation for the work and effort of the participants; demonstrating a broad-based, collaborative approach to policy development; and documenting the range of expertise and authority within the organisation. These acknowledgments will lead to broader acceptance and trust for the policy among the organisation's members.

- *Identification of the individuals or agencies responsible for managing the copyright policy.*

Many organisations may appoint a copyright officer, who may be the organisation's legal counsel or will work closely with legal counsel. Many libraries are beginning to appoint this position, often under titles such as 'Scholarly Communications Librarian', 'Electronic Resources Librarian' or even 'Intellectual Property Librarian'. This person, who may head a department or unit, has responsibility for administering the policy; keeping up to date on current legislation and information uses that may require revisions or exceptions to the policy; and generally providing guidance on appropriate use of information resources within the legal copyright framework. In any event, it is critical within the copyright policy to provide at least one point of contact for the organisation's members who have questions or need further guidance.

- *A process for continued evaluation and revision of the copyright policy.*

Copyright laws and legal interpretations of copyright laws change frequently. Policies also may require revision after they have been put into practise, since exceptions and omissions generally arise with use. A good copyright policy is a living document and should provide opportunities for feedback, questions and ongoing evaluation and revision, on at least a semi-annual basis.

- *Definitions and links to further information.*

It is important to explicitly define terms such as 'copyright-protected resources', 'work made for hire' and 'substantial use of organisational resources'. Links to copyright and other relevant laws, other information use policies within the organisation and tutorials or information sheets on copyright should also be provided. It should be clear that the organisation's copyright policy references, and conforms to, national and local intellectual property law and that it operates within the framework of accepted body of practise for the type of organisation, such as the academic library, public library, archive or corporate domain.

Further information

Sources providing guidance on creating a copyright policy and references for sample copyright policies are provided in the bibliography at the end of this book.

Document rights holders and appropriate use

A significant issue, with serious repercussions for the reuse of copyright-protected information, is the difficulty in identifying and locating rights holders to request permission to reuse resources. Libraries can address this issue in two ways:

- *Documenting the rights holder.*

Libraries are frequently responsible for managing unpublished and published resources created within the organisation. In a university setting, for example, these resources include theses and dissertations; faculty preprints or postprints; lectures; presentations and other unpublished documents; the papers, correspondence and other source documents of prominent persons; official university documents, etc. Care should be taken to document the rights holder, including the most recent contact information and the rights to reuse the resource, as determined by the rights holder in a permissions agreement or as transferred to the library in a deed of gift. Locating rights holders is a significant barrier in the reuse of copyright-protected resources. Although contact information changes, and rights may transfer, the library can at least provide an effective starting point for copyright research. While libraries should obtain the most expansive and durable deeds of gift or licenses for use from copyright holders, they can also play a role in encouraging further impact for resources, by enabling publishers to contact authors for reprint rights, etc. More guidance is provided on documenting the rights holder in Chapter 6.

- *Educating the rights holder.*

The library can also educate the depositor about the importance of his/her copyright-protected resources for future scholarship. Most copyright owners may not give much thought to the fact, or even be aware, that copyright remains in force and effect many years after the creator's death. Libraries have a significant role to play in educating copyright owners in the establishment and negotiation of licenses that allow reuse of resources and in the importance of providing continuing contact information, in the case of address changes or rights ownership transfers, so that the creative work can continue to have impact throughout its useful life. Many creators would appreciate that their work continues to be useful and have impact past its viable commercial life. Librarians have an important role to play for ensuring that creators understand fully their obligations and opportunities to ensure that their works will be useful throughout the copyright protection period.

Scholarly publication, whether book or journal, generally requires a contractual license or transfer of copyright so that the publisher is remunerated for the expense of publication and distribution, A significant issue for academic faculty and others who publish in scholarly journals or with commercial presses is that the agreement with the publisher generally involves a transfer of rights that may not support subsequent republishing or open access deposits. The publisher or the faculty member may also lack records of agreements for published works, particularly for older publications.

Libraries can also encourage authors to register their copyright, or to encourage their publishers to register their copyright, in those countries that provide copyright registration. Registration of copyright increases the likelihood that a rights holder can be identified and contacted, and a copyrighted resource can be republished or otherwise reused and distributed, thus increasing the long-term scholarly impact of the intellectual content.

The Zwolle Group, a collaboration of publishers, authors and university policy-makers worldwide, was formed to define policy and practices, collectively known as the Zwolle principles, to support a balance between publishers and authors to increase equitable access to information. Although the Zwolle Group has completed and archived its work, the Zwolle principles remain a useful tool for evaluating the publishing agreements of scholarly and commercial publishers. The Zwolle principles are available from the SURF Foundation, which sponsored the Zwolle Group.[71] SURF and JISC, two European organisations that support education and research, have created a *Copyright Toolbox* based on the Zwolle principles to provide guidance to both authors and publishers in developing an equitable, balanced license for published works.[72]

A very useful tool for libraries with institutional repositories and for faculty authors is the *SHERPA/RoMEO Publisher Copyright Policies & Self-archiving*. SHERPA is a consortium consisting of UK higher education institutions, the British Library and the Arts & Humanities Data Service (AHDS), which formed collaboratively to support the development of open access repositories. The *SHERPA/RoMEO Publisher Copyright Policies & Self-archiving* is a searchable database of publishers' policies and permissions for self-archiving of scholarly publications by the authors of those publications.[73]

SPARC, the Scholarly Publishing and Academic Resources Coalition, is 'an international alliance of academic and research libraries working to correct imbalances in the scholarly publishing system.'[74] SPARC has developed an author addendum that faculty in all disciplines can append to their publishing agreements to secure further rights for reuse of their articles, including depositing their work in institutional repositories, posting on personal or course websites, etc. SPARC has further launched an author rights initiative to educate authors on their rights to reuse and reproduce their works via SPARC's educational website.[75]

Making copyright-protected works available is not only an issue for the works of researchers, authors and artists. Photographs, correspondence and memorabilia created by individuals and families today are the artifacts of tomorrow's history. Many creators of today's digital creative works and artifacts are sharing their works freely on the web without any knowledge of the copyright status of their work. Other valuable resources, such as photograph albums and correspondence in analog form that are personally cherished today can be useful contributors to the permanent historical and social record tomorrow. However, the copyright on these resources will outlast the physical ability of their creators to manage and share them. Libraries, archives and museums can play an important role in securing availability of these artifacts for future generations. The New Jersey Digital Highway, the state-wide cultural heritage portal for museums, libraries and archives, provides guidance to the citizens of New Jersey on documenting and making available their personal photographs and artifacts for the edification of future generations of information seekers.[76]

Many libraries are engaged in digitising resources that may fall into a 'gray area' in terms of copyright protection. Published resources with a clear copyright date, within the timeframe of copyright protection, are clearly copyright protected and require permission from the rights holder to digitise and distribute. Unpublished, undated primary resources with no evident commercial value may or may not be in the public domain. In some cases, the works are of unknown provenance and in other cases the creator may be known but unlocatable. Some countries provide policy and practise for orphan works, such as the Copyright Board of Canada's process to obtain a license to use works by unlocatable authors. In many cases, a library may wish to establish a risk management strategy for exploiting unpublished primary source materials with no locatable author. This risk management strategy is not a guarantee that the library will be within copyright compliance if the library is found to be infringing the rights of a copyright holder. However, the risk management strategy will at least demonstrate a good faith effort to locate the copyright holder and to make available only materials with unlocatable ownership and no evident commercial value, thus minimising any economic harm to the copyright holder. A risk management strategy should include the following:

- *A continuum documenting the range of risk to the digitising institution for copyright infringement —*

from resources that are in the public domain and can be digitised and freely distributed, through resources of uncertain parentage or copyright protection status, with no evident commercial value. The risk continuum should ensure that any work of doubtful copyright status is thoroughly reviewed before a decision is made to digitise and make it further available. It goes without saying that no work should be exploited for economic profit without a clear transfer of rights to the library, written permission from the rights holder for this use, or a determination that the work is in the public domain.

- *A documented practise for locating copyright holders and contacting them for permission to reuse the work.*

Every effort to identify, locate and contact a rights holder and obtain permission or a deed of gift to reuse a work should be standardised and documented so that the organisation develops a consistent and standardised methodology to demonstrate reasonable effort in obtaining permission and so that the organisation knows the time and effort generally required for permissions, for planning current and future digital projects. Metadata for documenting permission requests is discussed more fully in Chapter 6.

- *Licenses and deeds of gift should be employed whenever possible to obtain rights to digitise and make available copyright-protected works.*

These licenses and deeds of gift should be linked to rights metadata for each digitised collection and object to provide an evidentiary chain of permissions or ownership rights transfer. The term of copyright is long, so libraries have an obligation to provide a rights ownership chain of evidence for future scholars and researchers. Copyright ownership can only be transferred in writing, so the original signed documents should also be retained, with a clear link to the digitised documents.

- *A published copyright policy or disclaimer notice on any website providing access to one or more digital resources that may be copyright protected.*

If an organisation decides to digitise and make available a resource with uncertain copyright status or an unlocatable rights holder, the copyright policy or notice should encourage users with information about the creation of the resource to contact the organisation with this information. A copyright policy page should be provided for any website with digitised resources. The copyright policy page should provide information about the organisation's policy for resources with uncertain provenance or rights, documenting that the institution has made a good faith effort to locate the rights holders for all resources and encouraging website viewers to participate in this effort. In addition, the copyright policy page should also address the usage of external web links appearing in the website and provide guidance, such as attribution and contact information, for use of the website's copyright-protected resources by others. Good exemplars of copyright notices are often provided by national libraries, for example the Library of Congress[77] and the British Library.[78]

For US resources, as the many changes to copyright law are not retroactive, a risk management strategy requires being able to analyze the likelihood that a work is copyright protected, based on its age and circumstances of publication. This will be an issue for other countries that also do not apply provisions of copyright law retroactively. Many charts for accessing copyright status in the US are available. Two excellent charts available via the Web are Peter Hirtle's *Copyright Term and the Public Domain in the United States*[79] and Mary Minow's *Library Digitization Projects, US Copyrighted Works that Have Expired into the Public Domain.*[80]

Obtain permission to digitise and distribute copyright-protected resources

If the work is not in the public domain, and the creator or copyright holder can be identified, you will want to obtain a license for permission to digitise and make the work publicly available, or a deed of gift transferring ownership and rights for the resource to your organisation, to enable the library to reproduce and distribute in the method and manner of its choosing.

There are two major issues with seeking permission:

- *Copyright holders are difficult to find*, particularly if the creator of a work is deceased and the heirs must be located. Registration is no longer required, and older registration and copyright renewal records may not be available online. Some countries, such as Australia, have no copyright registration system. Agreements between authors and publishers may be lost, and even if the author and publisher can be located, it is quite possible that neither party knows who retains the copyright for a published work.
- Even when copyright holders can be identified, *contacting them and receiving a response in a reasonable time frame can be difficult*. Multiple letters may be required before a response is received, and then the request may be denied or the response may be too ambiguous to be useful. Given the difficulty of locating and corresponding with copyright holders, it is critical that the permissions request be carefully written with a well-crafted deed of gift or permission license included.

Locating copyright holders can be very difficult. For a published work, guidance can often be found on the title page and verso of a text, or on the container or credit frames for an audiovisual work. The publisher can often provide guidance on current copyright ownership for a work, if the publisher has complete records or is still in existence. Many publishers have disappeared or were subsumed by other publishers. It can require significant research just to identify the current publisher. If the author holds the rights, the publisher can sometimes provide contact information for the author or author's agent. Webmasters can usually provide guidance on rights for materials published on a website. For photographs, the photographer or firm is generally the rights holder. Collective rights agencies, such as the Copyright Clearance Center in the United States, will sometimes provide copyright ownership research in addition to rights clearances.

Most governmental agencies responsible for administering copyright provide guidance on locating copyright holders. These agencies may also provide copyright search services, generally for a fee. Many copyright collective agencies – within specific countries and internationally – provide permissions and licenses to use copyright-protected resources for a wide range of rights holders. Check the web pages for the agency responsible for administering copyright in the country where the resource was created or published for guidance in locating the copyright holder. Government agencies, such as the Canadian Copyright Office and the US Copyright Office, provide searchable databases of registered copyrights, an added incentive to register any copyrightable works. Audiovisual works, particularly if commercially produced, may include watermarks that identify the provenance and rights ownership. Watermarks are discussed in detail in Chapter 7.

Further information

Sources providing guidance on identifying copyright holders and obtaining permission to use copyrighted resources, including sample permission letters and deeds of gift, are provided in the bibliography at the end of this book.

Basic 'rules of thumb' for the permissions request letter:

- Be aware that obtaining permission to reuse a resource can require a significant amount of time, even when the rights holder can be identified and easily located. Determine well in advance of a project that rights for a resource will be needed and begin the permissions process very early in, preferably well in advance of, the digital project.
- Be very clear about the resource to be digitised. Provide a full citation, if possible, including any identification numbers such as ISBN, ISSN or ISAN, or otherwise describe the work so that the identity of the work is unambiguous.
- Describe the context of use – current and potential. Describe the digital project or collection that will include the resource. If this is an existing project, provide a link to the website for the project or collection. Copyright holders are most likely to grant permission to copy and distribute resources if the use is non-commercial and educational and particularly if they can evaluate the impact of the potential use in advance.
- Be clear about the usage rights requested – whether public distribution, excerpting, adapting, translating, etc. Being clear about the nature and context of use can increase the likelihood that your organisation receives the permissions it is requesting.
- Provide a deed of gift or permission license that the copyright holder can complete, sign and return.
- Provide full contact information, including telephone number and email, so that you can address any questions or concerns the rights holder may have.

- Provide a self-addressed, stamped envelope for return of the license or deed of gift.

In order to reproduce and distribute a work, a library or archive must obtain either a **deed of gift**, which transfers all rights ownership to the organisation, or a **license**, which provides permissions for reproduction and distribution, preferably unconditional and permanent, but does not transfer rights ownership. Institutional repositories, for example, will frequently require a permanent, non-exclusive license of rights but will not require that copyright be deeded to the repository or to its parent organisation.

Basic 'rules of thumb' for a deed of gift or permission license to be signed by the rights holder:

- Clearly identify the resource to be digitised. Provide a full citation, if possible, or otherwise describe the work so that the identity of the work, including its physical instantiation, is unambiguous.
- Unambiguously state the terms of the deed of gift or license. Identify whether physical ownership and copyright are being permanently transferred from the donor to the organisation or whether a permanent or time-bounded license to reuse the resource is being sought.
- Include all current or future reuse of the resource in the deed of gift or permission license. Do not use limiting terminology that restricts a resource to a current technology (e.g. web access) or current use (e.g. for use in the online exhibit, 'The Italians of Jersey City'), unless the rights holder explicitly requires such limitations. Although you want to explain the current context of use in your permissions request letter, in order to obtain permanent rights to disseminate a copyrighted work, you want to be very inclusive (e.g. 'the right to make available

to anyone in any media now known or later developed') and not tie the hands of future archivists and librarians for continuing to make the resource available.

- Ask the copyright holder to assert that he or she is the copyright owner and is legally able to grant the right to digitally reproduce and disseminate the resource in question. You may want to ask the copyright holder to indemnify the organisation against any legal remedies for copyright infringement, if an accusation of infringement is successfully pursued. This indemnification is unnecessary in most cases, unless the resource has clear commercial value; the identity of the rights holder is questionable; or the organisation has paid a fee to purchase duplication and distribution rights.
- If the work includes multiple creators, be sure to identify the role and contribution of the copyright holder addressed by this deed of gift or license. For example, a work may include written text by one creator and illustrations by another. Each rights holder must generally provide separate permissions, and the deed of gift or license must clearly indicate what portion of the work is addressed as well as the role of the rights holder (e.g. 'illustrator') providing the license for reuse.
- Be clear about the continuing rights of the copyright holder to reuse the resource. You will have a better chance of securing permissions if you are requesting the **non-exclusive** right to digitise and disseminate a resource, so that the copyright holder can continue to exercise his or her rights to copy, distribute and otherwise exploit the resource. You can either request a permanent non-exclusive license to use the resource, or request a transfer of all rights but grant the copyright holder in return a non-exclusive permanent license to reuse the resource.

- Depending on the nature of the resource, you may want to offer attribution to the donor or copyright holder for the resource. Most copyright holders want attribution, and it is sound practise to provide attribution, both in metadata and in the web display of the resource. The project website or metadata should also provide provenance, context and guidance for citing the resource for users and maintain records of copyright ownership for ongoing rights management of the resource. Some copyright holders will not want attribution, so you will probably want to offer this as a 'check off' option on the deed or license.
- If the rights holder wants attribution, ask for guidance about how the rights holder would like the work to be attributed and cited.
- Your deed of gift or license is a legal document and should be prepared by, or under the guidance of, legal counsel – the organisation's intellectual property attorney or an intellectual property attorney employed for this purpose. The deed of gift/license should be digitised with access properly restricted to library staff, to protect the privacy of the donor. The original must also be retained in a secure, documented location for future reference. The digital surrogate and the location of the original document should be documented in metadata to maintain the evidentiary chain.

A deed of gift or license may be in physical form, to be signed by the rights holder, or in digital form. If in digital form, use at least one method of verification to ensure that the license was granted by the rights holder. This can involve a digital signature, digital certificate or other verifiable authentication practise. Authentication practises are discussed in detail in Chapter 5. The digital license should be stored in a digital audit trail, to document that the rights holder did sign or 'opt in' for the license and to document the terms of the license, as archives and libraries will change the terms of their licenses and agreements over time. Digital licenses should have assigned version numbers and dates, so that the library and archive can document their digital licensing terms and practices over time.

Involvement in the larger rights arena

Libraries should actively support open access efforts in local, national and multinational arenas, from encouraging creators within their organisations to provide the broadest possible access to their creations to participating in consortia that promote open access, such as the Open Content Alliance.

Most countries are involved in ongoing copyright treaty development, particularly under the auspices of the WIPO. In addition, national laws are often proposed to address intellectual property rights that will have a direct impact on the library's ability to manage and make available copyright-protected resources to its users. Libraries should be active in the rights arena, educating government representatives on the impacts of copyright legislation; lobbying for or against relevant legislation; responding to requests for comments for proposed legislation; and ensuring that the library's users and other stakeholders are aware of and responsive to important legislative proposals. Library organisations, particularly at the national level, frequently provide updates, including websites, email lists and RSS feeds (web feeds of frequently updated content that require a feed reader to view), on important copyright issues. They can also provide opportunities for libraries to become actively involved in copyright issues of national importance.

More than most legislation, copyright legislation has a direct impact on the library's business model. It is important for every librarian to be aware of proposed or pending legislation and to work within the context of national and international library and archives organisations to specify, respond to and lobby for needed legislation. Rights holders in the commercial arena have been aggressive in their efforts to frame the copyright debate. But copyright is intended to be a balance between the needs of the creator to exploit his/her work and the needs of society to profit from the wide availability of information. Libraries and archives are critical representatives for the public good, and playing an active role in both international and national legislation can help to restore the balance between the rights of creators and the rights of society.

Legislation can include changes to term limits or use exceptions, such as the expansion of the fair dealing exceptions. Also critical but often overlooked is the need for mandated record keeping and records availability by national agencies, so that copyright registrations may be easily searched and rights holders readily identified and contacted. Libraries and archives understand the mechanics and the frustrations of identifying and locating rights holders – an issue that will only intensify with the longer-term limits that are becoming the norm for many countries. Libraries and archives should collaborate with national agencies and publishers on strategies to ensure the long-term availability of rights-holder information as another avenue for ensuring access to the broadest range of information for the public good.

Notes and references

1. *Berne Convention for the Protection of Literary and Artistic Works of September 9, 1886, completed at Paris on May 4, 1896, revised at Berlin on November 13, 1908, completed at Berne on March 20, 1914, revised at Rome on June 2, 1928, at Brussels on June 26, 1948, at Stockholm on July 14, 1967,*

and at Paris on July 24, 1971, and amended on September 28, 1979. Geneva: World Intellectual Property Organization. Amended 28 September 1979. Last accessed 18 March 2008. *http://www.wipo.int/treaties/en/ip/berne/trtdocs_wo001.html*

2. *Title 17 United States Code*. Washington, DC: US House of Representatives. Last accessed 20 March 2008. *http://uscode.house.gov/download/title_17.shtml*
3. Sheldon & Mak Inc. (1989) *Coping with the Berne Convention*. Pasadena, CA: Sheldon, Mak, Rose, & Anderson PC. Last accessed 18 March 2008. *http://www.usip.com/articles/bernec.htm*
4. *Universal Copyright Convention*, as revised at Paris on 24 July 1971, with Appendix Declaration relating to Article XVII and Resolution concerning Article XI 1971. Paris: United Nations Educational, Scientific and Cultural Organization, 24 July 1971. Last accessed 18 March 2008. *http://portal.unesco.org/en/ev.php-URL_ID=15241&URL_DO=DO_ TOPIC&URL_SECTION=201.html*
5. *WIPO Copyright Treaty, adopted in Geneva on 20 December 1996*. Geneva: World Intellectual Property Organization, Last accessed 18 March 2008. *http://www.wipo.int/treaties/en/ip/wct/trtdocs_wo033.html#P66_786\5*
6. *International Convention for the Protection of Performers, Producers of Phonograms, and Broadcasting Organizations*. Done at Rome on 26 October 1961. Geneva: World Intellectual Property Organization. Last accessed 18 March 2008. *http://www.wipo.int/treaties/en/ip/rome/trtdocs_wo024.html*
7. *WIPO Performances and Phonograms Treaty*, Adopted in Geneva on 20 December 1996. Geneva: WIPO. Last accessed 18 March 2008. *http://www.wipo.int/treaties/en/ip/wppt/trtdocs_wo034.html*
8. *Trade-Related Aspects of Intellectual Property Rights*, signed in Marrakesh, on 15 April 1994. Geneva: World Trade Organization. Last accessed 18 March 2008. *http://www.wto.org/english/docs_e/legal_e/27-trips_01_e.htm*
9. World Trade Organization. *Understanding the WTO: The Agreements, Intellectual Property: Protection and Enforcement*. Geneva: World Trade Organization. Last accessed 18 March 2008. *http://www.wto.org/english/thewto_e/whatis_e/tif_e/agrm7 _e.htm*

10. Wikipedia. *Agreement on Trade-Related Aspects of Intellectual Property Rights*. St. Petersburg, FL: Wikimedia Foundation, Inc. Last modified 6 March 2008. Last accessed 18 March 2008. *http://en.wikipedia.org/wiki/TRIPS*
11. World Trade Organization. *Doha Development Agenda: Negotiations, Implementation and Development.* Geneva: World Trade Organization. Last accessed 18 March 2008. *http://www.wto.org/english/tratop_e/dda_e/dda_e.htm*
12. World Trade Organization. *The Doha Declaration Explained.* Geneva: World Trade Organization. Last accessed 18 March 2008. *http://www.wto.org/english/tratop_e/dda_e/dohaexplained_e.htm*
13. World Intellectual Property Organization, Standing Committee on Copyright and Related Rights. (2007) *Non-paper on the WIPO Treaty on the Protection of Broadcasting Organizations.* Geneva: WIPO. Last accessed 18 March 2008. *http://www.wipo.int/edocs/mdocs/sccr/en/sccr_s2/sccr_s2_paper1.pdf*
14. Library Copyright Alliance. (2007) *Library Concerns with the WIPO Broadcast Treaty*. Library Copyright Alliance. Last accessed 18 March 2008. *http://www.keionline.org/misc-docs/librarycopyrightalliance.pdf*
15. World Intellectual Property Organization. (2008) 'Member States Consider Future Work of Copyright Committee.' *WIPO News & Events.* Geneva: World Intellectual Property Organization. Last accessed 18 March 2008. *http://www.wipo.int/pressroom/en/articles/2008/article_0013.html*
16. *Directive 2001/29/EC of the European Parliament and of the Council of 22 May 2001 on the harmonisation of certain aspects of copyright and related rights in the information society.* Luxembourg: EUR-Lex, EU Publications Office. Last accessed 19 March 2008. *http://europa.eu.int/smartapi/cgi/sga_doc?smartapi!celexapi!prod!CELEXnumdoc&lg=EN&numdoc=32001L0029&model=guichett*
17. European Commission. *The EU Single Market, Fewer Barriers, More Opportunities, Documents*. Last update 26 April 2007. Last accessed 21 March 2008. *http://ec.europa.eu/internal_market/copyright/documents/documents_en.htm#directives*

18. UK Intellectual Property Office. (2006) *Copyright Acquis*. Newport: UK Intellectual Property Office. Last accessed 19 March 2008. *http://www.ipo.gov.uk/policy/policy-issues/policy-issues-copyright/policy-issues-copyright-acquis.htm*
19. European Commission, *The EU Single Market, Fewer Barriers, More Opportunities, Studies*. Last update 13 February 2008. Last accessed 19 March 2008. *http://ec.europa.eu/internal_market/copyright/studies/studies_en.htm*
20. Europa. (2008) 'Performing artists – no longer be the "poor cousins" of the music business' – Charlie McCreevy.' *Europa Press Releases*. Brussels: Europa. Last accessed 19 March 2008. *http://europa.eu/rapid/pressReleasesAction.do?reference=IP/08/240&format=HTML&aged=0&language=EN&guiLanguage=en*
21. Mitchell, Henry C., Jr. (2005) *The Intellectual Commons: Toward an Ecology of Intellectual Property* (Lexington Studies in Social, Political and Legal Philosophy). Lanham, MD: Lexington Books.
22. *Statutory Instrument 2003 no 2498: The Copyright and Related Rights Regulations 2003*. London: Office of Public Sector Information, Prepared 3 October 2003. Last accessed 19 March 2008. *http://www.opsi.gov.uk/si/si2003/20032498.htm*
23. *UK Copyright Service* [home page]. Didcot, UK: UK Copyright Service, c2008 Last accessed 19 March 2008 *http://www.copyrightservice.co.uk/*
24. *Copyright Designs and Patents Act 1988 (c.48), Part I, Copyright*. London: Office of Public Sector Information, c1988. Prepared 20 September 2000. Last Accessed 19 March 2008. *http://www.opsi.gov.uk/acts/acts1988/Ukpga_19880048_en_1.htm*
25. *Statutory Instrument 1997 no. 3032, The Copyright and Rights in Databases Regulations 1997*. London: Office of Public Sector Information, prepared 13 January 1998. Last accessed 19 March 2008. *http://www.opsi.gov.uk/SI/si1997/ 19973032.htm#end*
26. Dunning, Alastair. *Copyright and Other Rights Issues in Digitisation*. London: Arts and Humanities Data Service. Content updated 28 March 2006. Last accessed 19 March 2008. *http://www.ahds.ac.uk/creating/information-papers/copyright-introduction/index.htm*

27. UK Intellectual Property Office. (2006) *Performers' Rights.* Newport: UK Intellectual Property Office. Reviewed 22 September 2006. Last accessed 19 March 2008. *http://www.ipo.gov.uk/copy/c-claim/c-otherprotect/c-otherprotect-performer.htm*
28. UK Intellectual Property Office. (2007) *Copyright, Rights in Performances, Publication Right, Database Right: Unofficial, Consolidated Text of UK Legislation to 3 May 2007.* Newport: UK Intellectual Property Office. Last accessed 19 March 2008. *http://www.ipo.gov.uk/copy/cdpact1988.pdf*
29. UK Intellectual Property Office. (2006) *Fair Dealing.* Newport: UK Intellectual Property Office. Last accessed 19 March 2008. *http://www.ipo.gov.uk/copy/c-manage/c-useenforce/c-useenforce-use/c-useenforce-use-exception/c-useenforce-use-exception-fairdealing.htm*
30. Cornish, Graham P. (2004) *Guidelines on the Recent Changes to Copyright Law.* London: Museums Copyright Group/The Libraries and Archives Copyright Alliance. Last accessed 19 March 2008. *http://www.museumscopyright.org.uk/copyreg.pdf*
31. Copyright Licensing Agency. *Find the Right Licence.* London: Copyright Licensing Agency. Last accessed 19 March 2008. *http://www.cla.co.uk/licenceinformation_typesoflicenceavailable.php*
32. Copyright Licensing Agency. *Library Sticker Scheme.* London: Copyright Licensing Agency. Last accessed 19 March 2008. *http://www.cla.co.uk/Library_sticker_licence.php*
33. UK Intellectual Property Office. (2007) *About the Copyright Tribunal.* Newport: UK Intellectual Property Office. Last accessed 19 March 2008. *http://www.patent.gov.uk/ctribunal/ctribunal-about.htm*
34. *Agency for the Legal Deposit Libraries.* [home page] Diweddarwyd, UK: LIGC/NLW. Last updated December 2007. Last accessed 19 March 2008. *http://www.llgc.org.uk/aldl/*
35. Gowers, Andrew. (2006) *Gowers Review of Intellectual Property.* Norwich: Her Majesty's Stationery Office. Last accessed 21 March 2008. *http://www.hm-treasury.gov.uk/media/6/E/pbr06_gowers_report_755.pdf*

36. British Library. (2006) *Intellectual Property: a Balance, the British Library IP Manifesto*. London: British Library. Last accessed 19 March 2008. *http://www.bl.uk/news/pdf/ipmanifesto.pdf*
37. UK Intellectual Property Office. (2007) *Taking Forward the Gowers Review of Intellectual Property: Proposed Changes to Copyright Exceptions*. Newport: UK Intellectual Property Office. Last accessed 19 March 2008. *http://www.ipo.gov.uk/consult-copyrightexceptions.pdf*
38. UK Intellectual Property Office. (2008) *Proposed Changes to Copyright Exceptions*. Newport: UK Intellectual Property Office. Last accessed 19 March 2008. *http://www.ipo.gov.uk/about/about-consult/about-formal/about-formal-current/consult-copyrightexceptions.htm%20*
39. Australian Government, Department of Foreign Affairs and Trade. *Australia-United States Free Trade Agreement: Intellectual Property.* Sydney: Department of Foreign Affairs and Trade. Last accessed 19 March 2008. *http://www.dfat.gov.au/trade/negotiations/us_fta/outcomes/08_intellectual_property.html*
40. Australian Copyright Council. (2008) *Duration of Copyright.* (Information Sheet G023v14) Strawberry Hills, NSW: Australian Copyright Council. Last accessed 19 March 2008. *http://www.copyright.org.au/publications/G023.pdf*
41. Australian Copyright Council. (2007) *An Introduction to Copyright in Australia.* (Information Sheet G010v15) Strawberry Hills, NSW: Australian Copyright Council. Last accessed 19 March 2008. *http://www.copyright.org.au/publications/G010.pdf*
42. Australian Copyright Council. (2007) *Fair Dealing.* (Information Sheet G079v04) Strawberry Hills, NSW: Australian Copyright Council. Last accessed 19 March 2008. *http://www.copyright.org.au/publications/G079.pdf*
43. Australian Copyright Council. (2007) *Research or Study* (Information Sheet G53v07) Strawberry Hills, NSW: Australian Copyright Council. Last accessed 19 March 2008. *www.copyright.org.au/pdf/acc/infosheets_pdf/G053.pdf*
44. Australian Copyright Council. (2006) *Libraries: an Introduction to Copyright* (Information Sheet G049v09)

Strawberry Hills, NSW: Australian Copyright Council. Last accessed 19 March 2008. *http://www.copyright.org.au/publications/G049.pdf*

45. *Copyright Amendment (Digital Agenda) Act 2000 No. 110, 2000.* An Act to amend the Copyright Act 1968, and for related purposes Australian Government, Attorney-General's Office: ComLaw, Commonwealth of Australia Law, prepared date 2 August 2002. Last accessed 19 March 2008. *http://www.comlaw.gov.au/ComLaw/Legislation/ActCompilation1.nsf/0/DD0BF9419056F596CA256F7100564D03?OpenDocument*
46. Australian Copyright Council. (2007) *Copyright Amendment Act 2006* (Information Sheet G096v06) Strawberry Hills, NSW: Australian Copyright Council. Last accessed 19 March 2008. *www.copyright.org.au/pdf/acc/infosheets_pdf/g096.pdf*
47. Australian Copyright Council. (2008) *Private Use: Copying: Time-, Format-, and Space-Shifting.* (Information sheet G097v01) Strawberry Hills, NSW: Australian Copyright Council. Last accessed 19 March 2008. *http://www.copyright.org.au/g097.pdf*
48. *Copyright Act, R.S., 1985, c. C-42 Copyright Act.* Act current to 6 February 2008. Ottawa: Department of Justice. Last updated 17 March 2008. Last accessed 19 March 2008. *http://laws.justice.gc.ca/en/ShowTdm/cs/C-42*
49. Canadian Intellectual Property Office. *A Guide to Copyrights: Copyright Protection.* Gatineau, Quebec: Canadian Intellectual Property Office. Last modified 12 March 2008. Last accessed 19 March 2008. *http://www.ic.gc.ca/sc_mrksv/cipo/cp/copy_gd_protect-e.html#11*
50. Copyright Board of Canada. *Copyright Collective Societies.* Ottawa: Copyright Board of Canada. Updated 9 January 2008. Last accessed 19 March 2008. *http://www.cb-cda.gc.ca/societies/index-e.html*
51. Access Copyright. (2003) *2003 AUCC Agreement.* Toronto: Access Copyright. Last accessed 19 March 2008. *http://www.carl-abrc.ca/projects/copyright/pdf/2003_licence-e.pdf*
52. Library and Archives Canada. *Legal Deposit: Preserving Canada's Published Heritage.* Ottawa: Library and Archives, Canada. Created 26 September 2001. Last updated 3 January

2007. Last accessed 19 March 2008. *http://www.collectionscanada.ca/6/25/s25-200-e.html*

53. Copyright Board of Canada, *Unlocatable Copyright Owners*. Ottawa: Copyright Board of Canada. Updated 7 July 2001. Last accessed 19 March 2008. *http://www.cb-cda.gc.ca/unlocatable/brochure-e.html*
54. Anderson, Nate. (2007) *DMCA-Style Laws Coming to Canada, Switzerland.* Ars Technica. Last accessed 19 March 2008. *http://arstechnica.com/news.ars/post/20071129-dmca-style-laws-come-to-canada-switzerland.html?rel*
55. *Copyright Act 1994: 1994 No. 143.* (2004) Wellington, NZ: Parliament of New Zealand. Last accessed 20 March 2008. *http://interim.legislation.govt.nz/libraries/contents/om_isapi.dll?clientID=81126&infobase=pal_statutes.nfo&jump=a1994-143&softpage=DOC*
56. *Copyright Council of New Zealand* [home page]. (2006) Parnell, Auckland: Copyright Council of New Zealand. Last accessed 20 March 2008. *http://www.copyright.org.nz/*
57. *Copyright (New Technologies and Performers' Rights) Amendment.* (2007) Wellington: House of Representatives. Last accessed 20 March 2008. *http://www.parliament.nz/NR/rdonlyres/FCCEC06B-15EA-41D0-8169-438F48FA83A4/59845/DBSCH_SCR_3848_5268.pdf*
58. United States. *Constitution of the United States.* Washington, DC: National Archives and Records Administration. Last accessed 20 March 2008. *http://www.archives.gov/exhibits/charters/constitution_transcript.html*
59. US Copyright Office. *eCO Beta-Test Announcement.* Washington, DC: US Copyright Office. Revised 19 March 2008. Last accessed 20 March 2008. *http://www.copyright.gov/eco/beta-announce.html*
60. Besek, June M. *Copright Issues Relevant to Digital Preservation and Dissemination of Pre-1972 Commercial Sound Recordings by Libraries and Archives.* Washington, DC: Council on Library and Information Resources and Library of Congress, December 2005.
61. US Copyright Office. *How to Investigate the Copyright Status of a Work.* (Circular 22) Washington, DC: US Copyright Office. Revised July 2006. Last accessed 20 March 2008. *http://www.copyright.gov/circs/circ22.html*

62. American Library Association. (2007) *DMCA: Digital Millennium Copyright Act.* Chicago: American Library Association. Last accessed 20 March 2008. *http://www.ala.org/ala/washoff/woissues/copyrightb/federallegislation/dmca/dmcadigitalmillenium.cfm*
63. US Copyright Office. *Statement of the Librarian of Congress Relating to Section 1201 Rulemaking.* Washington, DC: US Copyright Office. Revised 22 November 2006. Last accessed 21 March 2008. *http://www.copyright.gov/1201/docs/2006_statement.html*
64. American Library Association. (2008) *Distance Education and the TEACH Act.* Chicago: American Library Association. Last accessed 20 March 2008. *http://www.ala.org/ala/washoff/woissues/copyrightb/distanceed/distanceeducation.cfm*
65. Register of Copyrights (United States). (2006) *Report on Orphan Works: A Report of the Register of Copyrights.* Washington, DC: US Copyright Office. Last accessed 20 March 2008. *http://www.copyright.gov/orphan/orphan-report-full.pdf*
66. (S.2913, *A Bill to Provide a Limitation on Judicial Remedies in Copyright Infringement Cases Involving Orphan Works) S.2913.* (2008) Washington, DC: Thomas, Library of Congress. Last accessed 29 April 2008. *http://thomas.loc.gov/cgi-bin/bdquery/D?d110:46:./temp/~bdVLwe::|/bss/d110query.html|*
67. (*H.R.1201, the Freedom and Innovation Revitalizing U.S. Entrepreneurship Act of 2007*) *H.R.1201* (2007) Washington, DC: Thomas, Library of Congress. Last accessed 20 March 2008. *http://thomas.loc.gov/cgi-bin/bdquery/z?d110:HR01201:@@@L&summ2=m&*
68. (S.522, *Intellectual Property Rights Enforcement Act*) *S.522.* (2007) Washington, DC: Thomas, Library of Congress. Last accessed 21 March 2008. *http://thomas.loc.gov/cgi-bin/bdquery/z?d110:SN00522:@@@L&summ2=m&*
69. (*H.R.4279, Prioritizing Resources and Organization for Intellectual Property Act of 2007*) *H.R.4279.* (2007) Washington, DC: Thomas, Library of Congress. Last accessed 30 April 2008. *http://thomas.loc.gov/cgi-bin/query/D?c110:2:./temp/~c110BDDXlW::*

70. National Institutes of Health. *Revised Policy on Enhancing Public Access to Archived Publications Resulting from NIH-Funded Research: Notice Number: NOT-OD-08-033*. Bethesda, MD: National Institutes of Health. Release date 11 January 2008. Last accessed 20 March 2008. *http://grants.nih.gov/grants/guide/notice-files/NOT-OD-08-033.html*
71. SURF. 'Zwolle Principles' *Copyright Management for Scholarship*. Utrecht, The Netherlands: SURF. Last update July 2006. Last accessed 21 March 2008. *http://www.surf.nl/copyright/zwolle_principles.php*
72. SURF and JISC. *Copyright Toolbox*. Utrecht, The Netherlands: SURF Foundation. Last accessed 21 March 2008. *http://www.surf.nl/copyrighttoolbox/*
73. SHERPA. (2006) 'SHERPA/RoMEO Publisher Copyright Policies & Self-archiving' *SHERPA, Opening Access to Research* [home page] University Park, Nottinghamshire, UK: University of Nottingham. Last accessed 21 March 2008. *http://www.sherpa.ac.uk/romeo.php*
74. SPARC. (2007) 'About' *SPARC, the Scholarly Publishing & Academic Resources Coalition* [home page]. Washington, DC: SPARC. Last accessed 21 March 2008. *http://www.arl.org/sparc/about/index.html*
75. SPARC. (2007) 'Resources for Authors' *SPARC, the Scholarly Publishing & Academic Resources Coalition* [home page]. Washington, DC: SPARC. Last accessed 21 March 2008. *http://www.arl.org/sparc/author/*
76. New Jersey Digital Highway. *Your Personal Story: Document and Preserve Your Family's History.* New Brunswick, NJ: New Jersey Digital Highway. Last updated 19 January 2007. Last accessed 21 March 2008. *http://www.njdigitalhighway.org/personal_story_ever.php*
77. Library of Congress. (2006) *Legal.* Washington, DC. Last accessed 21 March 2008. *http://www.loc.gov/homepage/ legal.html*
78. British Library. *British Library Website Copyright Statement.* London. Last accessed 21 March 2008. *http://www.bl.uk/copyrightstatement.html*
79. Hirtle, Peter. (2007) *Copyright Term and the Public Domain in the United States*. Ithaca, NY: Cornell University Library.

Last updated 1 January 2008. Last accessed 21 March 2008. *http://www.copyright.cornell.edu/training/Hirtle_Public_Domain.htm*

80. Minow, Mary. *Library Digitization Projects: US Copyrighted Works that have Expired into the Public Domain.* Los Altos, CA: LibraryLaw. Revised 15 April 2004. Last accessed 21 March 2008. *http://www.librarylaw.com/DigitizationTable.htm*

3

Privacy and other rights

This chapter addresses other rights – legal and ethical – beyond copyright that must be considered by libraries in the context of DRM. I begin with intellectual property rights that are complementary to copyright.

Related rights

Related rights concern the rights of entities that contribute in some form to a copyrighted work but are not identified as the creator. Related rights are also called neighboring rights and are sometimes explicitly addressed in copyright law, and in other cases are addressed in national law, local law or contractually. Related rights broadly include:

- *Contributors to the content of a copyright-protected work*. These contributors include the creators of underlying works, such as the composer of a musical score in a cinematographic work, the agents involved in sharing the work, particularly broadcasters and producers, and agents contributing to the work, such as actors, musicians or dancers in a performance work. Rights of producers and performers are explicitly supported in copyright treaties such as the *International Convention for the Protection of Performers, Producers of Phonograms and Broadcasting Organisations* (Rome Treaty) and the WPPT (*WIPO Performances and Phonograms Treaty*), particularly the right for performers and producers to authorise live performances to be fixed as phonograms, broadcast or otherwise publicly shared, and the right of producers to control the rebroadcast or other public sharing of phonograms. The rights of broadcasters are currently under further consideration in the forthcoming WIPO *Treaty on the Protection of Broadcasting Organizations*.

- *Packagers and disseminators of a copyright-protected work, including the publisher*. In the UK, for example, the typographic arrangement of a work is protected by copyright for a term of 25 years. UK copyright law also provides a publications right for a term of 25 years for anyone publishing an unpublished work that is no longer copyright protected. The intellectual property rights of producers of phonograms, as noted above, are explicitly protected in the Rome Convention and WPPT. As of this writing, WIPO is currently drafting the WIPO *Treaty on the Protection of Broadcasting Organizations* that would address the rights of broadcasters to control the rebroadcast and reproduction of broadcasts. More information is provided in Chapter 2.

Related rights vary by country. Treaties that address related rights, such as the WPPT, can be ambiguous about whether and how remuneration must be provided to performers, producers or both, often leaving such decisions to member states. Related rights are complicated by the fact that contracts may address the remuneration (residuals or royalties) paid for performances, scripts, sound tracks and other underlying or contributory rights within a work. Publishers and broadcasters may negotiate the transfer of a creator's rights as part of a contract to publish, broadcast or otherwise distribute a work. Underlying rights for musical scores within a moving image are particularly complex, as these underlying rights are generally separate from the cinematographic resource and often must be separately negotiated with a music licensing agency for the score itself and with the producers and also sometimes the performers for the recording and the performance that is fixed in the recording.

Libraries should identify the underlying works in a complex work and be prepared to negotiate reproduction and access permissions, beginning at the highest level and working down. Rights holders at each level of the work may be helpful in identifying related rights holders and providing contact information. Licensing agencies are another useful source for identifying the rights holders for underlying works, in particular. In some cases, licensing agencies may be authorised to provide public performance or reproduction rights for all entities with rights in the work. Rights metadata should document all the rights holders of a work and their roles in contributing to the work. Rights metadata for related rights is discussed further in Chapter 6.

Patent

The European Commission, in its *Bio-glossary*, defines a patent as 'a government grant of temporary monopoly rights on innovative processes and products.'[1] Patent is defined in Wikipedia as 'a set of exclusive rights granted by a state to an inventor or his assignee for a fixed period of time in exchange for a disclosure of an invention.'[2]

Patents are applied to inventions that include designs, manufactures and processes as well as improvements on existing designs, manufactures and processes. Patents are intended to promote the creation of novel and useful new inventions and provide to the patent holder the right to exclusively exploit the patent or to license or sell (i.e. transfer) the patent to others during the period of patent protection. Patents generally have a shorter term of enforcement than copyright. Patents do not guarantee the patent holder the right to manufacture or sell any products resulting from the patent. A patent may involve regulated products, such as biotechnology or pharmaceuticals, for example, which generally have stringent conditions for manufacture and sales. A patent simply prevents others from exploiting the described product or process contained within the patent during the patent protection period.

Patent is governed by national law as well as international treaty, with the World Intellectual Property Organization (WIPO) and World Trade Organization (WTO) serving as the predominant international bodies responsible for managing treaties related to patents. Relevant treaties include the *Paris Convention for the Protection of Industrial Property* (20 March 1883, last amended 28 September 1979), the *Patent Law Treaty* (Geneva, 1 June 2000) and the *Patent Cooperation Treaty*, which established an international patent filing system. The TRIPS treaty discussed in Chapter 2 also addresses patent issues, particularly within the context of multinational commerce. The *Strasbourg Agreement Concerning the International Patent Classification* (24 March 1971, amended 28 September 1979) governs the IPC classification system, used to standardise the identification of patents across the international arena.[3]

Libraries are most concerned with patents in two areas: managing resources that may include patented or patent pending information that are deposited with a library, perhaps in a digital repository, and inventions or processes that a library may want to exploit that are encumbered by patents. Each of these issues is discussed in turn.

Managing resources with patent issues

Academic library repositories, in particular, may receive dissertations or technical reports that include novel ideas or processes that the author may intend to patent. The author may request that access to the resource be restricted or completely disallowed until the patent has been granted or at least is pending approval. Libraries can prepare for this situation in the following ways:

First, the library should establish and publish an information access policy that reflects the library's mission and goals for its institutional repository. If the mission of the institutional repository is to provide open and unfettered access to information, then the library may want to inform authors in advance that resources with restricted access will not be accepted. In some cases, the needs of a significant collection may outweigh the library's open access policy. One obvious example is an electronic theses and dissertations collection maintained within an institutional repository. Dissertations, particularly in technology areas, may include patentable ideas and inventions. Many graduate programs and libraries have traditionally allowed the authors to request an exemption from public access for a limited time frame, generally 1–2 years. The library should examine such exemptions and weigh the competing demands for safeguarding the university's intellectual property and maintaining a complete collection against its stated mission of open access to information resources. Exceptions to a repository's open access policy should be explicitly identified, as well as whether the library will consider additional exceptions on a case-by-case basis.

A library may support restricted access to an information resource yet still choose to make its user community aware of the existence of the resource through a metadata record that indicates the title and nature of the resource, as well as a brief description of its content, but which also notes that the resource is embargoed from access for a specified period of time. This can support a range of information needs, including the needs of graduate students who are searching the dissertations and theses collection to validate that the research idea they are considering is unique.

Utilising patented inventions or processes

There are many patents in the information technology field that may have a direct impact on libraries that wish to exploit those technologies. A recent example is the slow adoption and commercial availability of the MPEG-4 audiovisual encoding standard, which supports a range of video streaming applications, from low-bandwidth web applications to high-definition broadband streaming. MPEG-4's technologies were heavily patent encumbered, despite the requirements of the Moving Picture Experts Group, which oversees the MPEG standards, that patented technologies within any MPEG standard must be made readily available at reasonable terms to any developers. The initial patent terms offered for MPEG-4 involved ongoing payment for use of the technology for encoding and playback and thus delayed MPEG-4 deployment by standard streaming server vendors, such as RealNetworks and QuickTime, until the licensing terms became more reasonable.

One particularly relevant example for DRM involves the suite of patents owned or applied for by ContentGuard, the developers and owners of the XrML (eXtensible Rights

Markup Language) specification. ContentGuard began as a Xerox PARC initiative and today is principally owned by Microsoft, Thomson and Time Warner. ContentGuard describes its intellectual property holdings as 'significantly greater than any other in the industry' containing 'over 187 issued patents and more than 300 patent applications in various stages of patent prosecution worldwide.'[4] In its FAQ for XrML is 'Do I need a license to use XrML and digital rights languages?' ContentGuard's response states, 'claims in the [ContentGuard DRM] patents cover the distribution and use of digital works and the use of a grammar in connection with the distribution of digital works.'[5] ContentGuard's patenting of the concept of a rights expression grammar generally rather than XrML specifically is an area of considerable controversy in the DRM arena and has a potentially chilling effect on the creation and distribution of any openly available rights expression languages or DRM technologies. ContentGuard's broadly stated patent claim to a rights expression language has not as of this writing been tested through any judicial decisions. XrML, which is discussed further in the chapter on rights expression languages, may require that a library wishing to use XrML obtain a license from ContentGuard for its use.

Trademark

The United States Patent and Trademark Office defines trademark as 'a word, phrase, symbol or design, or a combination of words, phrases, symbols or designs, that identifies and distinguishes the source of the goods of one party from those of others.'[6] A service mark has the same definition except that it applies to services rather than goods. Trademark requires registration for the protection of a trademark or service mark. Internationally, trademark is administered by the Madrid System for the International Registration of Marks, which was established by the *Madrid Agreement* (1891) and the *Madrid Protocol* (1989), with oversight by the WIPO. The Madrid System supports a single international trademark registration that 'is equivalent to an application or a registration of the same mark effected directly in each of the countries designated by the applicant. If the trademark office of a designated country does not refuse protection within a specified period, the protection of the mark is the same as if it had been registered by that Office.'[7] Trademark registrations may vary from a fixed term of years to a permanent registration, depending on the issuing country. Trademarks may also be abandoned if they are unused for a period of time or if the term or phrase becomes a generic term. Abandonment of trademark depends on the trademark laws in effect in the country of registration.

Libraries are concerned with several aspects of trademark. A library may choose to trademark a logo or phrase used to identify the library or a library project. Even if the library does not choose to register its logo or phrase, the library must be careful not to use a logo or phrase that has been trademarked by another individual or organisation. Trademarks require a national or international application and are generally evaluated based on distinctiveness (i.e. is the logo, design or phrase distinctive enough to identify the organisation or object to which it is applied?) and uniqueness (i.e. is the trademark already in widespread use, so that it has become representative of a class of goods and thus has become a *de facto* generic term?). Trademark registration may involve a trademark already in use or a trademark that the registrant intends to use, in which case the registrant may be required to use the trademark actively and successfully respond to any challenges to the trademark during the initial registration period, for trademark protection to remain in effect.

A library may be part of a larger organisation with one or more trademarked logos or designs associated with it. The library may wish to use the trademark, which might be a name, design or logo, in order to self-identify its relationship to the organisation. Generally, permission must be sought from the organisation's public relations department, which administers trademarks and logos to brand the organisation to the public. A library may also want to reference trademarked names, for example trademarked names for publishers' products, in research guides or other library publications. The library must seek permission from the publisher, unless guidance is provided on the publisher's website or in other documentation. The trademark symbol in use by the trademark owner must be included in any permitted publication of a trademarked name.

The other area in which libraries interact with trademarks is in the digitisation of resources that may include trademarks. Libraries will need to research any trademarks, which may be marked with a trademark indication, such as 'TM' or 'SM' in superscript, or the symbol ® in the United States. Any distinctive name, font or logo should be investigated for possible trademarking before digitisation is undertaken. It is important to realise that trademark protection exists independently of copyright. When requesting permission to digitise a resource that includes a trademark, the permission request letter and accompanying license should include a request to digitise the trademark.

Trademarks can be assigned and administered at the local, national or international level, which can make research difficult. Each country can have different terms of trademark and trademark renewal, as well as different record keeping, although the Madrid international trademark registration will help to standardise searching of records internationally. If a company is purchased by another, the owning company may not even know the status of any associated trademarks for the original company. In a worst-case scenario, an organisation may choose to remove or obscure a trademark, perhaps replacing it with the notice, 'trademark removed', before digitising a resource that includes a trademark, particularly if the trademark removal does not substantially affect the useful information contained in the resource.

An interesting case in the United States involving trademark, *Dastar v. Twentieth Century Fox Film Corp.*, was settled by the US Supreme Court in 2003. Dastar repackaged television series content produced by Twentieth Century Fox Film Corp. that had fallen into the public domain and sold the repackaged video content to consumers. Twentieth Century Fox, unable to claim copyright infringement, sued for trademark infringement, under the concept of 'reverse passing off', where the infringer uses a trademark belonging to another without attribution. Fox won in the lower courts, but the Supreme Court reversed the decision, noting that copyright is intended primarily to protect the content creator, and that when copyright expires, the consumer may freely use the information without attribution. Trademark, on the other hand, is intended to protect the consumer against confusion when purchasing a product. In this case, the consumer was not harmed by the repackaging and sale of the public domain video footage, so the US Supreme Court overturned the lower court's decision for the plaintiff, Fox. The United States is somewhat unique in not requiring attribution (a moral right), except for visual arts works, so no attribution was required for work that had fallen into the public domain.[8]

Moral rights

Moral rights, also known as *droit moral*, are legal rights that ascribe to creators, rather than copyright holders, and include the right to attribution and the right to the integrity of the creator's work, which enables the creator to determine how, or whether, his/her work can be altered. Moral rights are particularly concerned with alterations that are perceived as mutilating or derogatory, as moral rights are intended to protect the honor and reputation of the creator, rather than the creator's commercial interests. Moral rights apply to the creator, regardless of whether the work is sold, and generally cannot be transferred to another, even if copyright in the work is transferred. Moral rights are included in Article *6bis* of the *Berne Convention*, as described in Chapter 2. Moral rights are also legislated at the national level, for example the *Copyright Amendment (Moral Rights) Act 2000* in Australia. The duration of moral rights varies, by country and by type of moral right, with right of attribution generally lasting the duration of copyright, while right to the integrity of the work often terminates with the death of the creator.[9] In the United States, moral rights are limited to visual artists, as defined in the *Visual Artists Rights Act* of 1990 (VARA), which applies only to a limited set of visual works, specifically paintings, drawings, prints and sculptures, or still photographs for exhibitions, produced in a single copy or limited edition of 200 or fewer signed and numbered copies (17 U.S.C. § 106A).[10]

Indigenous peoples

Another important area of rights involves enabling indigenous peoples to determine how and whether religious and cultural artifacts can be displayed and used. The August 1993 *Draft United Nations Declaration on the Rights of Indigenous Peoples* identifies several protections for the historical, cultural and religious artifacts of indigenous peoples. Article 12 states that indigenous peoples have 'the right to maintain, protect and develop the past, present and future manifestations of their cultures, such as archaeological and historical sites, artifacts, designs, ceremonies, technologies and visual and performing arts and literature, as well as the right to the restitution of cultural, intellectual, religious and spiritual property taken without their free and informed consent or in violation of their laws, traditions and customs.' Article 13 states that indigenous peoples have 'the right to maintain, protect, and have access in privacy to their religious and cultural sites; the right to the use and control of ceremonial objects; and the right to the repatriation of human remains.' The draft declaration is currently moving through the UN hierarchy toward General Assembly review and approval.[11]

Indigenous rights may be governed by national laws, such as the United States *Native American Graves Protection and Repatriation Act* (1990) or by recommendations from organisations that work with indigenous cultural issues, such as the Aboriginal and Torres Strait Islander Library and Information Resources Network (ATSILIRN), author of the *Aboriginal and Torres Strait Islander Library and Information Resources Network Protocols*,[12] which provide recommendations for working with Aboriginal cultural and historical artifacts. Libraries wanting to make available the cultural and historical artifacts of indigenous peoples should identify any relevant national laws and also work closely with representatives or descendants of the relevant indigenous population to ensure that the digitisation, description and dissemination of indigenous artifacts reflects their cultural and religious traditions and practises. A website for the indigenous population can be a good starting point for finding appropriate contacts, as can any national or local agency or society that manages indigenous treaties or works with indigenous peoples.

Privacy rights

Beyond copyright, the right that has the most application within a DRM strategy is the right to privacy, which impacts primarily on the *users* of digital information.

Privacy as a right is safeguarded in international treaty, national constitutions and national law. Privacy is a broad term with many published definitions. Definitions of privacy focus on the right of individuals and groups to manage the access and use of their personal information. Another aspect of privacy involves the right of people to engage in activities, such as use of information or personal communications, without such activities being monitored or recorded. Privacy International, in its *Overview of Privacy*, identifies multiple aspects of privacy: information privacy, bodily privacy, privacy of communications and territorial privacy.[13] The aspects that most concern librarians and archivists are information privacy, defined as 'the establishment of rules governing the collection and handling of personal data' and privacy of communications, 'which covers the security and privacy of mail, telephones, e-mail and other forms of communication.'[13]

With copyright, the rights of the creator of information predominate, even though the fair use of information to benefit the public good is an important exception. Privacy rights are generally concerned with the rights of the user of information. Privacy protections will safeguard the personal identity of a user and also keep confidential the information practises of the user – both the nature of the information accessed by the user and the use of that information.

Privacy is governed by a plethora of treaties and laws. Privacy International identifies two types of laws: comprehensive laws, which are laws that cover the broad spectrum of personal information – an oversight body for the protection of privacy rights is generally mandated by comprehensive laws; sectoral laws, by contrast, are specific to certain circumstances, industries or technologies.[13] Some countries, such as France, include privacy in their constitutions as an explicit right guaranteed to citizens. Other countries have overarching, comprehensive laws, such as the UK's *Data Protection Act 1998 c.29* and Australia's *Privacy Act 1988 (Cth)*.

The UN has addressed the issue of privacy for its member states in two landmark documents. The *Universal Declaration of Human Rights, Article 12* states, 'No one shall be subjected to arbitrary interference with his privacy, family, home or correspondence, nor to attacks upon his honour and reputation. Everyone has the right to the protection of the law against such interference or attacks.'[14] Privacy is addressed in similar terms in Article 17 of the UN's *International Covenant on Civil and Political Rights*, which came into force on 23 March 1976.[15]

Another important multinational agreement is the *OECD Guidelines Governing the Protection of Privacy and Transborder Data Flows of Personal Data* of the Organisation for Economic Co-operation and Development (OECD). The *OECD Guidelines* were adopted in 1960 and represent 'minimum standards which are capable of being supplemented by additional measures for the protection of privacy and individual liberties.'[16] The OECD comprises 30 countries that have come together to develop policies and share statistics on economic and social issues.[17] The *OECD Guidelines* provide shared 'core principles' that enable OECD member nations to articulate policies and directives with regard to privacy and personal information, particularly the sharing of personal information across state borders. The principles state that personal data collection should be limited, obtained by 'lawful and fair means' and, 'where appropriate', with the consent of the person about whom the data are collected. Data collected should be relevant to the purpose for which they are collected and this purpose should be provided in advance to the relevant person, about whom the data are collected. Personal data collected should not be disclosed and should be protected from involuntary disclosure. The individual who is the subject of data collection should be able to confirm from a data collector that personal information about the individual exists and should further be able to obtain this information in a reasonable time and manner from the data controller. The *OECD Guidelines* also call for a data controller to oversee management of these personal data through compliance with the *OECD Guidelines*.[16]

In November 2004, the APEC Privacy Framework was published by the Asian Pacific Economic Cooperation members – 21 economic entities, from Chile to Singapore, including China and the United States. The work of APEC is to develop consensus and best practises rather than treaties or agreements with the force of law. The nine principles of the APEC Privacy Framework are:

- Preventing harm
- Integrity of personal information
- Notice
- Security safeguards

- Collection limitations
- Access and correction
- Uses of personal information
- Accountability
- Choice[18]

The Privacy Framework has been criticised as 'OECD lite'. In particular, it is criticised as weak on accountability and recommendations for data export.[19]

European countries are covered by comprehensive laws through multiple EU and EC directives. Important directives include the *EU Charter of Fundamental Rights of 7 December 2000; Council of Europe 1981 Convention for the Protection of Individuals with regard to Automatic Processing of Personal Data; Treaty on the European Union (TEU): Article 6; European Convention for the Protection of Human Rights and Fundamental Freedoms 1950 (ECHR): Art. 8; Directive 95/46/EC of the European Parliament and of the Council of 24 October 1995 on the Protection of Individuals with Regard to the Processing of Personal Data and on the Free Movement of such Data; Directive 2002/58/EC (Directive on Privacy and Electronic Communications).*[20]

These directives form a body of privacy legislation that ensures harmonisation across national laws and consistency of application for privacy regulations. Important concepts that are articulated in this body of legislation include requirements that personal information that is collected must be: relevant to the purpose of the organisation or industry; accurate and up to date; secure; transparent and accessible to the subject; and kept only as long as it is useful to the purpose for which it was collected. Oversight and enforceability are also mandated in the body of EC/EU legislation, with every European Union country required to designate or establish an individual or agency to enforce privacy rules.[21]

Directive 2002/58/EC... *Concerning the Processing of Personal Data and the Protection of Privacy in the Electronic Communications Sector* contains one controversial provision that reflects the growing importance of national security after the 11 September 2001 attacks on the World Trade Center in New York City. The Directive allows member states to mandate the retention of information for purposes of national security or for protection from, or prosecution of, criminal acts (Council Directive 2002/58/EC, art.15(1)).[22]

Many countries address privacy at the state or provincial level and through national legislation. Legislation may address governmental information practises, such as Canada's 1982 *Privacy Act*, which governs the use of information stored by federal agencies, government departments and statutory corporations, or legislation may address commercial practises, such as Canada's *Personal Information Protection and Electronic Documents Act* (PIPED), which covers the gathering and disclosure of personal information by commercial entities.[23]

In the United States, privacy is addressed tangentially in several amendments to the US Constitution, perhaps most notably in the 14th Amendment, which provides for the 'privileges or immunities' of citizenship, including the instruction that citizens not be deprived of 'life, liberty, or property, without due process of law.' (US Const. Amend. 14, § 1)[24] and the 4th Amendment, which grants 'The right of the people to be secure in their persons, houses, papers, and effects, against unreasonable searches and seizures.' (US Const. Amend. 4).[25] There is considerable debate among Constitutional scholars concerning the extent to which privacy is explicitly protected under the umbrella of the US Constitution.

The United States lacks a comprehensive body of privacy legislation, although legislation has been enacted into law that addresses aspects of privacy, such as the *Privacy Act of 1974*, which addresses records maintained on individuals, particularly by federal government agencies (5 U.S.C § 552A)[26] and the *Electronic Communications Privacy Act of 1986* (P.L. 99-508, *Electronic Communications Privacy Act of 1986)*,[27] which governs all aspects of use and disclosure for wire and electronic communications.

Recent controversy over privacy rights in the United States has centered on the passage of the *USA Patriot Act of 2001*, which expanded the ability of the Federal Bureau of Investigation (FBI) to obtain personal information records from libraries and other agencies under the Foreign Intelligence Surveillance Act (FISA). Among other provisions, the law allows FBI agents to obtain ' "any tangible thing", which includes books, records, papers, floppy disks, data tapes, computers and their hard drives, and any type of record in any format.'[28] In addition, libraries are not allowed to notify patrons that their records have been released to federal investigators.[28] The USA Patriot Act was reauthorised in March 2006 as the *USA PATRIOT and Terrorism Prevention Reauthorization Act of 2005*, also known as the *USA Patriot Improvement and Reauthorization Act.* Requirements for obtaining library records were tightened and now require investigators to show 'reasonable grounds' that library and other types of records are relevant to an investigation *(P.L. 109-177, USA PATRIOT and Terrorism Prevention Reauthorization Act of 2005)*.[29]

Privacy and libraries

Libraries provide a wide range of information to users and may sometimes retain records of this information use.

In particular, libraries retain records of the circulation of library materials to individual users, in order to ensure the return of those materials to the library in a timely manner. To a great degree, the success of the library as a communal information broker depends upon the trust that the library has earned from its patrons. Based on a long history of practise and informal contract, patrons generally believe and expect that libraries will not reveal their information uses unless the library is legally compelled to do so. However, the longer that information is stored by a library, the greater the potential that this information can be inadvertently released or misused.

In recent years, libraries have engaged in virtual reference, which involves the use of digital technologies to receive and respond to patron information requests. These information requests may be sent as email requests or instant messages (IMs). Patrons may leave digital voice messages requesting information that may be stored indefinitely on a voicemail server that may not be under the direct control of the library. Desktop conferencing using technologies such as Skype are an emerging digital reference option. Virtual reference services may be provided by local applications or by subscription to a centralised service that maintains patron queries and responses on a remote server. The end result is that a digital audit trail of patron information queries, which may be linked to the patron's identity, is often available for review after the patron has concluded the information transaction, and may in fact be under the control of a parent organisation or a third-party service provider.

Libraries are active members of the digital information community and may deploy multiple websites that serve as gateways to the library's catalog and as portals to digital collections. Libraries also offer many digital resources, including databases and full-text resources, which are licensed from third-party vendors. Data regarding patron use may be collected and maintained by the library or by an information resource vendor. Libraries must carefully balance the need to understand how their patrons access and use information versus the patron's right to privacy of access and use. It is almost always sufficient to concatenate statistics of information use under a class or category of patrons rather than by an identified individual. Exceptions may occur when a library is charging for services to a patron and must document patron information use. Information on fee-based information use should be kept only as long as required to complete the financial transaction and any financial auditing requirements for the library or the customer. Libraries must also ensure that the patrons' right to privacy is safeguarded as part of the contracts or licenses that libraries negotiate with publishers or third-party information brokers. For example, libraries can and should add language to license agreements that publishers may not obtain or use patron-identifying information in use statistics.

Developing a privacy policy

Libraries should address privacy in terms of both principle and practise in a privacy policy that can be shared with users. A library should begin its privacy policy by articulating its principles for ensuring the privacy of patrons: protecting the identity of patrons, ensuring confidentiality of information use and ensuring that the personal information that a library collects about patrons is required for the library's business model, is kept only as long as it serves a useful purpose and is safeguarded from misuse by others. The library's privacy principles should form the core of the library's privacy policy and should be actively shared with patrons.

Many libraries are part of larger organisations that have identity management strategies to safeguard both personal and financial information for users, particularly for organisational business practises that may require the transmission or storage of user identifiers, such as the US social security number, or financial information, such as credit card account numbers or bank account information. Organisations such as universities or government agencies will publish identity management policies and also provide stringent safeguards for hardware and software to ensure that confidential personal and economic information is not compromised. Libraries should comply fully with institutional identity management policy and practise and should only utilise bank or credit card information for library fines and fees within the safeguards of the institution's identity management practises. If an integrated library system offers an application to accept credit card payment for library fines and fees, for example, the library should ensure that this application can operate within the institutional confines of hardened software and hardware that is protected against identity discovery or theft. At the very least, if institutional safeguards are breached, the library will be protected by the institution's risk management strategy for lawsuits or other imposed penalties resulting from identity theft. Exemplars of good institutional identity management policies are included in the bibliography at the end of this book.

Most national library associations have published professional codes of ethics or core values statements. A library will want to ensure that its privacy principles are congruent with those of the national organisation or library and may even choose to quote from the applicable national code of ethics. The International Federation of Library Associations and Institutions maintains a collection of professional codes of ethics and conduct, organised by country, at its website.[30] The most up-to-date codes of conduct can be found at the websites for each national library or national library organisation.

A library should first audit its current information practises to analyze all information collected about its users, and all observable information uses, to determine how this information is currently maintained, secured and used. Policy and practise should be examined and revised to safeguard the privacy of library users. Areas to examine and address within a comprehensive privacy policy include:

- materials circulation records, including overdue records, which may maintain the link between the patron and information resources indefinitely;
- interlibrary loan records;
- closed stack and offsite storage requests, including requests for resources from storage facilities shared by other libraries;
- registration for services, such as borrowing a laptop, wireless card or network cable;
- document and materials delivery requests;
- library website use, which may involve documenting visits to the website, pages viewed, objects downloaded, links visited and duration of visits;
- transaction logs, which may be linked to an individual's registration;
- authentication and authorisation strategies, including passwords, certificates and proxy servers;
- information cached on public access computers, including email logs, Internet logs or files that users may place on hard drives or library servers in 'information commons' areas;

- requirements of commercial resources, which may be licensed by the library, that may require or promote individual registration;
- third-party search and retrieval services, such as Google scholar;
- 'Ask a librarian' and other digital online reference services, which may capture and archive user queries and sessions;
- web-based feedback and survey mechanisms used as part of a library's evaluation strategy;
- subscriptions to library newsletters and RSS feeds;
- learning content management systems, which may maintain information about use of e-reserves and other library materials integrated into the management system;
- institutional data warehouses that a library may utilise for information (e.g. current faculty and registered students) and to which the library may provide information (e.g. delinquent students, for institutional fine collection);
- ancillary activities carried out within the library that may involve personal data sharing, such as voter registration, tax assistance, reading clubs, etc;
- network security, which may identify network use by IP address and maintain backup logs to trace and resolve unauthorised use and other network security violations;
- public workstations, which may allow a patron to be observed by others as they access and display information;
- commercial services, such as electronic serial vendors, and centralised information services, such as virtual reference, personal citation management, etc;

- web personalization for users (e.g. 'MyLibrary' implementations);
- Web 2.0 applications, such as blogs, patron tagging, etc;
- security cameras installed in the library.

The audit should identify all information collected about patron information use. It is important to be explicit about what is actually identified. For example, an IP address identifies a device, not a person. Even a computer behind a locked door may be available for use by a visitor or after-hours custodian. If enough attributes are collected and stored about a person, the person may be identifiable, even if the person's name or username is not identified. The role 'instructor in Economics 101, February 2006' may identify a specific individual or narrow the possibilities to a few persons. In addition to information identifying a use, the library should document the amount and type of information collected, where it is stored, how it is safeguarded from misuse, how long it is stored and how it is deleted. It is particularly important to ask, is the user-identifying information essential for our business workflow? Personal information is often collected as a safeguard against a potential problem rather than because the information is necessary for the business transaction. The library should do a risk analysis and weigh the risks of a problem occurring against the risk that the patron's identity could be compromised by the misuse of the information collected. Also, the library should ask if the consequences of a problem warrant the risk of identity theft. An example would be a library requiring a user to register to borrow a network cable to attach a laptop to a library network connection. The small expense of the cable should be weighed against the amount of staff and user effort, and the potential for identity theft, involved in the patron registration.

Libraries often employ multiple levels of data storage, including online, near line, physical backup media and offsite storage, all of which must be considered to ensure the security of stored information. Older information may also be unwittingly maintained, such as circulation cards dating back several decades still affixed to the insides of book covers. A library may wish to initiate the practise of looking for old book pockets and removing circulation cards at time of circulation or whenever a collection is physically inventoried or weeded. In addition, it is important to document other organisations that may be custodians of information about the library's patron. As noted earlier, this includes third-party service and resource providers but may also include the parent organisation and its contractors, for example the telephone provider who stores digital voicemails or the security firm that captures patron information use on security cameras. The library needs to understand and have a voice in the data retention and use policies for all organisations involved in documenting the information use of library patrons, for whatever purpose.

A privacy policy should be designed and maintained according to the following core principles:

- *Conformance to relevant law and organizational policy.* A privacy policy should reference, and reflect, national, state/territory and local law as well as identity management and privacy policy and practise within any larger, parent institution, such as a university or municipal government.
- *Public availability and dissemination.* The library's privacy policy should be widely disseminated, particularly at point of need for patrons. Privacy policies, or relevant excerpts, should be linked from the library's home page, posted at information and access desks and at

public workstations, and distributed to new users at registration or included in first-time user packets.

- *Supporting core privacy principles for disclosure, security and appropriate use.* The library's privacy policy should identify the kinds of information documented about users, the length of time the information is maintained, how it is used, and how it is safeguarded from inappropriate sharing or other misuse. Whenever possible, all personally identifying information should be stripped out and anonymous or aggregated information used for statistical analysis, etc. If patrons are able to opt out of any information gathered about them, the policy should identify such uses and provide an opportunity for patrons easily to 'opt out'. The library's privacy policy should also guarantee to users that the minimum information needed for carrying out the library's business is collected.
- *Ensuring the accuracy and currency of the information collected.* The library should ensure that any information collected is accurate and up to date, so that the information can serve the business practises of the organisation, such as sending overdue notices to a correct email or postal address, and so that information that is invalid or out of date and therefore serves no useful purpose is not retained.
- *Providing for review and the adjudication of complaints or disputes.* Privacy policies should be reviewed periodically to ensure that new technologies, revised practises and new legislation are accommodated. Patrons should be provided with opportunities to request the disclosure of any information maintained about them and to request removal of information, as appropriate, or to complain about suspected violations of privacy, such as

the patron who complains that his/her Internet use on a public workstation is being observed. A library should designate a person or committee to maintain the library's privacy policy and respond to user concerns. This person or group should work closely with the organisation's legal counsel to ensure that the privacy policy conforms to law and to organisational policy and should assist with any legal issues that arise from patron complaints.

- *Disclaimers for information the library cannot control.* Disclaimers should be provided for resources or information use the organisation cannot control, such as external links referenced on a library's website or data collection practises of commercial, third-party information resources or the documenting of patron activities on security cameras, in cases where patron safety has primacy over patron privacy.

The University of California Libraries provides an excellent website with guidance on conducting a privacy audit and constructing a privacy policy. The site includes examples of library privacy policies from libraries within the University of California system.[31]

Further information

More guidance on creating a privacy policy as well as examples of privacy policies is available in the bibliography at the end of this book.

P3P, Platform for Privacy Preferences

A standard that may be useful for implementing website privacy policies is P3P, the Platform for Privacy Preferences, which is a standard maintained by the W3C (World Wide Web Consortium) to enable the standardised expression of website data practises that can be read by persons but also interpreted and acted upon by browsers or other web-based applications to enable decision making about actions to take, such as browsing or registering at a site, without requiring a person to read a privacy policy personally. The W3C maintains a website on P3P, including software that may be employed to implement or interpret P3P policy expressions.[32] The CMU Usable Privacy and Security Laboratory at Carnegie Mellon University offers the software Privacy Finder, a search engine that indexes websites with P3P implementations and identifies resulting websites by high, low, medium or custom conformance to the user's privacy preferences.[33]

Privacy is also an important component of any authentication or authorisation practises that a library may employ as part of a DRM strategy. Authentication and authorisation are discussed in Chapter 5.

Privacy and publicity rights

In addition to the users of information, privacy rights also concern the subjects of information resources, as personal information, which may include the subject's likeness or other physical representation, is often included in information resources that a library may want to make accessible to users. Privacy and publicity rights with respect to the subjects of information resources are often conflated. The distinction that is generally made is that privacy refers to the right of a subject of an information resource to have his or her likeness or personal information kept private, while publicity rights generally refer to the right to control the commercial exploitation of the subject's persona or identity, as defined by the likeness, voice, image, name or personally identifiable mannerisms. Privacy rights often end with the death of an individual but publicity rights may continue beyond the lifetime of the individual and may be managed by the estate or heirs of the subject or by a representing agency.

Publicity rights may be protected by national or local legislation. Libraries should be aware of relevant legislation and should obtain publicity releases for any identifiable living subjects contained within an information resource that the library intends to disseminate, particularly in digital form. Publicity releases should reflect relevant statutes and may vary if the person involved is a minor, or an active participant in an event, rather than a bystander. The organisation's public relations department may have a sample publicity release that the library can customise, as needed. Publicity rights generally obtain to everyone by statute and not just to 'famous' individuals. Libraries should identify the duration of publicity rights, which may continue for some period after death, and apply them for identifiable subjects of information resources, particularly with regard to an identifiable likeness or voice within a resource.

Academic libraries may be involved in research projects that examine patron information use, or they may participate in the research projects of academic faculty members. Research involving human subjects, particularly grant-funded research, often requires clearance from an institutional review board that is tasked with ensuring that no harm, including violations of privacy, results for the research subjects. Libraries should be aware of the need for this review for research involving human subjects. Institutional review boards can also provide guidance on publicity releases and good surveying practices, such as providing 'opt ins' for personally identifiable information, such as email addresses for survey follow up.

Understanding and actively supporting rights – the rights of the creator, the copyright owner, the user and the information subject, are fundamental to developing a DRM strategy. A working knowledge of relevant rights is a necessary first step before beginning the work of identifying and managing the entities in a rights scenario – the resource itself and the agents (creators, rights holders and users) that participate in a rights transaction for access and reuse of the resource.

Notes and references

1. European Commission. "Bio-Glossary" Research: Biosociety and the Knowledge-Based Bio-Economy. Brussels: EC Research. Last accessed 30 April 2008. *http://ec.europa.eu/research/biosociety/library/glossarylist_en.cfm?Init=P*
2. Wikipedia. *Patent*. St. Petersburg, FL: Wikimedia Foundation, Inc. Last modified 19 March 2008. Last accessed 22 March 2008. *http://en.wikipedia.org/wiki/Patents*
3. *Strasbourg Agreement Concerning the International Patent Classification of March 24, 1971, as amended on September 28, 1979*. Geneva: World Intellectual Property Organization, 28 September 1979. Last accessed 30 April 2008. *http://www.wipo.int/treaties/en/classification/strasbourg/trtdocs_wo026.html*
4. ContentGuard. (2006–2008) *The Premier DRM IP Portfolio*. El Segundo, CA: ContentGuard. Last accessed 22 March 2008. *http://www.contentguard.com/ip.asp*
5. ContentGuard. (2000–2008) "Frequently Asked Questions" *XrML*. El Segundo, CA: ContentGuard. Last accessed 22 March 2008. *http://www.xrml.org/faq.asp*
6. United States Patent and Trademark Office "Trademark, Copyright or Patent?" *Trademarks: Basic Facts*. Washington, DC: USPTO. Last modified 22 March 2008. Last accessed 22 March 2008. *http://www.uspto.gov/web/offices/tac/doc/basic/trade_defin.htm*

7. World Intellectual Property Organization (WIPO) "Madrid System for the International Registration of Marks." *IP Services*. Geneva: WIPO. Last accessed 22 March 2008. *http://www.wipo.int/madrid/en/*
8. *Dastar Corp. v. Twentieth Century Fox Film Corp. et al* certiorari to the United States Court of Appeals for the Ninth Circuit No. 02-428. Argued 2 April 2003 – Decided 2 June 2003. Washington, DC: US Supreme Court, 2003. Last accessed 22 March 2008. *http://www.supremecourtus.gov/opinions/02pdf/02-428.pdf*
9. Caslon Analytics. "Moral Rights" *Caslon Analytics Intellectual Property*. Braddon, ACT, Australia: Caslon Analytics. Version of February 2007. Last accessed 22 March 2008. *http://www.caslon.com.au/ipguide18.htm*
10. *Title 17 United States Code*. Washington, DC: US House of Representatives. Last accessed 22 March 2008. *http://uscode.house.gov/download/title_17.shtml*
11. United Nations High Commissioner for Human Rights. (1996–2000) 1994/45, *Draft United Nations Declaration on the Rights of Indigenous Peoples*. Geneva: The Commissioner. Last accessed 22 March 2008. *http://www .unhchr.ch/huridocda/huridoca.nsf/(Symbol)/E.CN.4.SUB.2.RES.1994.45.En*
12. ATSILIRN (Aboriginal and Torres Strait Islander Library and Information Resources Network Inc.). (2005) *ATSILIRN Protocols, the Aboriginal and Torres Strait Islander Library and Information Resources Network Protocols*. Canberra: ATSILIRN, c2005. Last accessed 22 March 2008. *http://www1.aiatsis.gov.au/atsilirn/protocols.atsilirn.asn.au/index0c51.html?option=com_frontpage&Itemid=1*
13. Privacy International. (2004) *PHR2004: Overview of Privacy*. London: Privacy International. Last accessed 22 March 2008. *http://www.privacyinternational.org/article.shtml?cmd[347]=x-347-82589&als[theme]=Privacy%20and%20Human%20Rights&headline=PHR2004*
14. United Nations. *Universal Declaration of Human Rights*. New York: United Nations. Last accessed 22 March 2008. *http://www.unhchr.ch/udhr/lang/eng.htm.*

15. Office of the High Commissioner for Human Rights. *International Covenant on Civil and Political Rights: Adopted and opened for signature, ratification and accession by General Assembly resolution 2200A (XXI) of 16 December 1966, entry into force 23 March 1976, in accordance with Article 49*. Geneva: OHCHR. Last accessed 22 March 2008. *http://www.unhchr.ch/html/menu3/b/a_ccpr.htm*
16. Organisation for Economic Co-operation and Development. *OECD Guidelines on the Protection of Privacy and Transborder Flows of Personal Data*. Paris: OECD. Last accessed 22 March 2008. *http://www.oecd.org/document/18/ 0,3343,en_2649_201185_1815186_1_1_1_1,00.html*
17. Organisation for Economic Co-operation and Development. "About the OECD" Organisation for Economic Co-operation and Development [home page]. Paris: OECD. Last accessed 22 March 2008. *http://www.oecd.org/pages/0,3417,en_36734052_36734103_1_1_1_1_1,00.html*
18. APEC Electronic Commerce Steering Group. *APEC Privacy Framework*. Singapore: APEC. Last accessed 22 March 2008. *http://www.apec.org/apec/news___media/fact_sheets/apec_privacy_framework.html*
19. Greenleaf, Graham. (2003) *The APEC Privacy Initiative: "OECD Lite" for the Asia-Pacific?* Ultimo, NSW, Australia: Australasian Legal Information Institute. Last accessed 22 March 2008. *http://www2.austlii.edu.au/%7Egraham/publications/2004/APEC_V8article.html*
20. European Commission Directorate-General for Justice, Freedom and Security "Legislative Documents". *Data Protection*. Brussels: Directorate-General. Last accessed 22 March 2008. *http://ec.europa.eu/justice_home/fsj/privacy/law/index_en.htm*
21. European Commission Directorate-General for Justice, Freedom and Security. *Data Protection*. Brussels: Directorate-General. Last accessed 22 March 2008. *http://ec.europa.eu/justice_home/fsj/privacy/index_en.htm*
22. *Directive 2002/58/EC of the European Parliament and of the Council of 12 July 2002 concerning the processing of personal data and the protection of privacy in the electronic communications sector (Directive on privacy and electronic*

communications): 32002L0058 Luxembourg: EU Publications Office. Last accessed 22 March 2008. *http://eur-lex.europa.eu/LexUriServ/LexUriServ.do?uri=CELEX:32002L0058:EN:HTML*

23. Caslon Analytics. "Privacy in North America". *Caslon Analytics Privacy Guide*. Braddon, ACT, Australia: Caslon Analytics. Version of October 2004. Last accessed 22 March 2008. *http://www.caslon.com.au/privacyguide7.htm*
24. United States. *Constitution of the United States. Amendments 11–27*. Washington, DC: National Archives and Records Administration. Last accessed 22 March 2008. *http://www.archives.gov/exhibits/charters/constitution_amendments_11-27.html*
25. United States. *Constitution of the United States. Bill of Rights*. Washington, DC: National Archives and Records Administration. Last accessed 22 March 2008. *http://www.archives.gov/exhibits/charters/bill_of_rights_transcript.html*
26. US Department of Justice. *The Privacy Act of 1974*, 5 U.S.C. § 552a, as Amended. Updated page 26 September 2003. Last accessed 5 August 2007. *http://www.usdoj.gov/foia/privstat .htm*
27. *Electronic Communications Privacy Act of 1986*. H.R.4952, A bill to amend title 18, United States Code, with respect to the interception of certain communications, other forms of surveillance, and for other purposes, 21 October 1986 Became Public Law No: 99-508. Washington, DC: Thomas, Library of Congress. Last accessed 22 March 2008. *http://thomas.loc.gov/cgi-bin/bdquery/z?d099:HR04952:@@@L%7CTOM*
28. American Library Association. (2008) Office for Intellectual Freedom. *Analysis of the USA Patriot Act Related to Libraries*. Chicago: American Library Association, October 2005. Last accessed 22 March 2008. *http://www.ala.org/ala/oif/ifissues/issuesrelatedlinks/usapatriotactanalysis .htm*
29. *USA PATRIOT and Terrorism Prevention Reauthorization Act of 2005*. H.R.3199. *To extend and modify authorities needed to combat terrorism, and for other purposes*. 9 March 2006 became Public Law No. 109-177. Washington, DC: GovTrack.us. Last accessed 30 April 2008 *http://www.govtrack.us/congress/bill.xpd?bill=h109-3199*

30. International Federation of Library Associations and Institutions. *IFLA/FAIFE Professional Codes of Ethics/Conduct*. The Hague: IFLA. Latest revision 23 April 2007. Last accessed 22 March 2008. *http://www.ifla.org/ faife/ethics/codes.htm*
31. University of California Libraries. (2008) *Creating a Library Privacy Policy*. Last accessed 22 March 2008. *http:// libraries.universityofcalifornia.edu/privacy/audit.html*
32. W3C. "P3P 1.0 Implementations". *Platform for Privacy Preferences (P3P) Project*. Cambridge, MA: Massachusetts Institute of Technology: W3C. Last accessed 22 March 2008. *http://www.w3.org/P3P/implementations.html*
33. CMU Usable Privacy and Security Laboratory. *Privacy Finder FAQ*. Pittsburgh, PA: Carnegie Mellon. Last accessed 22 March 2008. *http://www.privacyfinder.org/?faq=1*

4

The resource in digital rights management

Overview

A publisher finds an article in an institutional repository that it wishes to republish in a book compilation. The repository includes the preprint and the published version of the article, which vary in slight but important ways.

A scientist wants to utilise a data set to develop a computational model that simulates actual experiments. The data set has been iterated through several stages of curation, including raw sensor data, automatic normalisation of the raw data and review by an editorial board, resulting in substantial changes to each iteration.

A student searches for a novel by a Russian author. His/her search retrieves the novel in the original Russian, an award-winning translation and an earlier translation with analytical essays by noted scholars.

The resource is central to the information transaction. At its heart, DRM involves an agreement or offer by a rights holder (or his/her intermediary) for the reuse of a resource by the requestor. The resource is the critical element – the thing of value that must be identified, authenticated and safeguarded through any digital rights transaction. As the three examples above illustrate, the concept of the resource is complex, often representing a cluster of related resources that differ in important ways, with a relative value depending on the information user's context.

What are the critical issues for managing the resource to enable digital rights transactions? The first issue is *precise identification of the resource.* Identification requires that a resource be both uniquely and precisely identified – this resource and no other. A requester must be able to retrieve the exact resource that he/she wants and expects, not a similar or approximate resource. There are two important aspects of the identification of a resource. The first lies in the *definition of the resource* itself, which exists on a continuum from the overarching abstract creation through a specific physical copy. The second aspect is the *identifier*, a string that provides an unambiguous, unique and durable connection to the resource. Identifiers are critical enablers of resource use in the opaque digital world where things cannot be experienced until they are retrieved and cannot be retrieved without an identifier that links information about the resource to the actual resource itself. As Norman Paskin notes, 'nothing exists in any useful sense until it is identified.'[1]

The second issue concerns the *authenticity of the resource.* Authenticity involves two concepts: provenance and integrity. A useful definition is provided by Heather MacNeil, with regard to electronic records: 'An authentic record is one that is what it claims to be and that has not been corrupted or otherwise falsified since its creation.'[2] When a valuable painting is offered for sale, it is generally authenticated by provenance information that documents the lifecycle of the painting from its creation to the final sales transaction. It is also authenticated by a painstaking analysis of the characteristics of the painting to ensure that it originated with the artist in question. This assures the purchaser that he/she will be purchasing the authentic resource that is offered – the original painting by the known artist rather than a reproduction or a forged copy.

Authenticity also involves a comparison of the authoritative state of the resource – the resource as identified by owners or scholars – to the retrieved resource. The authoritative state, as documented in provenance metadata, is usually the creation or production state of the resource, but may be an authoritatively edited version, as might be the case with curated data, or the 'official' theatrical release for a motion picture. The authoritative, or 'canonical', resource could also be a painstakingly restored version, where a damaged resource is restored as faithfully as possible to its historical creation state.

The canonical state of a resource may represent the altered state in which a work has been experienced and documented throughout much of its lifecycle. Arms could be fashioned and attached – in the physical or a digital representation – to the *Venus de Milo*, for example, but the reconstruction would be so extensive that it would be widely recognised as being beyond a simple restoration to the actual creation of a new work altogether. The authoritative version of the *Venus de Milo* is universally acknowledged to be a statue of a woman with missing arms. An authoritative or canonical state of being depends largely on the context and consensus of those with the communally acknowledged authority to declare an authoritative or canonical state for a work.

In the digital environment, when the resource is 'born digital', the authoritative digital preservation version should either be the digital source object or as faithful a facsimile to the digital original as possible. For digital source objects in a proprietary digital format, the library may prefer to create a faithful digital surrogate in an accepted standard to serve as the canonical master file.

For analog source objects, the authoritative digital master object will also be as faithful a representation of the source as technology and community requirements dictate. When the authoritative digital resource represents an edited version of the source, each editing step should be fully documented so that the requestor knows exactly what he or she is retrieving, and how the authentic digital version differs from the source original. The authoritative resource can be a digital master that has been transcoded from one format (e.g. MPEG-4) to a newer format that offers more fidelity to the source information or equal fidelity with more functionality (e.g. M-JPEG2000). It goes without saying that as new digital formats emerge, the transcoding of an authoritative digital master from one format to another should be documented in digital provenance metadata for the end user and also for current and future resource managers.

Nature of information – the information model

How should a library approach resource management for digital rights? It is useful to begin with a common representation of the nature of information. It is difficult to identify and make available an authoritative information object without thoroughly understanding the object, from its abstract content properties to its concrete technical specifications.

IFLA FRBR conceptual information model

The International Federation of Library Associations and Institutions (IFLA) issued detailed specifications for metadata, the *Functional Requirements for Bibliographic Records* (*FRBR*), which included a conceptual information model with high-level entities in three groups. Group 1 entities reflect the information resource, or *work*, a highly abstract concept representing the creative content of the information resource.

The work is realised through an *expression* of the work. Without expression, the work could not exist in the physical space, where it can be experienced and understood by users. The expression is embodied by the *manifestation,* a concrete physical format that is then exemplified by a single or multiple items, as in the copies contained within the print run of a book. The *item,* or single physical instance of the manifestation, is a single entity occupying a unique point in space and time.[3] The IFLA FRBR model (Figure 4.1) is an extensible model that can accommodate a traditional library, where many items are representatives of a mass-produced manifestation, or a digital collection where each item is uniquely produced.

The FRBR information model is particularly useful within the framework of archival information management, where the focus is on the long-term preservation of information sources. An archive will generally conserve the original source object, which may be an analog artifact, and also ensure its long-term preservation by creating a digital preservation

Figure 4.1 **Example of the FRBR Information Model**

Work
Breaching Whale – Wyland
Is realized through
Expression
Working Sketch
Statue
Is embodied in
Manifestation
Bronze **statue** (large scale, unique)
Acrylic statue (mass produced)
Is exemplified by
Item
Foyer of an oceanographic institute building
Bookcase in home of purchaser in New Jersey
ABSTRACTION

master object that can be transcoded over time as technologies change and thus presumably will not suffer from the inherent fragility of the source object. The archive will generally also create a digital access or presentation copy that can be retrieved and displayed by end users. Each of these represents manifestations of the source object, where the technical specifications for each manifestation are documented through the technical metadata for each format. A digital preservation master, for example, will have encoding specifications that produce an object that is highly faithful to the source. A display or presentation copy tends to be lower resolution and thus accessible to a range of network bandwidths and display applications. The lower resolution access copy contains sufficient detail to represent the resource adequately to a wide variety of users but usually does not include sufficient detail for commercial reproduction.

MPEG-21 digital item declaration model

There are other useful object models, such as MPEG-21's digital item declaration model (DIDM), which is specifically designed for the digital object management space. MPEG-21 is a digital information system framework from the Moving Pictures Expert Group, which was developed to manage digital objects from creation to distribution for reuse by consumers. DRM is a major component of MPEG-21, so I will look at other components of this standard in future chapters. The MPEG-21 DIDM, which emerged from the digital multimedia world, is particularly designed to support complex objects, such as time-based consecutive media (video and audio) that can be subdivided into segments with meaning and value to end users, from the individual frame, to the clip, to the entire resource. Complex media are also frequently composed of many identifiable component objects, such as the video stream, the audio stream and the text track. The digital item, or the work, is defined as 'the thing that is acted upon (managed, described, exchanged, collected, etc.)' (Iverson, p. 1).[4] The digital item is further described as a 'structured digital object, including a standard representation and identification and meta data.' (Iverson, p. 3).[4] A container allows items or other containers to be grouped together to form packages for transport or for organisation onto virtual shelves for management. An item is a grouping of subitems or components bound to descriptors (metadata). A resource is an individual data stream. One or more resources described by descriptors are grouped together to form an item component. The MPEG-21 DIDM (Figure 4.2) thus supports complex objects (items), with multiple components, the binding of metadata about the item with the item itself or with its components, and the concatenation of items into meaningful groupings (containers) (Iverson, pp. 6–9).[4]

Figure 4.2 MPEG-21 Digital Item Declaration Model. Derived from Iverson *et al.*, p. 9.[4]

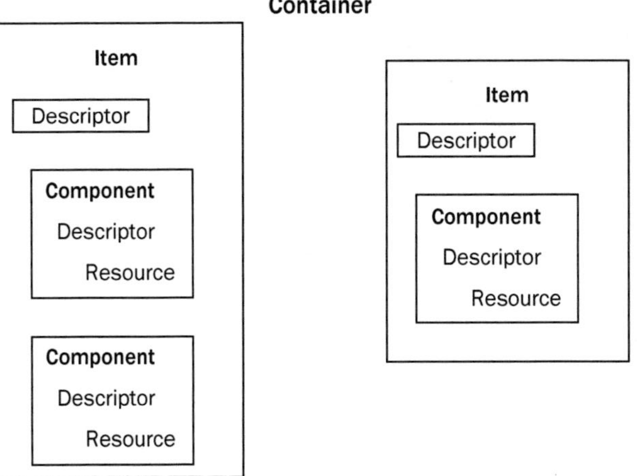

OAI-ORE: Open Archives Initiative – object reuse and exchange

A final interesting model to consider is the Open Archives Initiative object reuse and exchange (OAI-ORE) abstract data model. This data model, first introduced in 2007 and as of 2 June 2008 in beta (0.9) version, recognises that information objects on the web frequently consist of aggregations of multiple objects, each of which is related in some manner that can be semantically defined. An example would be the US Constitution as provided on the web by the National Archives and Records Administration, which consists of facsimile digital images related sequentially as individual facsimile pages and a text transcript. The resources within an aggregation can be defined by a controlled vocabulary of format or genre terms (e.g. 'facsimile', 'transcript') and the relationships between the resources can be similarly defined. (e.g. 'is page of' or 'is following page') The relationships are defined between the aggregation and each individual resource (e.g. 'is transcript of') and between each resource (e.g. 'is following page'). The Open Archives Initiative ORE protocol is designed to retrieve web-based resource aggregations. The ORE abstract data model 'makes it possible to associate an identity with aggregations of Resources and provide descriptions of their structure and semantics.'[5] An important entity in the model is the Resource Map (ReM), which encapsulates RDF triples or Atom syndication elements to express relationships among resources in the aggregation as graphs. 'The Resource Map is a Resource with information content that asserts that another resource is an Aggregation and describes that Aggregation.'[6] The aggregation is further instantiated with an associated URI (Uniform Resource Identifier), metadata about the aggregation, enumerated constituent resources and described relationships among

Figure 4.3 Relationship between a source map and an aggregation. Reprinted, with permission, from, Lagoze and Van de Sompel. *ORE Specification – Abstract Data Model*. Open Archives Initiative, 10 December 2007. http://www.openarchives.org.ore/0.1/datamodel

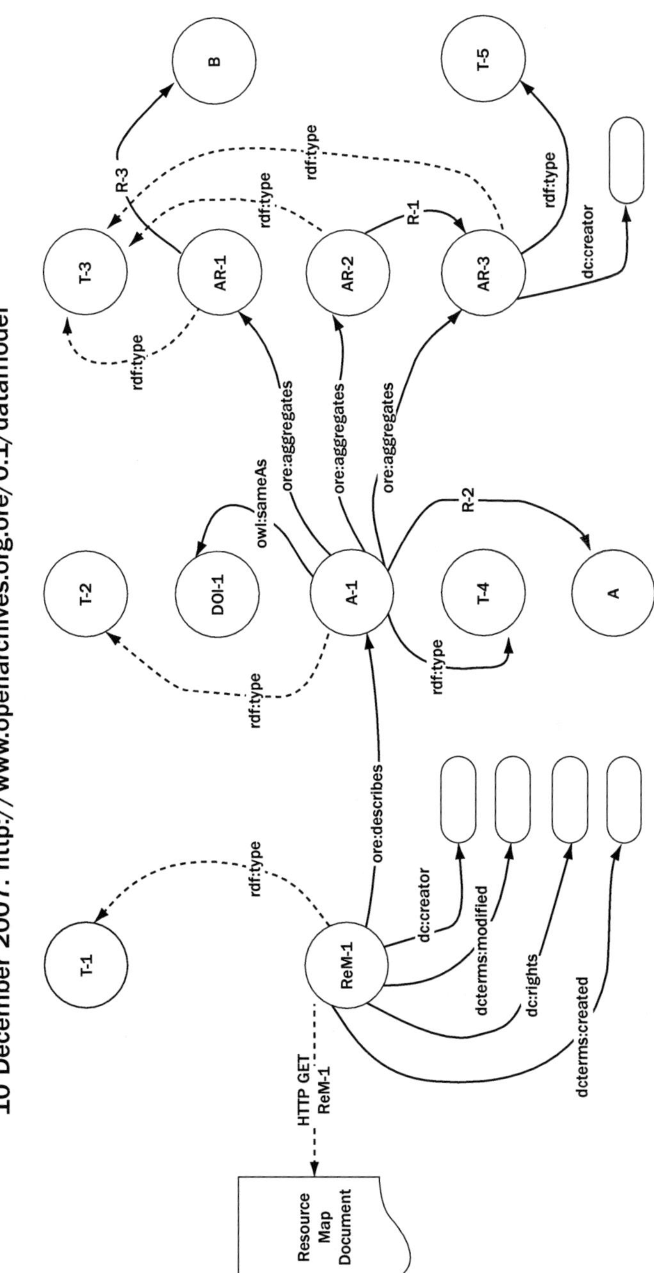

those constituents. The ReM also describes the relationships that the aggregation has with other resources on the web. The abstract ORE data model is still in development, but the draft model in Figure 4.3 shows the operation of the relationship between the resource map and the aggregation as of December 2007.

As the IFLA FRBR, MPEG-21 DIDM and ORE demonstrate, a good data model documents common data relationships – the different instantiations of a work as well as the components and relationships among components that make up the entire creative entity, or work. A critical aspect of a good DRM strategy is to develop or apply an information model that represents the resources you are managing. As the above discussion indicates, no information model is an objective and absolute representation of reality. Instead, a resource information model should be viewed as a working concept that represents the way resources are understood and used in the context of your digital initiative or organisation.

Identification of the resource

In order to identify the resources under its control, the library should first decide what it is identifying, and for what purpose. The library electronic resource management system developed by North Carolina State University, for example, concatenates all manifestations of a serial title under a 'work ID'.[7] This enables the library to provide an integrated display of all manifestations and physical instances of a resource, e.g. a single work ID for a serial that exists in paper, microform and digital formats. A resource can be identified at any or all levels of abstraction, from the enveloping work, to each expression and manifestation, to the individual item that exists in a unique space and time, to the components that make up the resource, or as OAI-ORE demonstrates, to aggregations of physically or semantically related resources. Supporting metadata should define for the user precisely what is being identified.

Once the library has determined which information entities it is offering to users, and how entities, such as components or format manifestations, are related to each other and will be offered to users, based on one or more information models such as the IFLA FRBR, MPEG-21 DIDM or OAI-ORE models, the next step is to select a systematic method for assigning and managing each identifier – the unique string that serves as a durable name and link to the resource itself. There are many identifier systems to consider, including identifiers that may have already been assigned to a resource by a third party, such as an ISBN that appears in a book the library is digitising and making available via the Web to its users. Although the library may want to supply the ISBN within its metadata to establish provenance by identifying which manifestation of the work was digitised by the library, the library will also want to provide a unique and persistent identifier that references the digital resource itself, as represented by the manifestation (digital format) and the unique item (this digital file and no other) so that the library distinguishes between the source object and the digital surrogate created by the library.

Before beginning an identification strategy, a library should first articulate its policies for resource identification and management. These policies should reflect any agreement(s) with the creators of the digital resources about the level of management and control that the libraries will provide for the resources it collects. In many cases, the creators will retain copyright of the resources, while delegating stewardship of these resources to the library. What assurances can the library offer the creators with respect to both authenticity and access to resources? What control over storage and access decisions will the creator retain? Under what conditions can a creator withdraw a resource deposited in the institutional repository managed by the library, for example? Will some or all resources have restricted access? If so, what are the policies and parameters for both open and restricted access, and how will such access be managed? As we will see, the identifier stategy is influenced by all of these policy decisions.

The library should determine its level of commitment to authentic information, and how it will respond to corrupted resources or to challenges to the authenticity of its resources. The library also needs to determine its commitment and support for iterated versions of a resource, over the lifecycle of the work. For example, a preprint may be published in the library's repository that is heavily cited by other works. However, significant errors are subsequently corrected and, as a result, a corrected postprint version is also deposited in the repository. What is the library's policy and practise with regard to both versions, each of which has established connections with third-party works that cite and build upon the preprint and postprint versions? Libraries can begin this research by examining the policies of other libraries, with regard to similar applications, such as institutional repositories, image collections, etc. It is important to have at least rudimentary policies in place, which may change with practise, before beginning the ingest and management of resources that are not under the sole ownership and control of the library.

Identification strategy

Identifiers can range from a simple method for uniquely naming resources to a complete identification system that includes policies and management for global uniqueness, as well as associated applications that make identifiers actionable, so that they provide a permanent path to the resource itself.

Characteristics of a robust identification strategy include:

- *Policy support.* The identification strategy a library adopts should support the library's policies for identification, access and resource management. The policy should document what the library will identify, e.g. the source, manifestations of the resource, individual copies of the resource or a digital package, such as a METS document (Metadata Encoding and Transmission Standard, a resource and metadata packaging standard described later in this chapter), MPEG-21 DIDL or OAI-ORE aggregation that includes all the manifestations of the resource and its metadata. If the library uniquely identifies each manifestation or component of a complex resource, the policy should document how the manifestations or components will be durably related to each other.
- *Global uniqueness.* Identifiers, particularly in the digital space, should be globally unique, which means that the uniqueness of the identifier exists beyond the library's context to any conceivable context of discovery and use. Each globally unique identifier will be created only once (i.e. will not be duplicated) and will represent one defined entity – this entity may be a single resource or an aggregation, group or class of resources, but this entity will be defined only once for the purpose of associating a unique identifier.

Global uniqueness can be assured in two ways. First, the identifier can be assigned by a global registry that ensures the uniqueness of all identifiers within its system and with regard to any other identifier systems. The registry can supply a unique identifier upon demand, e.g. through a global public name space that provides a web-based identification utility to assign identifiers to individual resources upon request. The Online Computer Library Center (OCLC) maintains a public default namespace for creating persistent URLs, or PURLs, for individual resources using an open web form.[8] A global registry can also supply a unique collective identifier, to identify the organisation assigning the identifiers (the 'naming authority'), which serves as a unique prefix that combines with a locally supplied suffix to create a globally unique identifier for each resource. This is the strategy employed by the Handle® System, for example. Finally, a global registry may issue a block of unique identifiers to a requesting organisation.

The second method for creating globally unique identifiers, without reference to an external registrar, is the computational method, which combines a unique prefix, often a node ID [such as the unique media access control (MAC) address of the hardware system creating the identifier], with a precise time stamp and clock sequence to create an identifier with very high probability of global uniqueness. This is the strategy employed by the Internet Engineering Task Force specification, UUID (Universally Unique Identifier).[9]

- *Persistent.* The identifier will persist through space and time, even though the entity it references ceases to exist. The identifier will not be reassigned to a new entity or resource. If the identified resource should cease to exist, the persistent identifier will ideally reference historical information concerning the formerly available resource, such as a metadata record that indicates the current unavailability status of the resource.
- *Unambiguous.* The identifier should serve as a surrogate to one and only one precisely defined entity. As noted above, the identifier may reference multiple resources,

such as a collection, an aggregation or even a choice of resources, but the definition for what the identifier references will be defined once, defined explicitly and will not change over time or in different contexts.

- *Interoperable.* An identifier should be usable and meaningful beyond the context of its creation and immediate use. An interoperable identifier should be transportable and able to be integrated into multiple contexts, including a shared digital environment, such as an information commons. An identifier should be able to be expressed in a common digital syntax, such as within an XML data element, and referenced by common protocols, such as HTTP. An interoperable identification system will also be able to incorporate legacy identifiers that may have utilised another scheme, and it should also be mappable to current and future identification schemes, both for collaborative data sharing today and to provide a migration path for tomorrow.
- *Consistent.* An identification strategy should have consistent rules for identifier creation and assignment to ensure that all identifiers conform to specifications. Consistency is critical for developing identifiers that are functional and useful over time.
- *Scalable.* The identification strategy should enable single and large-scale creation of identifiers, so that, as the organisation scales up its resource creation and management efforts, the identifier strategy does not become a workflow bottleneck. The identification strategy should also support large numbers of resources, from the thousands to the hundreds of thousands. The best identification strategies will have no practical limit in the number of identifiers that can be assigned.

In addition to these basic selection criteria, an identifier system may provide more functionality, depending on the needs of the library:

- *Actionable.* An identifier may be durably bound with a behavior or action. In most cases, this action is defined as *resolution*, in which the identifier resolves to the actual location of the resource. Generally, resolution involves linking the identifier to an entry in a database or registry that either references the current location of the resource or references metadata, which provides the current link to the resource. The resolver thus links the persistent identifier to the current location of the resource, so that the user transparently retrieves the resource. An actionable identifier provides location independence as the resolver database or registry always provides a link to the current location of a resource. The resource location may change frequently, but the entry in the resolver database, to which the actionable identifier points, will not change.

Actionable identifiers arose to support the requirements of digital storage management, which dictates that resources must often be moved for efficient space reallocation. Changes to location would require that location-bound identifiers are also changed, and thus are not persistent. Identifiers may be referenced in many contexts, so a change to the location-bound identifier means that many references become invalid. An actionable identifier that resolves to a permanent entry in a resolver registry will remain valid and thus persistent.

One issue with actionable identifiers is that they often rely on HTTP redirection, in which the user 'clicks' the permanent actionable identifier and the identifier changes during resolution to reflect the HTTP redirection to the current location. If the user copies the current address as it appears in his or her browser location window, the current but impermanent location may be referenced for future use, for example in a web bookmark or a journal article footnote, and yet the cited identifier is not permanent. This is known as the 'downstream citation' problem. Libraries utilising persistent, actionable identifiers should determine whether HTTP redirect is used and develop a strategy to address the user's misperception that the HTTP redirected address is the viable, permanent address for the resource.

- *Granular.* A library may wish to create hierarchical identifiers that include component suffixes for identifying parts of a resource. This can have practical application if the identifier is utilized as the organisational principle for managing hierarchical resources. However, libraries may prefer the flexibility of utilising associated metadata to document hierarchical relationships rather than explicitly referencing the whole-part relationship within a permanent identifier.
- *Intelligible versus opaque.* Intelligible identifiers provide meaningful information about the resource. This information may include the country of publication and the publisher, such as information included in the ISBN (International Standard Book Number); information about volume, issue and component (e.g. article) such as the components of Serial Item and Contribution Identifier or SICI string; and even title identification, as provided by the ISBN. Proponents of intelligible identifiers note that the identifier can provide some level of resource verification before the user commits to retrieving the referenced resource. Intelligible identifiers can also capture a relationship between the source artifact and the digital surrogate, for users who wish to trace the digital

object back to its source, as for example when an identifier for a digital book includes the ISBN number assigned to the printed source. They can also provide meaningful information to applications, such as article retrieval systems, which can identify the journal title, ISSN, volume and issue number from an intelligible SICI-based resolver, for example.

Opaque identifiers are recommended by some authorities to avoid 'identity rot', which can occur when parts of the identifier become meaningless over time, such as the resource-managing agency or the country of origin. Intelligible identifiers are also faulted for being more difficult to develop and assign and for being language and context specific, to the detriment of global information use. Opaque identifiers are generally assumed to be more durable and simpler to assign, with a higher probability of global uniqueness. However, opaque identifiers can be difficult for patrons to use as they provide no mnemonic characteristics to enable a user to easily remember and recreate the identifier. A library should carefully consider its identifier creation practises in terms of its own context, the context of its significant partners and the shared global information space. Either strategy can be appropriate, as long as the library carefully considers, tests and documents its identifier strategy.

- *Maintained as an international standard.* An international standard has the benefit of defined rules of application, so that identifiers can be consistently developed and applied. International standards also generally conform to stringent requirements for versioning and compatibility with previous versions and with other standards. Applications, such as resolvers, are often available for international standards. Using an international standard also implies some level of interoperability with other organizations using the same standard. If a library chooses to develop its own identifier specification, the library should ensure that it can achieve the requirements of consistency and interoperability that are part of a robust identification strategy and thus are generally addressed by international standards.

Identifier standards

The good news for libraries is that identifiers have long been recognised as a critical issue for resource management, in both the commercial publishing and the library arenas. Many open-source and low-cost strategies that address all or most of the requirements for a robust identifier system have been developed. This section looks at some of the more prominent and readily available identification strategies available for libraries. This list is not exhaustive, but represents the current 'state of the art' for identifier assignment and management:

The 'I' standards: ISBN, ISSN, ISAN, ISWC, ISRN, ISTC, etc.

The International Standards Organization (ISO) played an early and important role in developing standard identifiers that could be deployed internationally to support commercial publishing and subsequent resource management by libraries and bookstores. Many of the ISO identification standards have become fixtures in commercial information resources. The library will want to create a unique identifier for the digital manifestation that the library creates, using one of the strategies for locally assigned identifiers described later in this section. However, the library will want to reference the identifier for the published source object, such as the ISBN for a book or the ISSN for a serial, either through a cross-reference within the identifier, as the XRI (eXtensible Resource Identifier, described below) provides, or within the metadata describing the object, to provide a durable link between the published source object and the library's digital manifestation.

Representative ISO standards include:

ISBN

ISBN was created in 1970 and codified as ISO Standard 2108. Each component of the ISBN numeric string (formerly 10 digits, now 13) has significance, as opposed to an opaque identifier that cannot be deconstructed and interpreted. The parts of the ISBN are: the group or country identifier, publisher identifier, title or edition identifier and the check digit.[10] ISBNs are assigned by publishers to books at the manifestation level, so that a hardcover edition of a book would have a different ISBN than the soft cover edition. The 10-digit ISBN was an identifier success story, enabling publishers, book dealers, bookstores and libraries to manage, inventory, purchase, distribute and catalog books. The 10-digit ISBN reached capacity, and a 13-digit strategy, ISBN-13, utilizing the 978 EAN prefix for the book industry conforming to the GTIN (Global Trade Item Number), was adopted in 2005 to expand ISBN capacity and was required for use as of 1 January 2007.[11] ISBN is currently not actionable, but a central database with associated metadata and actionability are being considered to extend ISBN functionality further.[12] ISBN currently does not support automatic relationships among manifestations of a title or identification for component parts of a title, such as the chapter or a contribution within a book anthology or compilation.

ISBN is managed by the ISBN International Agency and by ISBN group agencies at the national or consortial level.

Ultimate management rests with the publishers who assign ISBNs to their book titles.[13] ISBN has broad penetration into book purchasing, distribution and inventory systems, as well as bibliographic utilities and library catalogs.

ISSN (International Standard Serial Number)

ISSN was developed in 1975 as ISO standard 3297. Unlike ISBNs, ISSNs are not managed by the individual publishers. The ISSN International Centre in Paris manages an international central database, the ISSN Register. National management is provided by designated ISSN national agencies. ISSN is an opaque identifier and does not represent the country, the publisher or the title within the components of the eight-digit numeric string. Like the ISBN, an ISSN is specific to a manifestation, i.e. the medium in which the title is issued. Changes to a serial title, such as a name change, require the assignment of a new ISSN.[14] A revision in 2005, the 't-issn', provides title-level identification to enable co-location of different manifestations (media versions) of a title, e.g. the print, microform and digital versions. The first ISSN assigned will serve as the co-locating, top-level 't-issn'. The t-issn occupies a separate namespace from the ISSN.[15]

ISAN (International Standard Audiovisual Number)

ISAN, unlike ISBN and ISSN, applies at the work or expression level. ISAN is applied to the same work regardless of its format or means of transmission (broadcast, streaming medium, etc.) ISAN became ISO Standard 15706 in 2002 and is managed in a central database by the International ISAN Agency. The ISAN is an opaque or 'dumb' identifier because it does not represent the country, publisher or title in a meaningful and explicit string.[16]

ISWC (International Standard Musical Work Code)

ISWC was adopted as ISO Standard 15707 in 2001, under the auspices of CISAC (International Confederation of Societies of Authors and Composers). ISWC provides identification at the work level, not at the expression or manifestation level. As the ISWC International Agency notes, 'the ISWC will uniquely and accurately identify each specific musical work.'[17] An ISWC number begins with the letter 'T' followed by a dash, nine digits, a dash and a concluding check digit. An ISWC is assigned only after all the creators have been uniquely identified. Descriptive metadata assigned to each ISWC includes the title of the work and all composers, authors and arrangers, each uniquely identified by a CAE/IPI number (a rights management number assigned to musical works, where the CAE represents rights holders, 'compositeur, auteur, editeur', and the IPI number is assigned to each 'interested party' with a right in the work) and a role code, making this identifier standard unique in its equal attention to creator and title. A centralized database is maintained by CISAC in conformance to agreements with national management agencies.[17]

Other ISO identifier codes include the ISRN, or International Standard Technical Report Number (ISO 10444), used by research and scientific organisations to identify technical reports, and the ISTC, the International Standard Text Work Code, which identifies textual works at the work level.

URI, URN and URL (including Info URI)

URI, or Uniform Resource Identifier, is defined as 'a compact sequence of characters that defines an abstract or physical resource.'[18] URI has been issued by the IETF (Internet Engineering Task Force), with the collaboration and support of the World Wide Web Consortium (W3C) in 2005 as RFC 3986, Std 66. While a URI can apply as an identifier to a resource in any context, the syntax was designed to conform to the 'Functional Recommendations for Internet Resource Locators' [RFC1736] and 'Functional Requirements for Uniform Resource Names' [RFC1737],[18] making this identifier scheme particularly relevant for identifying digital resources to be shared across the web environment. Components of the URI are delineated by slash ('/') question mark ('?') and hash sign ('#'). The generic URI syntax is a hierarchical sequence of components: scheme, authority, path, query and fragment, expressed as:

> URI = scheme ':' '//' authority '/' path '?' query '#' fragment.

Multiple subpaths may be separated by the slash ('/').[18]

An info URI scheme was proposed in 2003 by the library and publishing communities under the auspices of ANSI/NISO (American National Standards Institute/National Information Standards Organization) to extend legacy identifiers into the web information space through the assignment of 'lightweight' URI registrations that utilise placeholder namespaces until the legacy identifier system establishes a permanent namespace suitable for creating a permanent hierarchical URI string. Namespaces used in the info URI string must be registered in the info Registry. Examples include the Dewey decimal classification info:ddc/ and the OCLC numbers info:oclcnum/ The info URI scheme was published as IETF RFC (Internet Engineering Technology Forum Request for Comments) 4452 in April 2006.[19]

URLs, or uniform resource locators, are a subset of URI. URLs generally represent the location of the resource in a one-to-one relationship between identifier and resource location and thus may become obsolete as resource location changes.

URNs, or uniform resource names, refers to URIs that conform to the URN syntax (RFC 2141) and are designed to be globally unique, location-independent and persistent, even if the resource to which the URN refers ceases to exist. The generic URN syntax consists of the following:

<URN> ::= "urn:" <NID> ":" <NSS>, where NID represents the Namespace identifier and NSS represents the namespace-specific string. URN is often identified as a subset of the URI standard.[20]

Recent work within the W3C Technical Architecture Group (TAG) has focused on the concept of 'de-referencing' – abstracting URIs from simple web pages or web documents to acknowledge that a URI may reference a representation of a resource that may require applications to render the resource, such as a browser or a visualisation tool. The URI may also reference a resource that is not web accessible, such as a concept (e.g. 'unit of measure') or an analog resource. The httpRange-14 document addresses the de-referencing issue, where response codes returned in response to a URI could provide different information and redirections for the user, for example, to an entity 'representing' the resource, through code 200 ('an entity corresponding to the resource' is being returned) and code 303, which indicates that 'the response to the request can be found under a different URI' and also provides the URI.[21] httpRange-14 adds a level of abstraction to the simple 'one-to-one' correspondence between a URI and a web resource and acknowledges the increasing complexity of the digital information landscape.

IRI (Internationalized Resource Identifier)

A recent development in URI syntax is the creation of the IRI, or internationalized resource identifier (RFC 3987), which extends the URI character set to encompass the Universal Character Set (Unicode/ISO 10646). The IRI syntax is very similar to URI with the addition of the extended Unicode character set. IRI syntax can also support international differences in character scanning, e.g. right to left or up and down instead of left to right. The IRI syntax specifies mapping from IRI to URI to ensure that the use of IRI does not prevent resolution to the actual resource, particularly within the HTTP protocol.[22]

PURL (Persistent Uniform Resource Locator)

PURL is functionally a URL that achieves location-independence through a global registry supporting resolution to the current location of the identified resource. PURL consists of three parts: the protocol, the resolver address and a name (locally assigned string). PURLs are required to last longer than any associated URLs, and in fact, longer than the identified resource. The PURL schema was developed by the OCLC, which also serves as the global authority committed to maintaining the permanence of PURL identifiers. PURLs are allocated and managed within a top-level and subdomain hierarchical structure, with OCLC, as the global registration authority, overseeing the hierarchical management infrastructure. Registered users are granted a range of permissions, from creating PURLs to managing top-level domains. PURL servers may be installed worldwide, in any location. The resolver address identifies the PURL server responsible for resolving each individual PURL. PURLs may resolve to a localized hierarchy of URLs, rather than to a specific resource.[23]

Libraries or individuals may create or modify PURLs, domains or groups for their resources that will use the OCLC resolver to maintain persistence. OCLC also provides open-source PURL software that may be downloaded from the OCLC PURL site.[8]

UUID/GUID (Universally Unique Identifier)

A UUID is a computationally derived identifier with an extremely high probability of global uniqueness over time and space. UUIDs are also known as Globally Unique Identifiers or GUIDs. The UUID is a 128-bit number that 'is either guaranteed to be different from all other UUIDs/GUIDs generated until 3400 AD or extremely likely to be different (depending on the mechanism chosen)' (Leach, p. 2).[24] No centralized authority administers UUIDs, which can be locally assigned by any organisation. A 'unique value over space' is required for each UUID generation, which must be specified as an IEEE 802 address, which can be obtained from the IEEE registration authority or generated to be 'probabilistically unique' (Leach, p. 4).[24] UUIDs are fixed size identifiers that can be automatically generated in conformance to the requirements of the UUID version that the organisation chooses to adopt. UUIDs consist of 16 octets that include timestamp, clock sequence and a spatially unique node identifier. The unique node identifier in version one of the UUID was derived from the unique MAC or network address. Other versions use local domain identifiers, random numbers or cryptographic hash functions (MD5 or SHA1).[25] UUIDs can be used for both ephemeral and permanent resources. There are many available open-source UUID generators available on the web.

SMPTE UMID (Unique Material Identifier)

UMID, a standard (330M-2000) from the Society of Motion Picture and Television Engineers, is a 'unique identifier for audio-visual material that is locally created and globally unique.'[26] It can be generated at point of audiovisual resource creation – by a person, an application, or automatically by a UMID-enabled device. The UMID may be a base UMID, providing sufficient information to identify the material, or an extended UMID, which adds a set of metadata ('source pack') to the base UMID.[26] The UMID provides a permanent reference for an audiovisual content unit in a clip or shot so that the content unit can be identified and tracked through any context of reuse. The UMID is a critical component in the SMPTE AAF (Advanced Authoring Format) and MXF (Media Exchange Format) standards, which are intended to manage media assets through the entire media creation and use lifecycle in an interoperable, cross-platform manner.

CNRI Handle System®

The CNRI Handle System®, was developed, and is maintained by, the Corporation for National Research Initiatives (CNRI). It is a 'general purpose distributed information system that provides efficient, extensible, and secure HDL identifier and resolution services for use on networks such as the Internet. It includes an open set of protocols, a namespace, and a reference implementation of the protocols. The protocols enable a distributed computer system to store identifiers, known as handles, of arbitrary resources and resolve those handles into the information necessary to locate, access, contact, authenticate, or otherwise make use of the resources.'[27]

Handles are managed for global uniqueness and resolution through distributed local handle service implementations and a Global Handle Registry (GHR), maintained by CNRI. The GHR works like any other handle service, but also maintains the registry of distributed handle services, each of which has its own handle. Each local handle service incorporates one or more distributed handle sites and each site contains one or more handle services. Handle services are hierarchical in nature with a primary site and secondary sites for replication, creating a scalable distributed architecture. All individual handle services must be replicated within a handle site.[28]

The Handle System® is a secured system, requiring administrators with permissions for handle creation and maintenance that are secured by either secret key or public/private key access controls. Resolution clients enable users to contact the GHR to determine which handle service and server to contact for individual resource resolution. A handle is a globally unique, actionable identifier. The format of a handle consists of two parts: a globally unique naming prefix, which must be registered with the GHR, and the suffix, the local name which must be unique within the local handle service.

The CNRI Handle System® is complex to implement, as it requires the implementation of a client/server architecture and participation in the global naming registry. However, handles are in widespread use within the library community. Reference implementations for handles service are included within both DSpace and Fedora Commons open-source repository architectures, for example. The Handle System® provides persistent, globally unique identifiers, centralised management of the global handles registry, and the ability to resolve to multiple instances of a resource or multiple attributes of a resource (including different services or applications that apply to the resource). One issue with handles is that the originating organisation is 'hard coded' into the identifier, which can lead to confusion about resource ownership and management, should the digital resource change hands, as when an organisation ceases existence and transfers its resources to other organizations.

DOI® (Digital Object Identifier)

DOI® emerged under the auspices of the American Association of Publishers (AAP) but quickly became an international effort, eventually resulting in an international organisation structure, the International DOI Foundation (IDF), in 1998. The DOI® system was developed to support intellectual property management, specifically within the publishing arena, but its usefulness has expanded beyond publishing to any context of resource management and use. Like the Handle System®, DOI® is a complete system for the management of globally unique identifiers in the shared digital information space. Unlike the Handle System®, however, the DOI® system incorporates an identification strategy within a broader solution for managing intellectual property, including the support of different intellectual property communities sharing a common context.[29] The DOI® system consists of four component parts:

- *Numbering*. The IDF numbering schema was recently revised and codified as standard as ANSI/NISO Z39.84-2005, which addresses the composition and ordering of the DOI alphanumeric string. The DOI identifier string contains 'a set of components with minimal meaning.' (National Information Standards Organization, vii).[30] Each DOI string begins with '10', which identifies the identifier as belonging to the DOI Handle Service, within the Handle System®'s GHR. The next component is assigned exclusively to the DOI Registration Authority who created the DOI. This number does not reflect current ownership of the DOI, or of the resource identified by the DOI, but strictly the DOI originator. The final, or suffix, component, is an unspecified identifier that uniquely represents the entity that is identified by the DOI. This suffix component can be completely opaque (e.g. not identifying, through its composition, any descriptive information about the resource that is being identified). (National Information Standards Organization, vii).[30]

- *A data model and interoperable data dictionary.* The DOI® system includes a metadata implementation that utilizes the indecs Ontologyx framework and the indecs Data Dictionary (iDD). The metadata component of the DOI® system is intended to accomplish two objectives: support interoperability and semantic precision across DOI® system implementations and support DOI® system communities of use through data application profiles. Registration Authorities (RAs) are required to conform to the minimum requirements of the DOI® system data policy, including the ability to support, and produce, a kernel metadata declaration, composed of mandatory core data elements, for each DOI issued. Metadata that is shared among DOI® system participants should utilise the DOI® system Resource Metadata Declaration (RMD), a messaging protocol and schema for sharing metadata among all DOI® system registration authorities. Finally, registration authorities should map their proprietary data elements into the DOI® system iDD, in order to utilise the indecs event-based data model and ontology developed by Ontologyx for complete semantic interoperability across DOI® system RAs. The iDD is also under development as the repository of all metadata data elements and the information ('values') stored in those data elements, for kernels and for all RMDs.[31] The iDD has also been adopted as the basis of the MPEG-21 Rights Data Dictionary (RDD), discussed in the chapter on rights metadata.
- *Resolution*, through a Handle System® implementation.
- *A policy and governance infrastructure.* Unlike many other identification systems, the DOI® system relies on a fee-based membership business model, as well as mandatory participation requirements with regard to data, resolution

> and identifier creation. The DOI® system is managed by the IDF, a non-profit organisation created in 1998 with an elected Governing Board and a licensing strategy for long-term sustainability of the DOI® system.[29]

The DOI® system has widespread support within the publishing industry, including sponsorship by the EDItEUR and ONIX international publisher associations, as well as the AAP. The DOI identifier is perhaps most frequently used in a library setting within the context of OpenURL implementations for access to article-level full-text resources identified through indexing and abstracting services. The DOI® system provides a complete end-to-end management for intellectual property and a sophisticated, interoperable metadata strategy. A library must weigh the many benefits of a DOI® system implementation against the ongoing cost of DOI® system licensing and the complexity of its implementation.

ARK (Archival Resource Key)

ARK was developed by the California Digital Library and the National Library of Medicine and is now available as an IETF Internet draft. As noted by its lead developer, John Kunze, 'A founding principle of ARK is that persistence is purely a matter of service and is neither inherent in an object nor conferred on it by a particular naming syntax. The best an identifier can do is lead users to those services.' (Kunze, 2).[32] The ARK strategy identifies persistence as a multi-faceted issue that must include the organisation's stated commitment to persistence, which may change over time. ARK's actionability provides resolution to three things: the object, metadata about the object, and the current provider's commitment statement, which represents the provider's promise for persistence of the resource to which the ARK applies. The ARK string is a form of URL that supports a transfer of responsibility from one service provider responsible for making the resource available to another. ARK accomplishes this through a temporary or mutable component, the Name Mapping Authority Hostport (NMAH), which can be replaced as often as needed to reflect new management of the resource. The ARK identifier is a special URL consisting of temporary and permanent components:

http://NMAH/ark:/NAAN/name[qualifier]

The NMAH represents the current service provider for ARK resolution and resource management and is thus a temporary or changeable identifier component. The NAAN, or Name Assigning Authority Number, is a permanent component, which represents the originator of the ARK and thus the original service provider. As this reflects the historical provenance of the ARK and its associated resource, this is a permanent component, as is the name string, which is unique to each identifier. ARK resolution uses an algorithm to identify the current NMAH for an object. A NAAN may be obtained by any organisation wishing to implement ARK from the California Digital Library.[33]

A single question mark ('?') following the ARK identifier will produce metadata about the object. A double question mark ('??') will produce a commitment statement concerning the service provider's agreement or promise for persistence of the associated object. Entering the ARK into a browser followed by no question marks will resolve to the resource itself.

ARK uses *noid*, an open-source identifier minter utility, written in PERL and available as an open-source application. The noid (nice opaque identifier) utility creates identifier minters (i.e. generators) to produce consistent, globally unique identifiers. Noid is a lightweight database utility for identifier management that generates identifiers in random or sequential order and bindings to connect the identifiers to the relevant resource metadata elements and values. The noid utility can be run as a web service and also provides a resolver running behind a web server. Noid can be used to generate ARKs or used independently as an open-source application to generate consistent, actionable identifiers within a library's repository or other web-based resource service. Noid can be downloaded from the CPAN (Comprehensive PERL Archive Network) website.[34]

XRI (Extensible Resource Identifier)

XRI is a standard from OASIS (Organization for the Advancement of Structured Information Standards), a not-for-profit global consortium that focuses on the development and adoption of e-business standards. XRI is intended to identify any entity within an IT framework: resources, people and network assets. XRI is an expansion on URI and IRI. XRI is an actionable identifier. The resolution process converts the authority and path components of an XRI identifier to an XML metadata document, the XRI Descriptor (XRD), which documents the resource and the retrieval methodology. As with the ARK identifier, components of the XRI are designated as permanent 'primary' keys, while other components can be changed as the XRI's context changes. The basic XRI syntax is:

xri://authority / path ? query # fragment (Reed, p. 4)[35]

One of the most interesting characteristics of XRI is the ability to encapsulate cross-references. This enables a compound identifier, where the identifier contains part of its provenance and description within the identifier. Examples of cross-references include cross-referencing an ISBN within an XRI for a specific digital book surrogate and incorporating an email or website address as a cross-reference within an XRI for a person

(Reed, p. 5).[35] XRI also supports trusted resolution through SAML (Security Assertion Markup Language) assertions in XRD and HTTPS (Wachob, pp. 31–32).[36] XRI utilises the full Unicode character set specified for IRI, and provides automatic mapping to IRI, which can then be mapped to URI. XRI is characterised by fully structured and defined components, or subsegments, such as the ability of the assigner to specify that a subsegment is permanent or changeable.

XRI is a very functional identifier standard but is complex to implement. It leverages both the HTTP protocol and the XML semantic expression standard. Libraries considering this standard should weigh the initial investment in implementing the standard against the functionality that this feature-rich, highly interoperable identifier standard provides. There are open-source applications available that implement XRI, including client-server resolution and registration services. One useful implementation is the XRI 'i-name' identifier, which conforms to the LDAP directory schema (see Chapter 5 for details).[37] I feel that XRI has great potential particularly for identifying creators and rights holders in a digital rights implementation. XRI will be discussed further in Chapter 8.

Authenticity of the resource

The second issue with regard to resources in the DRM space is to ensure the authenticity of the resource. As we have seen in the previous section, a globally unique and durable identifier that will always reference and locate the expected resource is critical to the provision of authentic resources in the digital information space. However, this is only half the equation. The identified resource must be the resource that the user is expecting to retrieve. Particularly in a DRM transaction, the user has high expectations of the resource with regard to authoritativeness and responsiveness to the user's information need. Providing the expected resource to the end user is a fundamental element of the trust relationship that a library has with its users. The user also has expectations that the resource, when retrieved, will not be corrupted or modified from the source information, unless this modification has been documented and justified in administrative provenance metadata, and the modifications are understood and accepted by the user.

In the digital space, authenticity refers to the provenance and contextual information surrounding the resource, e.g. if the user expects to retrieve a facsimile of *Huckleberry Finn* with Mark Twain's handwritten notes in the margin, he/she will not feel that a transcription of *Huckleberry Finn* in an online text format is the authentic resource. Authenticity also refers to fidelity to the source information – a high-resolution facsimile providing the most fidelity and legibility to the source information will be more authentic than a poorly sampled, low-resolution version. Lastly, authenticity over time is based on permanence of information. A digital resource will be referenced and used many times over its lifecycle, and access to the unchanged resource, or to the version of the resource that was quoted, cited or reused, is critical for retaining the public's trust in the authenticity of the resource. Resources rarely exist in a dark digital vault. Generally, organisations preserve what they value, and this value is often based on the perceived usefulness of the resource to others. If changes occur to a resource, it is important to retain previous versions, which may have been cited or otherwise used, to reflect a durable and authentic link between resources related to each other by use.

How can authenticity be ensured for digital resources? One critical issue is that the digital resource is either the unchanged source data or a highly faithful facsimile of the source data. To achieve this, the digital master file should be created in a format that is accepted by the digital library community for the type of information, whether text, image, audiovisual or data resource. This format will generally represent a high-resolution digital facsimile in an open or widely available format standard, such as the TIFF format for digital image files. Most national libraries, archives and national or regional digitisation initiatives provide minimum digitisation standards for different analog formats and for born-digital resources. A digitisation project should seek to conform to standards provided by national initiatives or consortia in which the library currently participates or might in the future. An excellent source for prevailing standards for digital resource masters is the NISO *Framework of Guidance for Building Good Digital Collections*, currently in its third edition. The *Framework* includes a typology of formats with guidelines and recommendations for creating preservation digital master files (NISO Framework Working Group, pp. 28–36).[38]

After the resource is digitised to a recommended digital master standard, there are automated tools that can help a library maintain the physical authenticity of a resource. Recently, format registries and format validation frameworks as well as reference applications of those frameworks have emerged that identify digital file formats, document the characteristics of those formats, and automatically verify that ingested objects conform to the established reference formats. These framework applications can be used to validate and document the formats of digital files upon ingest into a library's repository, thus automatically providing technical metadata about file format types and characteristics. In addition, these applications can periodically validate that stored digital objects continue to conform to reference formats and thus are not corrupted, at least with regard to digital formatting.

These format validation application frameworks also support global migration of data from one format to another by validating each object after migration to ensure that the format conversion is error free. The forthcoming Global Digital Format Registry (GDFR) will serve as an authoritative format registry in the global information space.[39] JHOVE (JSTOR/Harvard Object Validation Environment) performs three format-related analytic activities on a digital resource: format identification (what is the format of the resource?), format validation (does the resource conform to the expected format?) and format characterisation (what are the salient format-specific properties of the object?). Each analytic action is performed by a different module, using a plug-in architecture that allows the user to analyze standard formats and also to add additional formats as needed.[40]

PRONOM, a technical registry of data formats and the software applications that produce them, is a product of the UK National Archives. PRONOM provides a metadata registry of information about formats, as well as the software that produces and displays them, and the requirements for formats and software. Information about file formats and software can be added by others through a web submission form. More detail about file formats will be added to PRONOM in the future.[41]

DROID (Digital Record Object Identification), also developed by the UK National Archives, is an application that performs batch file format identification, based on signatures in an XML signature file, generated from the PRONOM registry. DROID downloads signatures from the PRONOM registry, either in a manual or an automated process. DROID is written in Java and can be downloaded from SourceForge.[42]

In addition to ensuring that the resource is captured and maintained in an acceptable file format, a library will want to ensure that the resource, as captured in that format, remains unchanged throughout its digital lifespan. The digital resource may be transcoded to a new digital format over time, but as long as the file format storing the information remains viable, it should be unchanged. The most common strategy to ensure this persistence is to maintain multiple copies of the digital master (identical in every aspect, except, of course, storage location as two physical objects cannot occupy the same physical space). This ensures that if one digital copy is damaged or lost, another copy, identical in every respect, is available to take its place.

When a library has thousands of digital objects, perhaps organised in a repository, how can a library know if a digital file is corrupted or lost? A simple strategy that has been successfully employed by many libraries is the assignment of a checksum, which may be a cyclic redundancy check or a cryptographic hash. Essentially, a checksum works by adding the components or bits of a file and storing the result with the file, which can be compared against the file at any point in time or space. Discrepancies indicate that the file has been changed or corrupted in some manner. Common checksum formats include SHA-1 and MD-5. Although checksums are not foolproof, they do support a semi-automated way of checking files for errors. Open-source repository architectures such as DSpace and Fedora Commons include the assignment of checksums to files. There are also open-source applications that automatically assign checksums to digital files. Crawlers can then be used to sample files and report checksum errors to a repository manager or ultimately to establish an event chain that replaces the corrupted file with the most current backup copy.

A higher-level strategy for ensuring the unchanging integrity of a resource is the digital timestamp, which adds the concepts of time and referential integrity to the assurance of validity provided by a checksum or other cryptographic hash. Digital timestamps guarantee the integrity of a document through cryptographic information that guarantees the minimum and maximum age of a document. Digital objects are timestamped in a batch, and the timestamp is published in a manner that cannot be repudiated, such as in a dated newspaper issue. The entire batch of timestamped documents are also used to provide group support for the validity of content dating. The timestamp of a questioned document can be compared with other documents in the batch. If all dates contained within the batch are identical, this serves to validate the questioned document, as tampering with all documents is statistically improbable (Maniatis, p. 3).[43]

As discussed earlier in this chapter, formats that provide a more faithful surrogate for the source information may emerge, or the digital master file format may become obsolete and no longer supported by hardware and software applications. All digital objects in the superseded format will need to be identified, transcoded to a new, viable digital master format, verified for successful migration, and evaluated for quality and completeness. The format migration event needs to be documented in metadata, particularly for the benefit of users who may have utilised or cited the resource in its previous form and need to be aware of any changes, even a fairly transparent change to a new physical format.

Provenance information is important for documenting and maintaining the authenticity of the resource. Provenance includes information about the creation, ownership and ongoing management of a resource. Provenance provides the content authenticity for the resource, so that a user knows that he or she has retrieved the resource that conforms to the metadata description that he/she used to select the resource. Provenance metadata also provides a digital audit trail of any changes to the resource, so that the user also knows that the resource has not been edited or damaged in any meaningful way from the source original. Provenance metadata can also be used to document approved changes to the resource, as well as the rationale for those changes, so that a user knows the complete lifecycle of the resource.

The need for provenance metadata was first acknowledged in the Open Archival Information System (OAIS) model. The Consultative Committee for Space Data Standards developed a reference model for an OAIS that provides a framework for ingest, archiving, management, preservation and access to information contained within a digital repository. Metadata provides both the intelligence and the 'glue' that integrates the activities that maintain information across the information object's lifecycle within the repository, including its accessibility for users. The OAIS model identifies types of metadata important for managing and preserving information, including provenance, technical, and fixity information (Figure 4.4).

The OAIS reference model defines the collecting, maintenance and delivery of information to users. It documents the ingest and archiving of the resource, as well as providing descriptive information about the intellectual content of the resource. The OAIS Functional Model represents an end-to-end approach for managing digital resources within an archive, from ingest into the archive through storage and preservation within the archive, to delivery to the end user.

Three important entities in the OAIS model are the 'packages' that combine the information resource with the metadata relevant for each specific high-level task in a digital archive: submission, archiving and dissemination. The SIP,

Figure 4.4 **OAIS reference model for an open archival information system**

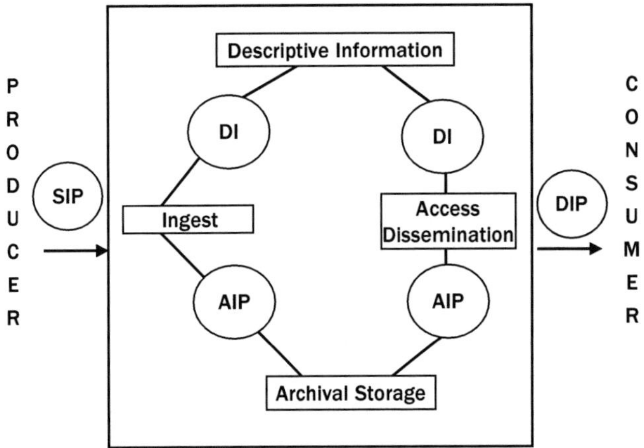

or submission information package, includes the information, or metadata, relevant to the provenance of the object before it is ingested into the repository, such as information about creation and ownership, and characteristics of the data. The AIP, or archival information package, contains information about its ongoing authenticity within the repository, for example its fixity, i.e. that the resource is unchanged, except for changes documented by the archive for ongoing management purposes, and its rights for dissemination. The DIP, or dissemination information package, includes the metadata needed to discover and interpret the intellectual content of the resource, the information needed to display the resource in a digital environment, and any information, such as rights metadata, needed to utilise the resource.[44]

The OAIS is a high-level model, not a reference implementation. Many standards have emerged to provide an OAIS implementation. Two standards of interest are PREMIS and METS. Both standards include provenance information about the resource.

What is meant, precisely by provenance? Clifford Lynch, in his article 'Authenticity and integrity in the digital environment', defined provenance as 'documentation about the origin, characteristics and history of an object, its chain of custody, and its relationship to other objects.'[45] Provenance is important for demonstrating the authenticity of a digital resource over time, as a digital resource may be modified, corrupted or otherwise drift from its origins, over time. Provenance information can document the authoritative version of information, in terms of its technical, custodial and intellectual characteristics, which may be compared with the resource to determine that the resource corresponds to its provenance.

How can you pull all the different metadata categories together to create an OAIS-compliant archive that provides for complete management of digital resources? Two useful examples follow.

PREMIS

OCLC and the Research Libraries Group brought together a working group in 2003 to develop a practical implementation of the metadata identified by OAIS as necessary to preserve digital objects. The Working Group developed a preservation metadata architecture, PREMIS (Preservation Metadata Implementation Strategies). Priscilla Caplan (Florida Center for Library Automation) and Rebecca Guenther (Library of Congress) co-chaired the Working Group, with the intent, as Caplan and Guenther noted, to develop a 'common, implementable core set of metadata elements for digital preservation.' (Caplan and Guenther, p. 111).[46] The PREMIS working group included representatives from libraries, museums, archives, governments and commercial enterprises in six countries. An international advisory board also provided guidance and input. The PREMIS Working Group included two subgroups: the Core Elements Subgroup and the Implementation Strategies Subgroup.

The Core Elements Subgroup defined the concept of 'core elements' for preservation metadata to be 'those elements that a working archive is likely to need to know in order to support the functions of ensuring viability, renderability, understandability, authenticity and identity in a preservation context.' (Caplan and Guenther, p. 115).[46] PREMIS developed its initial core elements by surveying organisations engaged in digital preservation activities, looking for commonly used data elements that could form a corpus of 'core elements' or semantic units. An activity that emerged from the consensus approach was the need to develop a data model that would add relationship, context and rigor to the development of core element subschemas.

The PREMIS data model consists of five entities. The definitions below are quoted directly from the Caplan and Guenther article:

- 'An event is an action that involves at least one object, agent and/or rights entity
- An agent is an actor associated with preservation events in the life of an object
- A right is an assertion of one or more rights or permissions pertaining to an object
- An intellectual entity is a coherent set of content that is reasonably described as a unit, for example a particular book, map, photograph or database
- An object is one or more sequences of bits stored in the preservation repository.' (Caplan and Guenther, p. 117).[46]

One of the important concepts behind PREMIS is the subdivision of an object into four physical subtypes:

- file, defined as 'a named, ordered sequence of zero or more bytes, known to an operating system and accessible by applications';
- a bitstream, defined as 'data within a file that cannot be transformed into a stand-alone file without the addition of file structures (headers, etc.) and/or reformatting in order to comply with some particular file format';
- 'a filestream is a contiguous set of bits within a file that can be transformed into a stand-alone file conforming to some file format without adding information or reformatting the bitstream';
- 'a representation is the set of files needed to provide a complete and reasonable rendition of an intellectual entity.' (Caplan and Guenther, pp. 117–118).[46]

An example of a bitstream is an image embedded in a TIFF. A filestream is a TIFF image within a TAR file (a file format frequently used to concatenate one or more files).

The data model also documents relationships. The relationships between objects, agents and events constitutes digital provenance.

The registration, or documentation, of a PREMIS semantic unit or data element within the PREMIS data dictionary provides the name of the unit; any components or subunits; rationale for the unit, the definition of the unit; the data constraint (controlled vocabulary, formatting principle); whether or not the semantic unit is a container or atomic subunit; the applicability to the four object subtypes and examples within each applicable subtype; the unit's repeatability; and its obligation for use within the schema (mandatory, optional, recommended), as well as notes on the creation and maintenance of the semantic unit and its usage. The PREMIS data dictionary is currently in version 2.0. The XML schema is currently in version 1.1, with version 2.0 in draft. PREMIS version 2.0 provides a number of significant additions, most importantly to rights metadata (discussed in Chapter 6) and also to extensibility, with an extension container provided for several semantic units, to enable one or more data elements from another schema to be used within PREMIS.[47]

PREMIS provides a model and XML schemas for each entity in the model, but a full implementation of an OAIS data architecture requires a *metadata system,* which consists of a metadata architecture and data model, metadata schemas for each metadata category (or model entity), and protocols and standards for binding the metadata together and making it actionable (able to be automatically acted upon by relevant computer applications). There are several metadata systems, particularly for digital multimedia, but the most common OAIS-compliant metadata system in libraries is the Metadata Encoding and Transmission Standard (METS). A number of organisations have developed METS profiles that incorporate the PREMIS data model and data dictionary.[48]

METS

METS was perhaps the first metadata system standard to codify an architecture, schemas and tools for implementing OAIS-compliant description encompassing all of the metadata categories required to describe and manage information objects. METS is a metadata system that provides encoding, a concatenating wrapper, and transmission of descriptive, administrative and structural metadata, expressed in XML. METS not only provides all the categories of metadata required to describe and manage the object, but it incorporates within the METS package the different physical instantiations of the resource, as well as procedures, or 'behaviors', that act upon the METS content.

An information object begins as source information, which may be an analog object, such as a photograph, or a digital object, such as a born-digital image. The source object is the *first generation* of the information object. Depending on the nature of the source object, an archive will create a digital preservation master, which is a high-resolution digital surrogate for the source information. This digital preservation master will be as faithful to the source object as possible. The archive will also create one or more access or presentation copies from the archival master, which are low-resolution digital copies that can be displayed on a range of computers and Internet connection bandwidths and that are less likely to be reproduced for unauthorised uses. The end user thus typically experiences the *third generation* of a resource.

METS accommodates all the physical instantiations, also called manifestations, of an information object. Physical manifestations of an information object have different technical characteristics. For example, a digital master image may be a TIFF image that was digitised at 600 dpi (dots per inch). An access copy may be a low-resolution, highly compressed JPEG image digitized at 72 dpi. Different manifestations may have different associated rights. A low-resolution image may be available for viewing at no cost, but a high-resolution image suitable for reproduction in a book may require the payment of a license fee for access. METS packages all the instantiations of an object, the structural components of an object (e.g. pages in a book), and all the metadata documents that comprise the descriptive and administrative metadata into a standardized package that may be ingested into a repository or transported across repositories. METS utilises the *file section* (*fileSec*) to document each object manifestation within a file group element (*fileGrp*), which identifies and locates each manifestation. The *structural map* (*structMap*) documents the hierarchical structure of an object, such as the pages in a book, and provides pointers to content so that users can navigate the information object. The *structural map linking* (*structLink*) links the component objects within the structure map.

METS metadata provides *descriptive metadata* for the intellectual content (*dmdMD*) and an administrative metadata section (*amdSec*) that concatenates the administrative metadata for the object: technical metadata (*techMD*) documenting the physical characteristics of the digital object, source metadata (*sourceMD*) documenting the provenance and characteristics of the information source (which may be an analog object), rights metadata (*rightsMD*), which documents the copyright status, permissions and restrictions associated with the object, and digital provenance (*digiprovMD*), which documents digital provenance ('preservation') events in the lifecycle of the digital object.

Figure 4.5 **Components of a METS document**

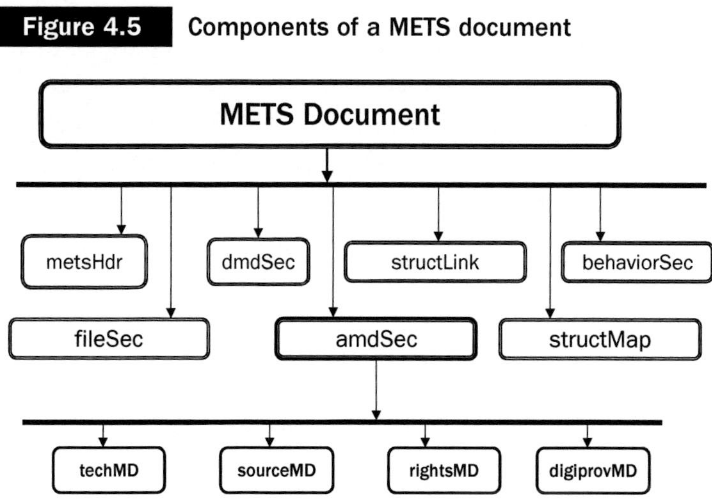

Metadata documents may be associated within the METS package with different object manifestations, such as different rights metadata documents, describing different permissions for a high-resolution and a low-resolution object within the METS package. METS also includes *behaviors* (*behaviorSec*), which are procedures that are executed against the content contained in the METS package and a *header* (*metsHdr*) to provide metadata about the METS document (Figure 4.5).[49]

Putting the pieces together

Systems and standards for identification, authenticity and transport of objects in the digital space are enabling research on the discovery, transport and reuse of objects across disparate repository and asset management architectures. Managing the object for authenticity is critical for managing rights to reuse the object. Both parties in a rights transaction must be in agreement about the identity of the resource in question. The resource must also be readily available once conditions for use are satisfied. The resource must be able to be authenticated against provenance statements that identify, among other things, the creator, the rights holder and the terms of use offered by the rights holder. Ensuring resources that are persistent and authentic is not trivial but is critical for maintaining the integrity of any rights transactions, including the common transaction within libraries of making a resource freely available for use in the open access environment.

Notes and references

1. Paskin, Norman. (2003) 'On making and identifying a 'copy'.' *D-Lib Magazine*, 9(1). Last accessed 23 March 2008. *http://www.dlib.org/dlib/january03/paskin/01paskin.html*

2. MacNeil, Heather (2000). 'Providing grounds for trust: developing conceptual requirements for the long-term preservation of authentic electronic records.' *Archivaria* 30, 53–76.
3. IFLA Study Group on the Functional Requirements for Bibliographic Records (1998). *Functional Requirements for Bibliographic Records: Final Report* (UBCIM Publications, New Series vol. 19, pp. 12–13). Munich: K.G. Saur. Last accessed 23 March 2008. *http://www.ifla.org/VII/s13/frbr/frbr.pdf*
4. Iverson, Vaughn, *et al.* (eds) *MPEG-21 Digital Item Declaration WD* (v 2.0). Singapore: International Organization for Standardization, ISO/IEC JTC 1/SC 29/WG 11, Coding of Motion Pictures and Audio, March 2001. Last accessed 23 March 2008. *http://xml.coverpages.org/MPEG21-WG-11-N3971-200103.pdf*
5. Lagoze, Carl and Van de Sompel, Herbert (eds) (2007) *ORE Specification – Abstract Data Model.* Open Archives Initiative. Last accessed 23 March 2008. *http://www.openarchives.org/ore/0.1/datamodel*
6. Lagoze, Carl and Van de Sompel, Herbert (eds) (2008) *ORE Specification – Abstract Data Model.* Open Archives Initiative. Last accessed 2 May 2008. *http://www.openarchives.org/ore/0.3/datamodel*
7. Antelman, Kristin and Davis, Susan (2005). 'Implementing a serial work in an electronic resources management system.' *Serials Librarian* 48(3/4): 287.
8. OCLC Programs and Research. *PURLS.* Dublin, OH: OCLC (Online Computer Library Center). Last accessed 23 March 2008. *http://purl.oclc.org/*
9. Leach, P., Mealling, M. and Salz, R. (2005) *A Universally Unique Identifier (UUID) URN Namespace (RFC 4122).* Sterling, VA: IETF. Last accessed 23 March 2008. *http://www.ietf.org/rfc/rfc4122.txt*
10. Bowker. 'Frequently Asked Questions about the ISBN.' *ISBN SAN ISMN.* New Providence, NJ: Bowker, c2008. Last accessed 23 March 2008. *http://www.isbn.org/standards/home/isbn/us/isbnqa.asp#Q4*
11. Wikipedia. *International Standard Book Number.* St. Petersburg, FL: Wikimedia Foundation, Inc. Last modified

28 April 2008. Last accessed 2 May 2008. *http://en.wikipedia.org/wiki/ISBN*

12. Vitiello, Giuseppe (2004). 'Identifiers and identification systems: an informational look at policies and roles from a library perspective'. *D-Lib Magazine* 10(1). Last accessed 23 March 2008. *http://www.dlib.org/dlib/january04/vitiello/01vitiello.html*
13. Bowker, 'Administration of the ISBN.' *ISBN, SAN, ISMN* New Providence, NJ: Bowker, c2008. Last accessed 23 March 2008. *http://www.isbn.org/standards/home/isbn/international/administration.asp*
14. ISSN International Centre. *What is an ISSN?* Paris, France: ISSN International Centre, c2006. Last accessed 23 March 2008. *http://www.issn.org/en/node/64*
15. CONSER (2005). 'Revision of the ISSN Standard Moves Forward' *CONSERLine* no. 26. Last accessed 23 March 2008. *http://www.loc.gov/acq/conser/conserline/conserline-26.html#ISSN*
16. ISO TC 46/SC 9 Secretariat. *Frequently Asked Questions about the ISAN Version Identifier for Audiovisual Works.* Ottawa: ISO TC 46/SC 9 Secretariat, last updated 11 July 2005. Last accessed 23 March 2008. *http://www.collectionscanada.ca/iso/tc46sc9/v-isan.htm*
17. ISWC International Agency. *FAQ*. Paris: International Confederation of Societies of Authors and Composers. Last accessed 23 March 2008. *http://www.iswc.org/en/html/FAQA.html*
18. Berners-Lee, T., Fielding, R. and Masinter, L. (2005) *Uniform Resource Identifier (URI): Generic Syntax* (RFC 3986). Sterling, VA: IETF. Last accessed 23 March 2008. *http://www.ietf.org/rfc/rfc3986.txt*
19. 'About 'info' URIs: Frequently Asked Questions' *'info' URI Scheme*. Dublin, OH: OCLC Office of Research, 24 May 2006. Last accessed 23 March 2008. *http://info-uri.info/registry/docs/misc/faq.html*
20. Moats, R. (1997) *URN Syntax* (RFC 2141). Sterling, VA: IETF. Last accessed 23 March 2008. *http://www.ietf.org/rfc/rfc2141.txt*

21. Lewis, Rhys (ed.) (2007) *Dereferencing HTTP URIs: Draft Tag finding, 31 May 2007*. Cambridge, MA: W3C. Last accessed 23 March 2008. *http://www.w3.org/2001/tag/doc/httpRange-14/2007-05-31/HttpRange-14*
22. Duerst, M. and Suignard, M. (2005) *Internationalized Resource Identifiers* (*IRIs*). (RFC 3987). Sterling, VA: IETF. Last accessed 23 March 2008. *http://www.ietf.org/rfc/rfc3987.txt*
23. Shafer, Keith, *et al. Introduction to Persistent Uniform Resource Locators*. Dublin, OH: OCLC. Last accessed 23 March 2008. *http://purl.oclc.org/docs/inet96.html*
24. Leach, Paul J. and Salz, Rich. (1998) UUIDs and GUIDs. (Internet-Draft). San Francisco: Open Group, Expires 4 August 1998. Last accessed 24 March 2008. *http://www.opengroup.org/dce/info/draft-leach-uuids-guids-01.txt*
25. Wikipedia. *Universally Unique Identifier*. St. Petersburg, FL: Wikimedia Foundation, Inc. Last modified 1 May 2008. Last accessed 2 May 2008. *http://en.wikipedia.org/wiki/UUID*
26. SMPTE (2003). *SMPTE 330M-200X: SMPTE Standard, Unique Material Identifier (UMID) (Private Committee Document) Version 5e*. White Plains, NY: SMPTE. Last accessed 23 March 2008. *www.irmaproject.net/Members/egoray/thesaurus-dictionnaire-metadata/s330m-umid.pdf*
27. Corporation for National Research Initiatives. *The Handle System*. Reston, VA: CNRI. Last updated 24 March 2008. Last accessed 2 May 2008. *http://www.handle.net/index.html*
28. Corporation for National Research Initiatives. 'Handle System Architecture.' *Handle System: Unique Persistent Identifiers for Internet Resources*. Reston, VA: CNRI. Updated 17 April 2007. Last accessed 23 March 2008. *http://www.handle.net/overviews/architecture.html*
29. Paskin, Norman (ed.) 'The International DOI Foundation, [chapter] 7.' *DOI Handbook*, doi:10.1000/182. International DOI Foundation, Updated 5 October 2006. Last accessed 23 March 2008. *http://www.doi.org/handbook_2000/governance.html*
30. National Information Standards Organization. *Syntax for the Digital Object Identifier, ANSI/NISO Z39.84-2005. An American National Standard developed by the National*

Information Standards Organization. Bethesda, MD: NISO Press, Approved 30 September 2005. Last accessed 2 May 2008. Available in PDF format via: *http://www.niso.org/kst/reports/standards/listing/process*

31. Paskin, Norman (ed.) 'DOI® Data Model, [chapter] 4' *DOI Handbook,* doi:10.1000/182. International DOI Foundation. Updated 5 October 2006. Last accessed 23 March 2008. *http://www.doi.org/handbook_2000/metadata.html*
32. Kunze, John A. *Towards Electronic Persistence Using ARK Identifiers*. Oakland, CA: California Digital Library. Last accessed 23 March 2008. *www.cdlib.org/inside/diglib/ark/arkcdl.pdf*
33. Kunze, John. 'Archival Resource Key (ARK).' *Inside CDL*. Oakland, CA: California Digital Library. Last reviewed 18 September 2007. Last accessed 24 March 2008. *http://www.cdlib.org/inside/diglib/ark/*
34. Kunze, John A. *Noid*. CPAN. Last accessed 23 March 2008. *http://search.cpan.org/dist/Noid/noid*
35. Reed, Drummond and McAlpin, Dave (eds) (2005). *Extensible Resource Identifier (XRI) Syntax V2.0. Committee Draft 02*. Billerica, MA: OASIS. Last accessed 23 March 2008. *http://docs.oasis-open.org/xri/2.0/specs/xri-syntax-V2.0-cd-02.pdf*
36. Wachob, Gabe, *et al.* (eds) (2006) *Extensible Resource Identifier (XRI) Resolution V2.0, Working Draft 10 (xri-resolution-V2.0-wd-10)* . Billerica, MA: OASIS. Last accessed 23 March 2008. *http://oasis-open.org/committees/download.php/17293*
37. Schleiff, M. (2006) LDAP Schema for eXtensible Resource Identifier (XRI) draft-schleiff-ldap-xri-01 (Internet-draft). Reston, VA: Internet Society (ISOC). Last accessed 23 March 2008. *https://opends.dev.java.net/public/standards/draft-schleiff-ldap-xri.txt*
38. NISO Framework Working Group (2007). *A Framework of Guidance for Building Good Digital Collections*, 3rd edn (A NISO Recommended Practice). Baltimore, MD: National Information Standards Organization. Last accessed 2 May 2008. *http://www.niso.org/publications/rp/framework3.pdf*

39. Harvard University Library. *Global Digital Format Registry*. Cambridge, MA: Harvard University. Last updated 7 October 2006. Last accessed 23 March 2008. *http://hul.harvard.edu/gdfr/*
40. JSTOR and Harvard University. *JHOVE: JSTOR/Harvard Object Validation Environment*. Cambridge, MA: Harvard University. Last updated 17 December 2007. Last accessed 23 March 2008. *http://hul.harvard.edu/jhove/*
41. National Archives. *PRONOM: the Technical Registry*. Kew, UK: The National Archives. Last accessed 23 March 2008. *http://www.nationalarchives.gov.uk/PRONOM/default.htm*
42. National Archives. *DROID: Digital Record Object Identification*. Kew, UK: The National Archives. Last modified 29 August 2006. Last accessed 23 March 2008. *http://droid.sourceforge.net/wiki/index.php/Introduction*
43. Maniatis, Petros, Giuli, T.J. and Baker, Mary (2001). 'Enabling the long-term archival of signed documents through time stamping.' Stanford, CA: Stanford University. Last modified 1 February 2008. Last accessed 24 March 2008. *http://arxiv.org/PS_cache/cs/pdf/0106/0106058v1.pdf*
44. Consultative Committee for Space Data Systems (2002). *Reference Model for an Open Archival Information System (OAIS): Recommendation for Space Data System Standards, CCSDS 650.0-B-1 Blue Book*. Washington, DC: CCSDS Secretariat, National Aeronautics and Space Administration. Last accessed 24 March 2008. *http://public.ccsds.org/publications/archive/650x0b1.pdf*
45. Lynch, Clifford (2000). *Authenticity and integrity in the digital environment: an exploratory analysis of the central role of trust*. Washington, DC: Council on Library and Information Resources. Last accessed 2 May 2008 *http://www.clir.org/pubs/reports/pub92/lynch.html*
46. Caplan, Priscilla and Guenther, Rebecca (2005). 'Practical preservation: the PREMIS experience.' *Library Trends* 54(1): 111–124. Last accessed 24 March 2008. *http://www.loc.gov/standards/premis/caplan_guenther-librarytrends.pdf*
47. PREMIS Editorial Committee (2008). *PREMIS Data Dictionary for Preservation Metadata: Version 2.0* Washington, DC: Library of Congress, March 2008. Last

Accessed 18 May 2008. *http://www.loc.gov/standards/premis/v2/premis-2-0.pdf*

48. 'Using PREMIS with METS'. *METS: Metadata Encoding & Transmission Standard, Official Web Site*. Washington, DC: Library of Congress, 28 January 2008. Last accessed 24 March 2008. *http://www.loc.gov/standards/premis/premis-mets.html*
49. Library of Congress. 'METS: an Overview & Tutorial.' *METS: Metadata Encoding & Transmission Standard, Official Web Site*. Washington, DC: Library of Congress, 13 September 2006. Last accessed 24 March 2008. *http://www.loc.gov/standards/mets/METSOverview.v2.html*

5

The agent in digital rights management

Overview

A rights transaction to use copyright-protected information involves, at a minimum, two agents – the rights holder, who controls the rights associated with reproduction and use of the information, and the end user, who wants to re-use the information. When the end user selects a resource, there are a number of questions he or she *should* ask. Is the resource copyright protected? If so, what uses are permitted for the resource? How can I obtain permission for any use that is not explicitly authorised? The user often does not know the right questions to ask and may not even realise that he/she should ask these questions. The library has an important role to play in enabling the user to obtain the appropriate digital permissions to access the resource, in a simple, intuitive and straightforward manner.

Enabling resource use is where the rubber truly meets the road for librarians, archivists and museum curators. The primary goal for DRM in the library or archives is to enable the authorised use of copyright-protected resources in a seamless and relatively transparent manner. Libraries manage a range of resources, from commercial subscriptions that are restricted by license through open access and public domain resources that are freely available. A crucial role for libraries in the digital rights arena is to mediate successfully all resources for their users so that the focus is on satisfying the information need and not on negotiating the permissions. Obviously this is easier said than done, but understanding the rights transaction from the perspective of the two primary agents – the rights holder and the end user – is an important first step.

In the last chapter, I looked at the importance of identifying the resource, to enable an authentic transfer of information in a rights transaction. Here I look at the two concepts for the agents in a rights transaction: *authenticity* (unambiguous identification) for both the rights holder and the user and *authority* (what permissions are provided to the end user and how can these be supported as seamlessly as possible).

The creator: establishing authenticity

As with resources, the first requirement for enabling digital rights transactions is to identify the authentic agent or entity. As already noted, the primary entities in a digital rights transaction are the copyright holder and the user. The first entity possesses something – the rights to the re-use of the resource – that the end user wants to obtain. Both agents play a critical role in a rights transaction. Rights ownership can be difficult to identify. A resource may have multiple, or uncertain, authorship. The creator of a resource may have transferred rights to a publisher or distributor. However, the creator is explicitly identified in copyright law as the initial rights holder, so the first step in identifying a rights holder is to begin with the creator of the work in question.

Authority control

Most resources are discovered by a search of *access points*, which are the indexed points of entry into a metadata record. Librarians and archivists have long recognised the value of an authoritative access point, or heading, to co-locate all resources created by the same person or organisation. Authority control began at the national level and then expanded into a collaborative effort across countries. Authority control has evolved from the concept of a single authoritative heading for each author, based on the nation of origin, to recognition that authoritative headings should be localised to each country, to support language and cultural differences that are important to local users. William Shakespeare can be established as an authoritative access point in English, for English-speaking countries, and in other languages for other countries. Another significant development for authority control has been the movement within the library's digital infrastructure to a modular authority file, generally created in a separate database, that links to metadata records. This enables authority records to provide, or link to, additional information, such as contact or biographical information, thus coming full circle, from the entity as the creator of the information, to the entity as an information resource in his or her own right. The core of authority control remains two pronged: an unambiguous and unique authoritative heading, often localised within a country, and the syndetic use of cross-references to co-locate all variants of the name, thus supporting the seemingly contradictory goals of uniqueness and completeness. Authoritative headings are thus critical for establishing authoritative rights holders to enable a digital rights transaction. I will now look briefly at some milestones of authority control in the digital information space.

Authority control still remains true to the principles articulated by Charles Ami Cutter in his groundbreaking work, *Rules for a Dictionary Catalog*, published in 1876, with subsequent editions in 1889, 1891 and 1904. Cutter emphasised alphabetical sorting to enable the user to browse headings, syndetic cross references to variant forms, and documentation of the sources consulted to provide credibility for the authoritative heading selected. He articulated the principles of completeness, or co-location, of all forms of an access point; uniqueness; and authority, as established by references that justify the access point selection. As he noted in the preface to the 4th edition (p. 6), 'The convenience of the public is always to be set before the ease of the cataloger.'[1] The International Federation of Library Associations and Organizations (IFLA) continues to promote these concepts in the international information space and has played a leadership role in the development of international rules for creating authoritative access points, through the publication of *Guidelines for Authority and Reference Entries* (GARE) in 1984 and the updated edition, *Guidelines for Authority records and References* (GARR) in 2001.

A working group, the IFLA UBCIM (Universal Bibliographic Control and International MARC Programme) Working Group on Minimal Level Authority Records and ISADN developed a core set of data elements for defining authoritative headings, as well as cross-references and supporting references. The group also examined whether a unique identifier, the International Standard Authority Data Number (ISADN), is necessary or desirable for managing authority headings and records. The report of the Working Group in 1998 strongly encouraged the international sharing of authority records through publication of authority records on the web in 'read-only' form by national agencies. The Working Group also articulated the need to support local language and cultural differences through country- and language-specific authoritative access points. The Working Group identified 19 data elements that are mandatory when applicable within an authority record and three additional data elements that are strongly recommended for use. The need for a unique identification number (ISADN) was not resolved by the Working Group, which had concerns about the expense and effort involved in international maintenance of an ISADN registry.[2]

While the Working Group was deliberating and preparing its report, the IFLA Study Group released the *Functional Requirements for Bibliographic Records* (FRBR), including the groundbreaking conceptual information model model (discussed in Chapter 4), which incorporated concepts of the *work* (the intellectual entity), the *expression* (a creative realisation of the work), the *manifestation* in a specific physical format, and the *item*, which represents one physical instance of a manifestation of the work.[3] In 1999, a new group was established to incorporate FRBR concepts into authority records and to build forward on previous authority work. The Functional Requirements and Numbering of Authority Records (FRANAR) Working Group was tasked with three responsibilities: (1) to define functional requirements for authority records; (2) to explore the feasibility of the ISADN; and (3) to serve as the IFLA liaison to promote interoperability and information sharing with organisations interested in authority control.

The FRANAR group developed a conceptual model for Functional Requirements for Authority Records (FRAD), which identifies an entity (person, family or organisation) associated with a work, expression, manifestation or item. The entity is known by a name and assigned a unique identifier, which is the basis for an access point, which is registered as an authorised or variant heading, which are governed by rules, which are supplied by an agency, which also creates or modifies the access points.

The conceptual model (Figure 5.1) distinguishes the entity, or agent, identified by a name and/or identifier, from the access point, which has relevance within an authority or reference record and represents a heading formulated by rules to represent the agent or entity.

The FRAD conceptual model identifies two broad classes of users: 'authority data creators, who create and maintain authority files and users who use authority information, either through direct access to authority files or indirectly through the controlled access points (authorized forms, references, etc.) in catalogues, national bibliographies, other similar databases, etc.' (IFLA Working Group, p. 50).[4] The model also identified user tasks appropriate to both user groups: find, identify, contextualise and justify. The model shows the relationships between the entities and their attributes and relationships in authority control and which attributes and relationships satisfy which user need. For example, the dates (birth and death) of a person satisfy the user needs to 'find', 'identify' and 'justify', where justify is defined as the authority data creator's 'reason for choosing the name or form of name on which a controlled access point is based.' (IFLA Working Group, pp. 50–51).[4]

The FRANAR Working Group also looked at the issues surrounding the development and use of a unique identifier, the ISADN. FRANAR identified concerns with the financial and staffing overhead for maintaining unique identifiers and also explored the issue of what would be identified – the authority record, or the access point(s) provided within the record? The concept of a single, unique authoritative access point has been supplanted with parallel access points that reflect language and cultural differences across countries, which further complicates the issue of what to identify.

Figure 5.1 **FRANAR conceptual model for authority data (International Federation of Library Associations and Institutions Working Group on Functional Requirements and Numbering of Authority Records *Functional Requirements for Authority Data*, Draft. 1 April 2007, 7)**

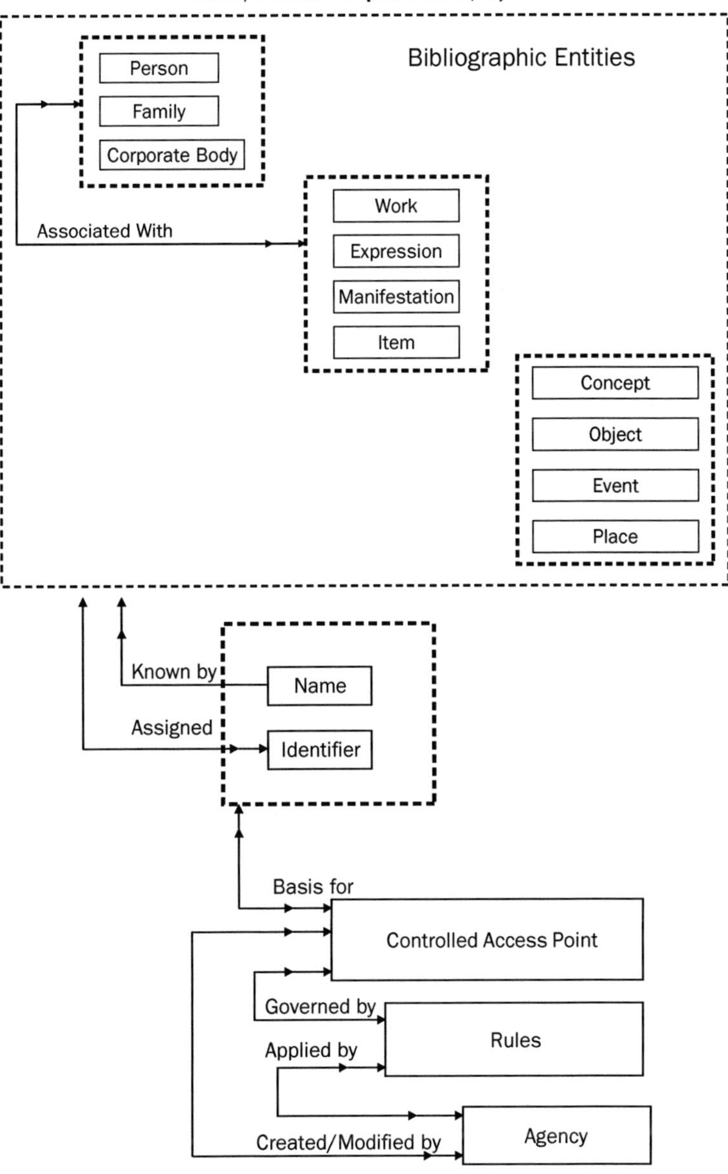

In addition, the Working Group concluded that no new number should be created, but instead existing numbers should be used. (Bourdon, p. 6).[5] Currently, the need for a unique authority identifier remains unresolved.

The archives community has recently provided leadership in 'next-generation' authorities work with the International Standard Archival Authority Record (Corporate Bodies, Persons, Families) [ISAAR (CPF)], released in a second edition in 2004. ISAAR (CPF) has been described as 'a real turning point in the theory and practice of archival description.' (Vitali, p. [2]).[6] ISAAR (CPF) specifies data elements for providing a rich collection creator description, as a separate and modular description that integrates with the finding aid or other descriptive record for the collection. ISAAR (CPF) specifies data elements for biographical information, cultural context relevant to the creator and relationships with other entities. A reference implementation, Encoded Archival Context (EAC), an authorities schema in XML, was released in beta form in 2004 by the *Ad Hoc* EAC Working Group, an international group of archivists. EAC is intended to complement the encoded finding aid standard, EAD.[7]

The Society of American Archivists Working Group on Encoded Archival Context received a grant from the Gladys Krieble Delmas Foundation to create and release version 1.0 of the Encoded Archival Context (EAC) standard, in the form of an XML schema. An EAC Working Group Meeting to launch the development of the standard will take place in May 2008.[8] Recent collaborations in authority control have focused on integrated access to international authority headings information. Noteworthy initiatives include:

- *Project AUTHOR*. This short-term project, which was conducted in 1997 and funded by the European Commission, explored the issues with sharing authority records among European libraries. The project was a collaboration of the national libraries of France, Portugal, Spain and the United Kingdom, with each library contributing a sampling of their authority records to a shared test database. The project was intended to identify interoperability issues in the construction of a shared authority database. The project involved working with five different languages, five variations of the MARC format and four bibliographic software applications. The project identified several key issues for interoperability, including the sorting and displaying of records in different languages and formats; the need for a multilingual search and display interface; difficulties with displaying notes; the need for required core data elements and best practise standards for creating records; and the need for an improved cross-database search and retrieval application.[9]

- *LEAF* (Linking and Exploring Authority Files) is a 3-year project of the Information Society Technologies Programme of the Fifth Framework of the European Commission. LEAF was begun in 2001 to develop a model framework and architecture for linking across distributed authority record databases and providing integrated access to the discovered authority records. LEAF stores query results in a 'Central Name Authority File' and links between authority records for the same entity. LEAF builds upon MALVINE, an international OPAC (online public access catalog) search and retrieval network. The LEAF demonstrator will extend the MALVINE search and retrieval service into a dynamic, multilingual information service about persons and corporations, based upon the user's selection of those entities for searching. The global authority file will thus be built dynamically, triggered by user searches.[10]

- *VIAF* (Virtual International Authority File) is a collaboration of Die Deutsche Bibliothek (German National Library), the Library of Congress and OCLC (Online Computer Library Center) to match and link name authority records in the authority files of the two national libraries. OCLC's software application for matching and linking authority records will be used to match and link existing records and OAI-PMH (Open Archives Initiative-Protocol for Metadata Harvesting) servers will be used to maintain the VIAF database. Users in each country will be able to view the matched and linked authority records in the language and format of the national library for their respective country. VIAF will thus focus equally on integrating multilingual authority records and on meeting region-specific user display needs. A prototype catalog is currently available.[11]
- *NACO* (Name Authority Program of the Program for Cooperative Cataloging) is a component of a national cataloging collaborative within the United States, coordinated by the Library of Congress, in which libraries contribute name, title and series authority records to the Library of Congress authority files. Authority records must be created to NACO minimum standards. Individual organisations may join NACO or may form a funnel project with a group of libraries to contribute authority records.[12]
- *WorldCat Identities. WorldCat Identities* is an OCLC user information service that completed its beta test in June 2007. *WorldCat Identities* mines data from the *WorldCat* database and other resources to provide a range of information about persons and organisations, including resources authored by the entity; resources and information about the entity, such as critical works and biographies; and collaborations engaged in by the entity. The goal of

WorldCat Identities is to co-locate all relevant information or links to information about a creator. *WorldCat Identities* demonstrates how authoritative entries can enable the searching and retrieval of information about creators, to support resource retrieval and also to acknowledge the creator as a primary source of useful information.[13]

- *The Names Project* is a JISC-funded project 'to scope the requirements of UK institutional and subject repositories for a service that will reliably and uniquely identify individuals and institutions' and then to 'develop a prototype service which will test the various processes involved. This will include determining the data format, setting up an appropriate database, mapping data from different sources, populating the database with records and testing the use of the data.' The Names Project is a joint endeavor of Mimas, a national data center for UK higher education and the British Library.[14]

The library's authority strategy

Identifying creators in a clear, unambiguous manner is important for a number of reasons, including:

- enabling users to find, or co-locate, all the resources by a creator;
- enabling the users of information to identify, and locate, the creator of a work to obtain rights to reuse the work;
- enabling users to find information about creators, including biographical and critical information, as creators are information sources in their own right, in addition to the resources they create;
- further establishing the authenticity of a resource through context ('the work created by this entity and no other').

Libraries should be familiar with the authority files maintained by their national library or other relevant bibliographic entity. Creators should be documented in library metadata with authoritative headings – either headings established in a national authority registry or headings created locally by the library according to rules and best practises for authority control in the library's country or region, which might then be contributed to a national authority registry.

Libraries developing institutional repositories or digital collections with local creators should establish authoritative headings for those creators and maintain an authority file, ideally a database that interacts dynamically with the library's metadata database. This will ensure that headings for creators are consistent and authoritative as well as guiding users from variant to authoritative headings, to ensure successful creator searches in the library's digital collection or repository. A creator may appear in multiple authority files – a library's local authority file, a national or regional authority file, or an authority file specific to a subject domain such as ULAN – the *Getty Union List of Artist Names*. A library's authority file should include the authoritative name, variant names and links, such as identifiers or URI links, to authority records for the creator in other authority files. This will enable interoperability with other authority files for definitive identification of the creator as well as co-location of information by and about the creator in the national or international information space.

Contact information for creators, if known, should be maintained in the authority file, together with the date last verified, to enable the library automatically to contact creators for updated information based on verification date. Valid contact information is difficult to maintain but an address and a verification date, even if outdated, provides an important starting point for locating a creator or his/her heirs.

Another important rights holder that often holds the rights to copyright-protected resources is the publisher or distributor, both of which should be identified in metadata. Publishers and distributors may be purchased by other corporations, may cease to operate, or may not retain older author agreements for resources that they do not deem economically exploitable. Nonetheless, they are important contact points for researching resource ownership. No centralised authority file exists for publishers and distributors, with contact information and a history of corporate ownership. Some sources for identifying and contacting publishers and distributors are provided in the bibliography at the end of this book.

The user: authentication and authorisation

As we learned in the last section, it is important to identify the rights holder authoritatively. It is equally important, and considerably more complex, to support the needs of the user, who may have to satisfy conditions established by a rights holder before he/she can access a resource to enable further use of the resource, e.g. read, copy, print, download or modify.

Common conditions that a user may have to satisfy include the payment of a fee for use, such as paying a per-item fee to download a music file to a personal audio player. A user may need to demonstrate membership in a group for which a group-licensing fee has been paid. This scenario often occurs in libraries that pay licensing fees for access to online databases and journals on behalf of an identified user base. Another common scenario is the issuing of individual licenses based on specified conditions of use, such as personal use only, or not-for-profit use of a resource. These uses may or may not be actively enforced via software applications but are often legally binding requirements that are generally explicitly identified for users via copyright usage notices or licenses published at the website where the resource resides. These permissions may also be satisfied in the digital space by web-based 'click-through' licenses, where a user agrees to terms and conditions by checking a mandatory license check box before he or she can access the resource. An example would be the copyright check box in a library institutional repository, where a faculty or student must assert that they hold the copyright to a resource before they can deposit, or 'self-archive', the resource. An open license for use may be published and linked to the resource, such as the Creative Commons license, which carries moral and legal weight but does not include digital enforcement. The Creative Commons license is described in Chapter 6.

Enabling the end user to obtain a copyright-protected resource in a digital rights transaction is a complicated dance with many steps. First, the user must be *authenticated* as having the identity he/she claims to own. A user is authenticated when credentials, such as a certificate or other information establishing the identity of the user, are made available to the rights holder or system requesting this authentication.

The authenticated user must then prove that he or she has the attributes required to obtain the resource. This may involve demonstrating membership in a group or demonstrating a role, such as 'instructor' or 'student', within a specific course. The user may need to satisfy a condition, such as payment of a fee, or prove that a use fee has previously been paid. Based on demonstrated attributes, the permissions that the user is entitled to exercise on the resource (read, copy, print, etc.) are enabled, i.e. the user is *authorised* to use the copyright-protected resource. Once authorisation has occurred, the resource will then be released for use. Michael Teets, Vice President, Global Product Architecture at OCLC, has developed an excellent diagram that documents all the steps of the access management process, which often occurs in the online environment in the space of a few seconds (Figure 5.2).

As Figure 5.2 illustrates, the *authentication* of a user as possessing the identity he/she claims to own, and the subsequent *authorisation* of the user to access a resource based on possession of attributes required for resource use, can be a complicated, multi-step process requiring different tools and protocols. This section will focus on the concepts, strategies and tools that can enable the access management process.

Strategies for access management focus on two broad categories of user: the *device*, which is used to access and display resources, and the person, or *user*, who will actually use the resource. Each is discussed in turn.

Figure 5.2 **Access management process (from Teets and Murray)[48]**

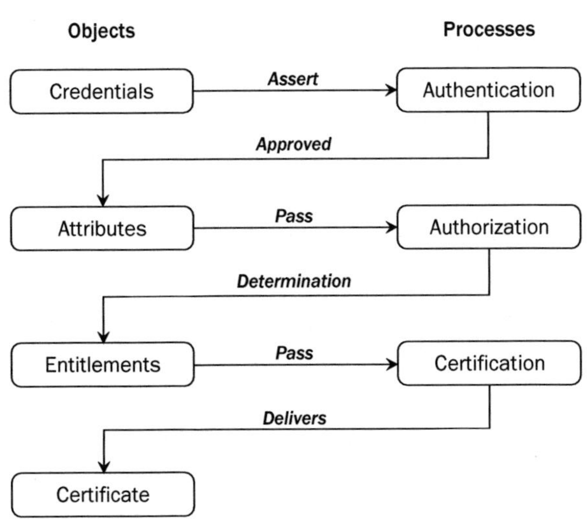

Device-based access control

Resources are often limited to members or employees of an organisation, such as a library, so a straightforward strategy for limiting resources to an organisation is to limit resource access to devices known to be on the premises of the organisation. This can be accomplished by providing the resource in its entirety to the organisation, such as the files of an electronic database, which the organisation then loads on a local server and limits access to nodes on the internal network of the organisation. This strategy was frequently employed in the early days of electronic resources, before the web became ubiquitous. Two common device-based access control strategies currently employed in the web environment are IP filtering and trusted systems.

IP filtering

A simple strategy that is often employed for group access to licensed resources is IP filtering. Devices, such as computer workstations, laptops, networked printers, etc., participate in a computer network through an IP (internet protocol) address that enables them to be recognised as nodes on the network. A simple method for ensuring that access to a copyright-protected resource is limited to an organisation is to limit access to the IP range or ranges that represent valid nodes on the organisation's network. This is a generally effective way to limit resource access to a specified group. The problem inherent with this strategy is that resource access control applies to hardware, but not to users. A workstation may potentially be used by anyone on the organisation premises, regardless of whether the user operating the workstation is a member of the organisation. This issue may be addressed by restricting all network devices to authorised users via workstation or network usernames and passwords or physical authentication devices, such as attached card readers. Controlling access to all devices on a network carries its own management issues, particularly for libraries that serve a large, distributed user base.

IP filtering will generally not support restricting resource access based on user attributes or roles, such as enrollment in a course. IP filtering also may exclude members of the organisation who are not on the organisation's premises, such as a member who is attempting to access resources from home or on the road. Fortunately, methodologies for obtaining IP addresses within the authorised IP range are generally employed to circumvent this restriction, including proxy servers and dynamic IP assignment using the dynamic host configuration protocol (DHCP). A proxy server is interposed between clients and the servers that provide resources or applications requested by the clients. The proxy server makes the requests to other servers on behalf of the client. A proxy server with a valid IP address can request IP-range restricted resources on behalf of the library's user as the proxy server's address falls within the authorised IP range. The proxy server could also cache the resources for the benefit of its authorised users, who may authenticate to the proxy server through a process such as a username and password. In this case, the IP filtering strategy 'hands off' to the proxy server for further authentication and authorisation to enable access to the cached resources.

A proxy server may use the 'referring URL', i.e. the URL from which the user is requesting proxy access, to authenticate the user automatically, so that entering a username and password at a login screen is not required. Access to restricted resources is thus transparent to the user. However, referring URLs only work based on the source URL or location where the user discovered a link to a restricted resource. If the user attempts to access the resource from a different URL, he or she may need to log into the proxy, thus providing inconsistent and confusing access to resources.

The proxy server may also hand off to a DHCP assignment process, to assign a dynamic IP address to the requesting user. A DHCP server provides a dynamic IP address to a requesting client, such as a user's workstation, to enable the user to meet the requirement that the requesting device falls within the organisation's designated IP range. The dynamic IP address generally remains valid as long as the user's session on the network is active.

Proxy servers are either accessed by users through configuration of the user's client to address the proxy server or through a rewriting proxy server, in which case each URL that is sent to the proxy server gets a proxy URL prefix, which leads to the proxy server, where the real URL is launched. A problem with both proxy URLs and referring URLs, which were previously described, is that the URL is not an independent URL and cannot be relied upon as a bookmark within a browser or included in a citation for others to use.

Restricting resource access to an IP address or range of IP addresses is a simple yet largely effective strategy to ensure that resource access is restricted to members of an organisation. It requires that the organisation utilise contiguous IP addresses within a definable range and limit unique IP addresses to members of the organisation in order to comply with most resource licensing requirements. The organisation must also accommodate resource access for valid users who are not utilising devices with IP addresses within the organisation's IP address range. With these caveats, IP address restriction has worked for many years to the satisfaction of commercial resource vendors.

Trusted system

Another 'device-dependent' authentication strategy in wide use is the trusted system strategy. In a trusted system, DRM applications or devices are installed within a user's device, which then communicates with systems and applications utilising the same DRM technology to enable the user of the device to access and use protected applications and resources. The 'trusted system' is a widely used DRM strategy. Many devices are sold with DRM technologies already on board. For example, HD-DVD and Blu-ray players support the High-Bandwidth Digital Content Protection (HDCP) DRM technologies, which will determine that an encrypted transmission is licensed for use on the device before decrypting the content for playback. Trusted system technology can also be enabled at first point of use, for example when a user downloads a multimedia player, which involves installing a DRM application on the user's client device that communicates with the corresponding DRM application on the remote multimedia streaming server or with encrypted DRM information on an optical medium, such as a DVD or Blu-Ray disc.

The trusted systems approach raises several issues of concern. First, the technologies are often embedded in the device before purchase or downloaded and stored in an encrypted area of the user's hard drive when an application or resource is first accessed, e.g. when a trial version of software is downloaded for use for a specified time period or when an e-book reader with content protections, such as print and download restrictions, is first downloaded. The result is that the owner of a device has no control, and often no awareness, of the DRM technology stored in the device. Another significant problem is that the trusted system often requires that all devices in the trusted system chain support the same

DRM technology. For example, in the case of the Blu-ray and HD DVD devices, if the playback device (PC or television) is not HDCP-enabled, the device with either fail to display the resource or, if the content provider has set an ICT (Image Constraint Token) flag, the content will be played back as a downsampled, low-resolution signal. Trusted systems are discussed in more detail in Chapter 7.

The most significant issue with both IP filtering and trusted systems is that the device is authenticated and authorised, but not the user. Unless a device is exclusive to a specific user, device authentication cannot generally address access that is customised to a user's needs, which requires role-based user access or support blanket licenses for educational or non-profit use. In addition, access restrictions at the device level can require the user to take additional actions, such as logging into a proxy server, downloading a DRM technology, or registering a device with a remote server to move resource access from one device to another. Resource transfer may also require that all resources share the same version of the same DRM technology. In today's connected environment, where a user may access information at work, at home or on the road, via a range of devices, such as workstations, laptops and mobile phones, restricting information based on the device can quickly become cumbersome.

Of even greater concern is the fact that device authentication is often not exposed to the end user, who may not be aware that he/she is participating in an authentication and authorisation process for access to protected resources. Access to copyright-protected resources generally involves a license or agreement for use. The end user is a participant in this agreement. However, the user, who is focused on the resource rather than the access methodology, may not realise he or she is a party to a resource usage agreement. An authorisation strategy that is hidden from the end user, while providing seamless access, also carries with it the danger that the user, who is ultimately responsible for resource use, may not be aware that there are any restrictions or obligations on the use of copyright-protected information resources. In addition, in the trusted system approach, the user may unwittingly install DRM applications that engage in encrypted digital conversations with third parties, without the user's knowledge or consent.

The best authentication and authorisation strategy will be unobtrusive but will actively engage the user, at the beginning of a session, in the authentication process so that the user is aware of the protected nature of the resources he/she is accessing and aware of the attribute(s) (e.g. 'registered user of public library X') that authorise(s) his or her access. Any system that is completely transparent, and thus hidden, from the resource user presents ethical issues. While smooth, seamless access to information is always a goal, the resource user is ultimately liable for any infringing use of copyright-protected materials. The user also owns the attributes of his/her identity that enable him/her to access protected materials, and he or she should be aware when those attributes are being queried. The library needs to enable swift, efficient access to resources while at the same time ensuring that the resource user is an informed participant in the resource access process. These somewhat competitive goals can only be addressed through a user-based authentication and authorisation process. A single sign-on, which is discussed later in this chapter, is an important user-based access control strategy because it enables the user to authenticate and authorise once in a simple but meaningful manner and then use any protected resources or services within a single web session. Single sign-on supports the parallel requirements for user awareness of the authentication and authorisation process and seamless access to information, and thus is a recommended strategy for any library or archive. Single sign-on will be discussed at length later in this chapter.

User-based authentication and authorisation

Basic concepts

User-based authentication and authorisation is founded on the core concept that the user must prove, to the satisfaction of the resource provider, that he/she has the identity and the attributes required for resource access. An intermediary, such as a library or an organisation's IT department, manages the process, but the user supplies the proof required to issue credentials attesting to the authenticity of his or her identity. I begin by examining the core concepts behind user-based authentication and authorisation strategies.

Authentication refers to the process that establishes that a person conforms to an expected identity. *Identity*, in information technology, refers to the establishment of a valid digital persona that uniquely identifies an entity (person, organisation, etc.) through a unique name or identifier, describes the entity through one or more attributes, and may provide supporting documentation, such as a photograph or fingerprints that validate, or vouch for, the authenticity of the entity represented by the digital *identity*.

Authentication is based on three broad authentication factors:

- something a user *is or does*, such as fingerprints, a retinal scan or a signature;
- something a user *has*, such as a computer with an allowed IP address or a smart card issued to an authenticated user;
- something a user *knows*, such as a password.[15]

Strong, or multi-factor, authentication requires the use of two or more authentication strategies that employ more than one authentication factor. For example, an application may require the use of biometrics, such as a fingerprint or a retinal scan ('what the user is'), and a password ('what the user knows'), or the use of a smart card or detachable USB token ('what the user has') and a password ('what the user knows'). A common strategy to authenticate a user for a secured transaction is to require a username and password and also to require the user to enter a one-time password (OTP) token ('what the user has'), in which a randomly generated sequence of alphanumeric characters is displayed on the screen and must be entered by the user before a resource or application can be accessed or an Internet purchase completed. This ensures that a person who can read and interpret a visible token, using the computer on which the token is displayed, is requesting the resource or transaction.

Authorisation refers to the permissions or rights that are granted to an agent (generally the resource requester) based on the authentication, or validation, of the agent's identity, as well as the attributes of that identity that are required for access to a service or a resource. *Attributes* are roles or characteristics of an identity, such as the role of 'instructor in course X' or 'registered member of public library Y'. An attribute may also be a characteristic such as a birth date that demonstrates that the user is 18 or older for access to resources that are restricted to adults. A person may be authorised to access resources by virtue of fulfilling a condition, such as payment of a fee, or by virtue of group membership, or by possessing another attribute. The fact that a person has fulfilled a condition is documented and tied to the identity of the person fulfilling the condition. This ensures that the person will be authorised to access the resource or exercise other conditional rights for the duration of the contract or agreement between the person and the rights holder.

Federation is a term used in the digital space to describe the bringing together of disparate entities (organisation, networks, databases, etc.) via common services or policies that apply to all entities. Applying a single search engine to more than one database is known as federated searching. Organisations may federate to share a common authentication and authorisation framework.

Identity management is a term used to establish and manage the life cycle of an identity, which will generally include:

- establishing and documenting the identity;
- tying the identity to an identity management system;
- vouching for the identity, as part of a trusted authentication and authorisation environment;
- revoking or terminating the identity at the end of its digital lifespan, which could be as short as a single Internet session, for an online purchase, or could represent a change in a critical attribute, as when a student graduates from a university and thus ceases to possess the role of 'enrolled student in institution X'.

The concept of *identity* is critical to the authentication process. An identity typically includes a unique identifier, which may be a name, a number or a combination of identifying attributes, such as name or address. *Identity* is often bound to a digitally signed certificate in which the identified entity and a trusted third party (generally the certificate issuer) both vouch for the authenticity of the identity. The identity establishes the authenticity of the user making the request, so that the user can be authorised, through conditions that have been met or attributes that entitle the user to access a resource. The organisation or service providing a resource to the user must be able to *trust* that the identity is associated with the correct user.

Trust is an important concept in authentication and authorisation, particularly in the federated web environment where physically distributed organisations must be able to trust each other. Trust is classically defined as being able to have confidence or faith in someone or something, such that you can rely upon that entity to provide reliable information or to perform in an expected manner. A service or resource provider needs to be able to trust the authenticating agency that supplies credentials. This trust is based on authentication practises whereby the authenticating agency assigns and manages identity and also on the security practises that ensure that an identity is not compromised. Organisations in a trusted relationship will either use an agreed-upon application and agreed-upon policies to authenticate and authorise or will be able readily to discover and evaluate the authentication and authorisation policies and practises of an entity in order to decide dynamically whether to trust that entity. Organisations can also agree to trust each other's policies and practises without knowledge of those policies and practises, based on a formal or informal agreement or simply on prior collaboration experience.

Level of assurance (LoA). LoA refers to the trust that can be placed on the authentication of the identity of the user. It is assigned to a service or resource provider and to an identity provider (IdP). Codes are used to represent level of security, with the objective to match LOAs for the resource/service provider and the identity provider. For the service/resource provider, the LoA is based upon the risk posed to the service provider or its resources if an incorrectly identified user is authenticated to the service, as well as the risks to the customers or users of the service provider if a user identity is compromised. Risk assessment should also take into account the likelihood of occurrence for misuse of a user identity.[16] For the IdP the LoA is based on the IdP's practises in authenticating and credentialing users. An IdP that requires in-person authentication with multiple forms of ID, such as a passport agency, would have a high LoA, for example. The intent behind LoA is to ensure that a high-risk transaction (e.g. a tax payment within a municipal government) has a very high LoA, while obtaining a library card from the public library agency within that municipal government might have a lower LoA. LoA enables users to engage readily in low-risk transactions where very little identity management is required and yet be protected in high-risk transactions where both the user and the service provider need to be protected against identity theft or misuse.

The US federal government requires that LoAs be assigned to all online government services based on low-, moderate- or high-risk factors. The four levels of assurance are:

- 'Level 1: Little or no confidence in the asserted identity's validity
- Level 2: Some confidence in the asserted identity's validity
- Level 3: High confidence in the asserted identity's validity
- Level 4: Very high confidence in the asserted identity's validity.' (Bolten, p. [4]).[16]

Single sign-on (SSO) applies both to a single integrated authentication and authorisation solution for all parties within an organisation or consortium and also to the ability to authenticate once and then to access a range of services and resources within a single session. A person utilising SSO would supply a username and password once within a session and could then access different applications (e.g. email) and resources (e.g. a commercial database) within a single session.

SSO should enable access to resources with different attribute requirements, such as access to a commercial database, which requires that the user be an enrolled student at the university, and access to an electronic reserves article, which requires that the user also be enrolled as a member of a specific course. SSO also requires standardised practises for identity management, access management and session control. A session may be continuous use of applications and resources within a single browser or at a single workstation, within an enterprise network, or within a community of trust across the Internet. Session control also includes decisions about timeout options, in which a session may be terminated after a period of inactivity for security reasons, to prevent identity misuse.

Tools and standards for authentication and authorisation

This section looks at tools and standards for authenticating the identity of a user and authorising access to applications or resources, based on that identity and on the possession of required attributes tied to that identity. The preferred strategy will include applying access controls through SSO to a range of applications and resources, applied in different scenarios, within a local network and in a federated web environment.

Username and password

The most basic authentication strategy, which is often a component in other strategies, is the use of the username and password. The username is generally an eye-readable identifier. This may sometimes be the user's email address. It is coupled to an encrypted password. The premise behind a username and password is simple: that the username will be paired with the password, requiring the user to know both identifiers, and that the password, in particular, is unique to the user and presumably known only to the user. As the password is encrypted so that it is not eye-readable, and only known to the user, the reasoning is that the person using the password must match the identity associated with the username and password. The reality, of course, is that passwords can be easily breached – perhaps discovered by computer applications that search for encrypted code within a web page or retrieved from the protected area where the password was stored on a server.

Passwords can be guessed by software designed to crack passwords through a method known as 'brute force' in which terms in a dictionary and commonly known numbers (e.g. '9112001') are tried in succession until the password is discovered. Brute force password-cracking applications can compensate for simple substitutions of numbers and symbols for letters in common words or dictionary terms. Passwords related to commonly known information about a user, such as pet name, nickname and date of birth, are also weak, particularly if this information is readily discoverable on the web, such as in user profiles on public social networking sites. Passwords may be assigned to a class of users, which increases the likelihood that the password will be commonly known or shared with unauthorised users. Common shared passwords, such as 'sysadmin' or 'guestuser' are easily discovered by unauthorised users. Users may also store passwords in cookies that are entered automatically when an application is launched, which can then be retrieved through the simple act by an unauthorised person of opening a cookie-enabled application on the user's computer or by harvesting the cookie from a user's browser. There are numerous strategies to reduce the inherent vulnerabilities of passwords – some of which may be employed by the organisation requiring the password and some of which must be applied by the password holder.

To begin with, the organisation should require a password that includes numbers or symbols in addition to letters. To increase the strength of the password, the organisation should use case-sensitive passwords and encourage users to mix upper-case and lower-case characters. An organisation may also apply password-auditing software to 'test' a user's password selection before accepting the password for use on the organisation's system. An organisation may also time out the password access application after several tries, requiring the user to contact the organisation for assistance. Password resetting should require at a minimum two-factor authentication. In a common password reset procedure, the user should know either the username or the password, or should answer one or more security questions about the user, where the user has supplied the answers in advance. ('what the user knows'). Once the user passes the first factor, the user will receive an email ('what the user has') allowing him or her to reset his/her password. The organisation can also store a 'hash', which is not the password but is based on the password through a matching algorithm. This reduces the likelihood that an unauthorised user can steal the password from the organisation. The transmission of a password should also occur in an encrypted communication channel, known as the Transport Layer Security (TLS) or Secure Sockets Layer (SSL), which further helps to ensure that the password will not be captured during an active session. In addition, use of the OTP token can ensure that a user who can view and type the OTP is supplying the password, rather than a software application.

Password crackers frequently use a tool known as the 'rainbow table', a pre-computed table specific to a hash function, such as MD5, that computes possible passwords based on a specific length and often on a specific character set. A rainbow table can greatly speed the password-cracking process. An organisation can guard against rainbow cracking by using a different hash function for each password generation and by requiring larger passwords.[17]

The password holder also has an obligation to select a password that is both memorable to the user (and only the user) but difficult to crack through a brute force attack. A common strategy is to use the first letter of each word in a memorable phrase or the first line of a poem, substituting numbers or symbols for one or more letters or and varying upper and lower case, e.g. T1Dtw1k@m (Toto, I don't think we're in Kansas anymore, where '1' substitutes for 'i' in 'I' and 'in', @ substitutes for the 'a' in 'any' and the word 'anymore' is treated as two words).

Any password that conforms to some logical arrangement as opposed to truly random can be cracked. Password strength is gauged in terms of the entropy factor – how random the password appears to the user. Password strength is also gauged in how much effort cracking requires, whether it is worth the time and effort required for the cracker to break the password. A user-created password should balance a stronger password that does not conform closely to a word or phrase against a word or phrase with simple number or character for letter substitutions. Although the former is more secure, the latter is more easily remembered and thus more easily safeguarded, as it is less likely to be written down and placed in an insecure place.

Passwords age over time, making it more likely that a password may be discovered and misused. Best practise for password management recommends changing them at frequent intervals, but not at such frequent intervals that the password becomes a serious obstacle to a user obtaining a resource, or that encourages the user to make poor choices for convenience, such as posting the password prominently on the users' computer, or in an unencrypted file-named 'passwords'.

X.509 certificate

The X.509 certificate is an ITU-T (ITU Telecommunication Standardization Sector) standard that is used to standardise authentication and encryption of information for an entity (person or organisation) to provide a secure method to conduct transactions, such as access to licensed information or an e-commerce transaction. Certificates emerged as a standardised way to package an identity, tied to a public key infrastructure, with generally a third party, the 'certificate authority' (CA) attesting via a digital signature that the certificate, and thus the identity it documents, is valid. A CA may be an organisation that supplies certificates for a fee, such as VeriSign, or an organisation that issues certificates as an authentication methodology, such as a university or corporation. The CA often vouches for the authenticity of the identity, using one or more of the three authentication factors, such as the private key ('what the user has') and another factor. A user may have to sign for a certificate in person ('who the user is') or use a smart card or other device issued by the organisation to authenticate his/her identity and obtain the certificate ('what the user has'). The value of certificates consists largely in their standardised approach to identity management and in the trust accorded to the verification practises of the CA.

Certificates are based on a public key infrastructure, which is an encryption methodology. Public and private keys are provided in pairs. A public key may be shared with anyone, but the private key is provided only to the owner. A public key infrastructure (PKI) allows entities without prior knowledge of each other to be authenticated to each other and to encrypt information to share with each other. The private key ('what the user has') is issued only to the certificate holder and, if carefully stored to maintain its integrity, can serve, in combination with another authentication factor (generally username and password), to provide a multifactor authentication to assert that the identity of the certificate holder is valid and trustworthy.

Certificates conform to the X.509 standard and contain the following components:

- *Version* of the X.509 standard being used.
- *Signature algorithm identifier*. Each certificate contains a digital signature based on the private key of the signer. The signature algorithm identifier identifies the algorithm used to sign the certificate.
- *Signature* attesting to the validity of the information in the certificate.
- *Serial number* – a unique identification number assigned to the certificate by the CA. The serial number is used to revoke a certificate when it expires or is compromised by publishing the number in a certificate revocation list.
- *Issuer name*. The name of the entity that signed the certificate, usually the CA. It uses the X.500 standard and can include the name, organisational affiliation and contact information, such as address, email and telephone number. The information is concatenated to form a 'distinguished name' or unique identification string that should belong to one entity and no other. X.500 is an OSI (open systems interconnection) protocol for directory information, often called the 'electronic phone book' standard. It is used to create electronic directory information, such as that appearing in virtual business cards.
- *Validity period*. A certificate should only have validity for a specified time period, which may be the length of an online session or may be tied to a meaningful time

frame, such as an academic year or semester at a university. Limiting the time frame for a certificate is a precaution against misuse, should the private key be compromised.

- *Subject name.* The subject name is the name of the entity whose public key is identified by the certificate. This is a distinguished name with X.500 attributes such as organisational affiliation, country, etc.
- *Subject public key information.* This is the public key and the algorithm identifier that specifies the cryptography system to which the public key belongs.

Certificates are often used in the SSL or TLS, which are cryptographic protocols using PKI to enable secured Internet transactions for activities such as e-commerce, email and web browsing. Certificates bring the concept of identity and authentication to encrypted transactions so that the transactions are not only private but also involve an entity – the certificate holder – that has been authenticated as possessing the identity described within the certificate.[18]

Kerberos

Another IETF (Internet Engineering Task Force) authentication technology that is in widespread use by such diverse applications as the Apache web server and microcomputer operating systems is Kerberos. Kerberos is a network authentication protocol that uses strong, or symmetric, encryption to enable two parties in a transaction to communicate securely with each other. Kerberos is distributed as an open-source application by the Massachusetts Institute of Technology. Similar to X.509 certificates, Kerberos uses encryption key technology – in this case, symmetric or strong key cryptography – and a trusted third party. Also similar to X.509 certificates, Kerberos enables two parties who do not know each other to communicate in a secure transaction. Unlike X.509 certificates, Kerberos uses strong or secret key encryption, where no public key is broadcast for use. Kerberos is a client-server application suite, where the client first authenticates itself to an authentication server. After authentication, the client requests a ticket from the ticket-granting server. The client receives the ticket and uses the ticket to demonstrate to the service server that it is authorised to receive the service. A strong or private encryption key is created for the client, using a hash of the client's password, which was first used to authenticate the client. This completes the symmetric keys required for the secured transaction. Kerberos is session based and thus temporary. Each session establishes its own private key encryption for both the client and the server. Kerberos is an effective methodology for session-based authentication and authorisation but carries significant overhead, including single points of failure if any Kerberos server is not available, which can be problematic when used as the sole authentication and authorisation strategy for an organisation.[19]

Cookies

A cookie is a small data file containing information, generally about the user, such as name, password and use preferences, that is generally specific to a website, and is stored by a web browser and retrieved in response to specific actions, such as log-ins or transactions at the website associated with the cookie. The completion of username and password for a website is accomplished through a cookie, for example. Cookies can also be used to collect information, such as the tracking of website use by an advertising service, such as DoubleClick. A user may actively choose to set a cookie, or a cookie may be set by a website in response to some action, such as a log-in. 'Hidden' cookies that are set by a third party without the user's knowledge have come under fire. Many websites have responded by asking permission to set a cookie or allowing the user to opt out from the cookie. Web browsers also allow users to establish cookie settings that range from rejecting all cookies through asking permission to set a cookie, to accepting all cookies.

Cookies are used in diverse applications where the information stored in a cookie can enable a user to navigate a website more efficiently or enrich the user's experience. 'My library' applications generally rely on cookies to capture user choices to customise the user's experience at the library's website, for example. Cookies play an important role in maintaining what is called 'client state', in other words maintaining dynamic information, such as the information filled out in a form, for the length of the session. Many cookies have short lifespans and many cookies live only for the length of a session, at which point they expire. As the report of the NISO MetaSearch Task Group on Access Management noted in a report ranking access management strategies, 'while a cookie is initially set in the browser as the result of a specific user's request, there is no inherent linkage of the cookie to [the] user ... furthermore ... subsequent presentation of the cookie is not guaranteed to be from the user to whom the cookie was originally granted.' (NISO Metasearch Initiative Standards BA (Task Group 1), p. 12).[20] The report further notes that cookies do not require basic security protections, such as encrypted password transmission, and do not provide a mechanism for initial authentication as they arise as a token in response to some action by the user (pp. 12–13).[20]

Pubcookie

A popular open source cookie application is Pubcookie, which is intended for intra-institutional website authentication. Pubcookie includes a standalone login server and modules for web server applications. Pubcookie can be used to integrate authentication services such as Kerberos and LDAP (lightweight directory access protocol) into a single sign-on for web servers within an institution. Pubcookie sends usernames to a secure login server to limit their exposure for unauthorised capture. Pubcookie works with Apache and IIS web servers. It was initially developed by the University of Washington and is currently a shared development by Carnegie-Mellon, University of Wisconsin and others. The open source license and software are available from the University of Washington. Pubcookie works as both an initial sign-on application as well as an SSO as the login information can remain valid for the length of a session and automatically authenticate a user whenever a pubcookie-enabled website is encountered. Pubcookie uses a shared symmetric key to encrypt some messages between the login server and each applications server. A key server application is incorporated in the login server to generate and manage the symmetric keys.[21]

NCIP (NISO Circulation Interchange Protocol) and SIP/SIP2 (Standard Interchange Protocol)

NCIP and its predecessor standard SIP are message exchange protocols that include client authentication and are used within integrated library systems (ILSs). SIP was originally developed by 3M to support the sending of circulation transactions from self-checkout stations to ILSs. Its utility for other transactions was quickly recognised, and the standard is now in common use for sending client information to the ILS or exchanging information within ILS applications. SIP has been superseded by NCIP, which offers greater functionality for supporting ILS transactions and utilises XML for messages, but SIP/SIP2 remains in wider use among ILSs. Neither protocol is intended for managing access to protected resources, but either protocol could be extended to support this application, particularly as ILSs continue to evolve to provide an integrated information platform that includes the catalog, third-party databases and the institutional repository. Technologies that foster interoperability, such as XML and web services description language (WSDL), are enabling open library systems to become platforms for information management and access beyond the library catalog. It remains to be seen whether NCIP has an important role to play in authentication for digital library collections in a DRM implementation (NISO Metasearch Initiative Standards BA (Task Group 1), pp. 20–22, 31–32).[20]

LDAP

LDAP is a protocol for accessing directory services via the TCP/IP protocol, making it ideal for organising and delivering directory-type information over networks and over the Internet. The LDAP directory structure is organized in a hierarchical tree, with attribute/value pairs used to define each directory entry. Each attribute has a unique identifier, its 'distinguished name' (DN), as well as a unique value. Each DN consists of a relative distinguished name (RDN), unique to the entry, followed by the parent entry's DN. LDAP attributes are organised in a schema. Attributes include standard directory information, such as 'sn' (surname), 'givenname' and 'telephonenumber'.[22] The attribute 'objectClass' is an important attribute that places the entity defined by the entry in a group with specified roles.[23] The objectClass, 'eduPerson', defined by the EDUCAUSE/Internet2 EduPerson Task Force, extends LDAP to establish data elements (attributes) that are widely used in higher education, to facilitate communications, such as role-based authorisation, within and between academic institutions. Attributes include common attributes, such as eduPersonAffiliation with permissible values of faculty, student, staff, alum, member, affiliate and employee.[24]

LDAP is used to provide access to information about network nodes, departments and individuals within an organisation or group of organisations. LDAP is an IETF standard currently in version 3 (LDAPv3), detailed in IETF Request for Comments (RFC) 4510.[25] The LDAP protocol supports many actions, or operations against directory entries, including:

- start TLS (initiates the transport layer security for a secured connection)
- search (search and retrieve directory entries)
- compare (test an entry for a specific attribute value)
- add a new entry
- delete an entry
- modify an entry.[26]

LDAP is used within authentication and authorisation services, such as Shibboleth®, discussed below, which includes a suite of applications and protocols. Other standards conform to LDAP in a reference application. An example is the XRI (extensible resource identifier, described in Chapter 4) implementation 'i-name' that conforms to the LDAP directory schema.[27]

XML authentication and authorization: SAML and XACML

A common need across the web is the desire for standards-based authentication and authorisation that can be utilised in a robust, interoperable manner. Organisations are often able to address SSO within the enterprise, but robust, interoperable authentication and authorisation across the web, particularly for use cases where the requesting user and service provider may be unknown to each other, has been a thorny issue. OASIS (Organization for the Advancement of Structured Information Standards) has developed two important XML standards to address robust, interoperable authentication and authorisation: SAML (Security Assertion Markup Language) and XACML (eXtensible Access Control Markup Language). OASIS is self-described as 'a not-for-profit consortium that drives the development, convergence and adoption of open standards for the global information society.'[28] OASIS membership includes corporations, academic institutions, not-for-profit organisations and individuals, but its work is supported in large part by its foundational members – large information technology companies such as IBM, SAP and SUN. OASIS has focused on the development of standards to support e-commerce, particularly in the digital rights arena. The two authentication and authorisation standards represent some of OASIS' most significant and useful work for enabling digital rights transactions.

SAML is currently available in version 2.0, although version 1.1 is more widely deployed. SAML is an XML language, protocols and bindings to enable the exchange of authentication and authorisation statements between two or more entities across the web. SAML entities are the identity provider, who produces assertions about a subject, and the service provider, who receives the assertions and issues an authorisation decision statement based on the assertions of the identity provider.

SAML consists of assertions, protocols and bindings to enable the exchange of authentication and authorisation information between SAML authorities (identity providers and service providers).

Assertions contain zero or more statements from a SAML authority or asserting party. Assertions belong to one of three types:

- authentication – asserting that a subject was authenticated by a specific means at a specific time;
- attribute – asserting that one or more supplied attributes are associated with the subject;
- authorisation decision – granting or denying access to a resource to the assertion subject (Cantor, p. 11).[29]

SAML assertions and statements are expressed in XML according to the SAML schema.

SAML protocols describe the packaging of SAML requests and responses and provide processing rules for SAML entities to produce and consume requests and responses. SAML protocols include queries for authentication, attributes and authorisation decisions, among others. SAML bindings map SAML protocol messages onto standard messaging formats for communicating queries and other SAML message exchanges over the web. Bindings include SOAP, HTTP and SAML URI bindings. SAML has profiles, which represent common use cases for the SAML specification, particularly the Web Browser SSO profile.[30]

XACML emerged as an extension to SAML, primarily to codify and enforce access policies within an XML schema language. XACML, currently in version 2.0, provides an XML schema for the 'expression of authorization policies in XML against objects that are themselves identified in XML.'[31] XACML describes policies that apply to targets, which may be resources, subjects ('users') or actions. A policy within XACML is a set of rules, an identifier for the rule-combining algorithm that combines decisions from multiple rules, such as separate applicable policies in a policy set, and optionally obligations that must be met to satisfy rules. Policy statements may refer to classes of resources, subjects or actions or may combine multiple or distributed policy statements that reference a shared target, such as separate policy statements for a single resource. XACML operates through multiple entities for policy definition and enforcement. The Policy Enforcement Point (PEP) performs the access control by sending decision requests and enforcing authorisation decisions. The PEP receives a request for a service or resource from a client and formulates a request, containing the user group to which the client belongs, the URI of the resource the user is requesting and the action(s) the user wants to perform on the resource. The Policy Information Point (PIP), which stores attribute values, is used to construct the request, which is sent to the Policy Decision Point (PDP). The PDP retrieves the appropriate policy, evaluates the applicable policy based on data elements in the request (subject, target, attributes) and renders an authorisation decision to the PEP. The PEP returns the decision to the requesting client.[32] A diagram of an XACML request process is provided in Figure 5.3.

The Policy Administration Point (PAP) creates a policy or policy set and the PIP serves as the source of attribute values. Attributes are characteristics of a subject, resource, action or environment and are used to locate applicable policies and to satisfy rules so that an authorisation decision can be made and enforced. Unlike SAML, which works with attributes and assertions in a fairly simple manner, XACML allows for much more nuanced access controls based on subjects, resources and enforceable policies. Complex situations that may involve multiple policies referring to the same resource, access policies for classes of subjects (e.g. 'students') or resources (e.g. 'licensed databases') are accommodated by XACML. XACML thus extends SAML and also utilises SAML protocols and bindings to support communications

Figure 5.3 **XACML request process**

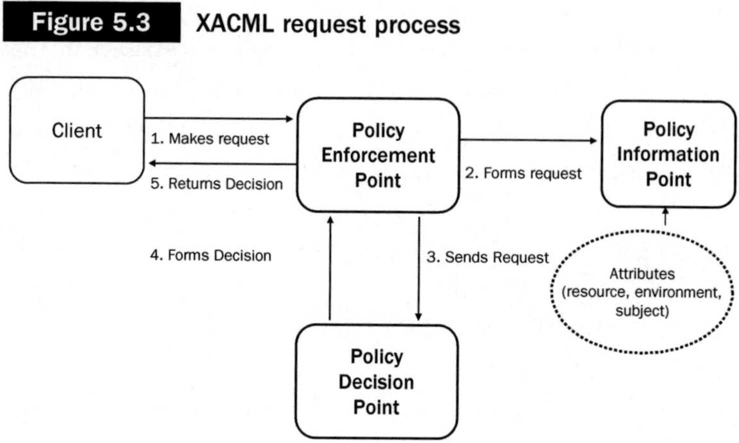

among the XACML entities.[31] XACML can be implemented within a repository architecture, to enable access communications among the policy entities. The open source repository architecture Fedora Commons employs XACML for resource access control enforcement, for example.[33]

Central Authentication Service (CAS)

CAS is an SSO protocol that provides unified access to web resources within a single institution, utilising a centralized authentication server. The CAS architecture currently exists in complete form in CAS 1 and CAS 2. The CAS server is currently in release 3.2.1. Many clients, including those of Java, JSP and uPortal, are available. The primary component of CAS is the CAS server, which is a standalone web application accessed through three URLs: the login URL, the validation URL and the optional logout URL. A CAS site may redirect users or provide a hyperlink to the login URL. When the client requests an application that is protected within CAS, the client is automatically directed to the CAS server for authentication, which will validate the client username and password or other specified credential against a directory database or other authentication process via the authentication handler. Applications that direct a user to the login URL must provide a service identifier. When the user is authenticated, the CAS creates a ticket that is associated with both the user and the service and serves as a one-time use credential that enables access to the resource. The ticket is then handed to the validation URL, which validates the ticket against a stored database to determine that the ticket, based on user and service, is valid. An optional session cookie may be created that enables SSO, or access to any CAS-enabled resource or application within the user session. As the website notes, 'when the cycle is completed, a web application has been able to verify a user's identity without ever having access to that user's password. Furthermore, in the case where the user's browser accepts cookies, it is left with a cookie that can re-identify the user to CAS so that the user does not have to enter his NetID and password in the future.'[34] CAS 2 extends CAS 1 to support a multi-tier architecture in which an agent may represent the user and must first authenticate itself and next demonstrate that it has been in contact with the user 'recently'.[35] CAS was originally developed by Yale University but was transferred to the JA-SIG group to become the JA-SIG Central Authentication Service. JA-SIG is the Java architects group that develops open standards utilising Java.[36]

CoSign single sign on

CoSign is an open source SSO system for web-based resource access. CoSign was originally developed by the University of Michigan and is currently part of the National Science Foundation EDIT software release. CoSign works in a web environment with cookies. If a user successfully authenticates at log in, a login cookie is associated with the user. The login cookie is then associated with a service cookie to provide user access to the server. The login cookie enables the user to access any services that require authentication without having to log in again. CoSign is now a module for the Drupal web content management system.[37]

OpenID

OpenID is self-described on its website as 'an open, decentralized, free framework for user-centric digital identity.'[38] OpenID is based on the concept that application and resource users can use a unique URI to authenticate with any OpenID-enabled website and thus access resources or applications across the web.

OpenID does not require standardised authentication practises for the identity provider, which makes OpenID easier to implement broadly but poses some risk to service and resource providers, who will probably want to know something about the authentication practises of the OpenID identity provider, particularly for transactions needing a higher level of security. OpenID does support encryption to support secured authentication transactions.

A user visiting an OpenID-enabled website ('the relying party') will be prompted for his or her identifier. The relying party will perform discovery on the identifier, depending on whether the identifier is an XRI or a URL, both of which return a XRDS document, an XML document that provides standardised discovery. In other cases, an HTML-based discovery is attempted. The user is provided with an OpenID Provider endpoint URL, a redirected URL back to the returning page of the relying party website. The relying party redirects the end user's user-agent (web browser) to the OpenID Provider with an OpenID authentication request. The OpenID Provider authenticates the user and redirects the user-agent to the relying party with an assertion that authentication is approved or a message that authentication failed. The relying party verifies the information, including the returned URL and provides access to the resource or service.[39] OpenID is a fairly simple application that supports authentication and the exchange of identity information between two OpenID-enabled sites through the OpenID Attribute Exchange specification. Retrieval and storage of identity information are supported in OpenID Attribute Exchange 1.0.[40] OpenID is gaining acceptance among websites and web-based service providers, including browsers such as Mozilla Firefox and web service providers such as Google.

OpenID's ownership is unclear although the OpenID Foundation exists in part to 'ensure that OpenID specifications are freely implementable'. Contributors who develop community-developed specifications must sign a license granting copyright for the specifications to the OpenID Foundation and agreeing not to assert a patent.[41]

XRI i-name

The XRI was discussed at length in Chapter 4. XRI, an OASIS standard, provides an identifier syntax and protocol for resolving URI identifiers over the Web. It is intended to be highly functional to support cross-domain usage and to support rich identification that can include cross-references to other identifiers, such as an email address or website specific to a person. A reference application has been developed for the 'i-name' XRI identifier that enables resolution to an OpenID XRDS document, to support OpenID authentication. The i-name XRI identifier is also interoperable with directory applications, such as LDAP. i-name is emerging as a highly functional option for identifying agents – users and resource creators/owners – within digital library applications.[42]

Federated authentication and authorisation

As the discussion on tools and standards demonstrates, there are many options that an organisation can consider to enable web-based authentication and authorization as well as SSO to allow its users to authenticate once and access many applications and resources. However, in the interconnected world, libraries are involved in many collaborative and consortial applications that require authentication and authorization, and even SSO, among disparate, geographically distributed entities. Organisations that enter into a relationship in order to authenticate and authorise the members of the participating organisations must be able to trust one another. As the definition of 'trust' provided earlier notes, organisations must (1) share a common platform for authentication and authorisation, or (2) be able to readily discover and evaluate the authentication and authorisation methodology of an organisation and determine whether to 'trust' the policies and practises of that organization, or (3) simply choose to trust the authentication and authorisation practises of federation members without knowing anything about those practises.

In the web environment, a shared platform is generally simpler and more transparent for the end user. Federated authentication and authorisation architectures can generally be employed within an organization but can also enable the organisation to join 'communities of trust' to extend access to applications and resources beyond those hosted by the organisation. Federated solutions may include a common technology shared among distributed servers, such as OpenID (described above). A common standard-based architecture designed to support research and higher education that is readily extensible to all types of libraries and archives is the Internet2 Shibboleth®, project.

Shibboleth®

In the open source space, particularly in higher education, Shibboleth®, has emerged as a *de facto* standard for federated authentication and authorisation. Shibboleth®, a product of Internet2/MACE (Middleware Architecture Committee for Education), is an open source authentication and attribute-based authorisation framework that includes a suite of applications and reference implementations. Shibboleth® is intended to support a 'community of trust' or federation, where multiple sites serve as service providers (sites holding Shibboleth-protected applications and resources) and as identity providers (where requests originate and requestors are subsequently authenticated). The core of Shibboleth® is a SAML implementation for managing communication between the requestor of resources, the identity provider (authenticating institution) and the service provider (resource-providing institution). Shibboleth®, also includes a handle server that generates attribute-based handles to maintain the active privacy of the end user, who can be identified as 'member of X University English 101 course' rather than as 'John Smith'. Identity provider sites maintain user credentials and attributes, which are delivered using SAML assertions supported in Shibboleth®. Service provider sites need to incorporate the Shibboleth®, plug-in with their applications in order to support discovery of the identity provider and accept authentication and attribute assertions.

Shibboleth®, is described as 'standards-based, open source middleware software that provides Web Single Sign On (SSO) across or within organizational boundaries. It allows sites to make informed authorization decisions for individual access of protected online resources in a privacy-preserving manner.'[43] Shibboleth®, includes both a policy framework and a technical architecture to enable participating organisations to join communities of trust, share policies and attributes, and authenticate and authorise users of each member organisation in the community. Shibboleth®, supports:

- *Active privacy.* Handles are generated to represent the requesting user, based on user role attributes, rather than on name or unique identifier. The unique identity of the user is protected from exposure.
- *Attribute-based authorization.* Shibboleth®, supports attribute-based authorisation, and much of the policy and application components of Shibboleth®, deal with attribute management, particularly the controlled dissemination of attribute information based both on institutional policies and on user preferences.
- *Reliance on open source standards and applications.* Shibboleth®, utilises open source standards, such as LDAP, SAML and SOAP (Simple Object Access Protocol), and leverages an institution's existing authentication and authorisation technologies.

Shibboleth®, is essentially an exchange of information between an Identity Provider (IdP) and a service provider (SP), on behalf of a user.

The *SP* consists primarily of three components: assertion consumer services (ACSs), resource manager (RM) and the Shibboleth daemon (shibd), which interacts directly with the identity manager.

The *IdP* consists of four primary components: the attribute query handler, the SSO handler, the directory service and an authentication mechanism. An authentication mechanism is provided with Shibboleth®, 2.0 but for earlier versions a local authentication mechanism is triggered.

1. A user initiates a request for a shib-protected resource through a browser to a service provider. As a member of

a Shibboleth®, organisation, the user has been able to specify which attributes can be released, through attribute release policies (ARPs) maintained by the IdP.

2. The SP can use a WAYF (Where Are You From) service to determine where to authenticate the user or it can issue an authentication request directly to an IdP. WAYF is used when the IdP may not be immediately known or if the SP wants to delegate identity provider discovery. WAYF can be provided by a third party or within the SP. WAYF can determine in two ways where to receive authentication information and attributes for the user. WAYF can map the user to an internal registry and can direct the query to the appropriate identity manager. The user can also tell the WAYF which organisation will provide authentication.
3. WAYF will redirect the user to the appropriate handle service within the IdP, which will check the SSO handler to determine if the user has already been authenticated.
4. If the browser user is not already authenticated, he/she will be asked to authenticate.
5. After authentication, a SAML assertion will be bundled in a handle and sent to the SP's assertion consumer service (ACS) URL.
6. The Shibboleth Daemon, shibd, will send a request to the IdP's attribute query handler with the handle mentioned in step 5, requesting all attributes the SP is entitled to know about the handle, which is the surrogate for the user.
7. The IdP consults the attribute release policies (ARPs) associated with the directory entry identified by the handle and queries the directory for attributes.
8. The IdP releases to the SP all attributes the SP is entitled to know.

9. The Resource Manager (RM) provides validation and analysis based on attribute acceptance policies (AAPs). The attributes are then either handed off to the application to grant access, or used internally for access decision making.[44]

The multi-step Shibboleth®, process is illustrated in Figure 5.4.

The above process may sound familiar, particularly after reading the description of SAML in the previous section on tools and strategies. Shibboleth®, incorporates the SAML suite of applications and protocols for enabling attribute-based access controls, as well as encouraging the use of LDAP for directory-based attribute storage and management.

Shibboleth®, is not trivial to implement, but it is uniquely positioned as a mature, communally developed architecture for federated authentication and authorisation, particularly within the higher education environment. Adoption has been gradual but widespread. Two interesting implementations are SWITCHaai, the authentication and authorization

Figure 5.4 **Shibboleth process**

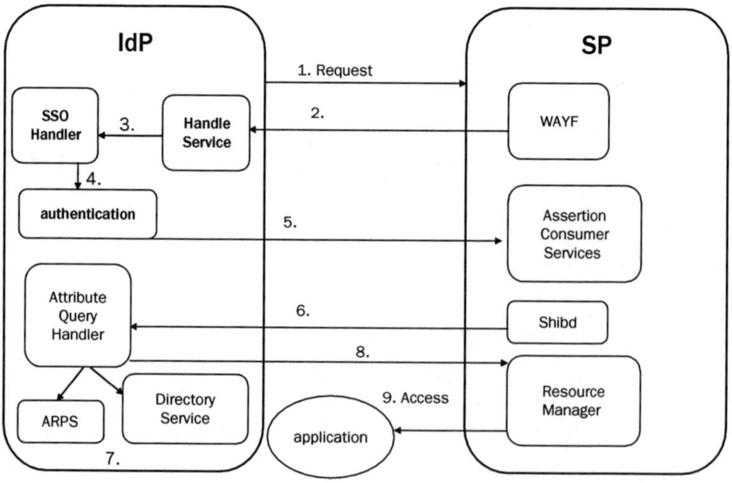

infrastructure of the Swiss Education and Research Network, a federation of universities that utilise Shibboleth®, for SSO access to web resources across member institutions[45] and DRAMA (Digital Repository Authorization Middleware Architecture), a component of the Australian RAMP project (Research Activityflow and Middleware Priorities Project). DRAMA incorporates Shibboleth®, within the Muradora repository application, which supports federated identity via Shibboleth®, authentication and flexible authorisation at the resource level utilizing XACML. The DRAMA Muradora Digital Repository Authorization Middleware Architecture (DRAMA Auth/Z Suite) is important because it overcomes a significant limitation of Shibboleth®,. Shibboleth®, is currently triggered by a browser-based user request. DRAMA is extending Shibboleth®, to support use of a web services interface rather than a browser.[46]

An interesting library implementation is the Virtual Library of Virginia's (VIVA) Public Broadcasting System (PBS) video collection, a licensed collection of more than 500 hours of commercial content available to all 70 higher education organisations that are members of the VIVA consortium. The VIVA consortium joined the InCommon Federation, a Shibboleth®, community of trust open to any US higher education institution for an annual fee. VIVA organizations use Shibboleth®, authentication and authorisation to enable access for organisational members to this licensed video collection.[47]

Implementing authentication and authorisation in libraries

Library users want seamless access to a wide range of information. The ease and convenience of the Internet have resulted in extremely low tolerance for roadblocks and delays in accessing information. Users are not particularly interested in the distinction between open access resources and copyrighted resources that may have legal restrictions on access. A good authentication and authorisation strategy is key to enabling users to browse among digital resources and select the information most responsive to their needs. In addition, most library workflow is digital and frequently involves distributed transactions across the web. A library's internal workflow frequently requires levels of authentication that may range from basic tasks performed by students or volunteers to administration of the entire workflow application. A nuanced authentication and authorisation strategy is critical to ensuring that digital resources in a repository are created and managed with efficiency and accountability, for example.

Libraries do not exist in a vacuum, and the information and services offered to authorised users rarely represent the complete range of resources that the user wants and needs. A library may be part of a larger government agency that might offer authorised users the opportunity to register their automobile and register to use digital library resources through the same citizen's portal. An academic library is part of a college or university that offers a range of services and information to authorised users, including the ability to register for courses, access a transcript and, for faculty and staff, to access personal benefit information. In addition, a library may be part of a consortium, based on geographic location or type of library. These consortia often negotiate shared commercial databases and provide interlibrary loan of books and articles among the members.

A critical first step in planning an authentication and authorisation or access management strategy is to investigate how the larger organisation manages the process. Many universities, for example, use an LDAP directory to authenticate users, which also serves as a web-based locator service on the university's webpage. It is important to recognise that the larger organisation represents an important context for the library's user. The user's workflow is frequently enabled by the larger institution, particularly in higher education where the institution enables enrollment, course management, transcripts, email and other services that represent the critical activities of faculty and students. Integrating the library into the institution's access management system not only provides expertise and support and an SSO within the institution but also enables the library to integrate its information and services into the organisational framework of the user.

Another important factor to consider is the range of services and resources present in the library or under development. These include integrated library systems, web content management systems, repository systems and course management systems. Each system incorporates some level of authentication and authorisation. Evaluating an application such as a content management system should include evaluation of the access management strategy, particularly to determine if the access management component can integrate easily with other library services. Libraries should expend the effort to understand the access management component of each application and to determine if an SSO strategy can integrate all the services under a single authentication and authorisation strategy. This is perhaps the most important service for supporting users as they search for information and participate in services such as signing up for RSS feeds, participating in a blog, or accessing licensed or copyright-protected resources.

A good access management strategy will include:

- Adherence to open standards.
- Transparency to the user, with a straightforward interface and clear explanations of the process so that the user is informed but not inconvenienced.

- Ability to provide an SSO strategy for web resources.
- Attribute-based authorisation, to enable a range of user types.
- Support for multifactor authentication.
- The ability to integrate different authentication mechanisms, such as username and password, X.509 certificates and LDAP is highly desirable. 'Authentication transparency' will enable the access management system to integrate across applications, departments and organisations.
- Multiple browser support to enable users to access services and resources through their browser of choice.
- Strong market penetration and an active user group to ensure that the authentication and authorization strategy will be sustained over time.

An SSO that enables users to make seamless use of services and resources within a session is critical for providing the level of service that information seekers want and expect. Ideally, this SSO will exist at the institutional level and enable the library to integrate its services and resources seamlessly into the workflow of the organisation's members. If an institutional SSO does not exist, libraries should advocate for this service. Many consortia provide economies of scale and cost-effective licensing of resources as well as interlibrary loan utilising commercial software. A critical next step is to develop a federated access management strategy, such as Shibboleth, to support the shared creation, management and access to resources in a digital community of trust, thus expanding users' access to information resources in a manner that is both seamless and scalable, but which also supports users in their need to know their obligations for responsible use of copyright-protected resources.

Notes and references

1. Cutter, Charles A. (1904) *Rules for a Dictionary Catalog: U.S. Bureau of Education, Special Report on Public Libraries Part II*, 4th edition, rewritten. Washington, DC: Government Printing Office. Available in pdf from Google Books. Last accessed 24 March 2008. *http://books.google.com/books?id=X078UC_a7IIC&printsec=titlepage&dq=rules+for+a+dictionary+catalogue+1st+edition&psp=1#PPA1,M1*
2. Tillett, Barbara B. *et al. Mandatory Data Elements for Internationally Shared Resource Authority Records: Report of the IFLA UBCIM Working Group on Minimal Level Authority Records and ISADN*. The Hague: IFLA. Latest revision 5 February 1999. Last accessed 24 March 2008. *http://www.ifla.org/VI/3/p1996-2/mlar.htm*
3. IFLA Study Group on the Functional Requirements for Bibliographic Records. (1998) *Functional Requirements for Bibliographic Records: Final Report* (UBCIM Publications, New Series vol. 19). Munich: K.G. Saur. Last accessed 24 March 2008. *http://www.ifla.org/VII/s13/frbr/frbr.pdf*
4. IFLA Working Group on Functional Requirements and Numbering of Authority Records (FRANAR). (2007) *Functional Requirements for Authority Data: A Conceptual Model, Draft*. The Hague: IFLA. Last accessed 24 March 2008. *http://www.ifla.org/VII/d4/FRANAR-ConceptualModel-2ndReview.pdf*
5. Bourdon, Françoise. (2001) *Functional Requirements and Numbering of Authority Records(FRANAR): to what Extent Authority Control can be Supported by Technical Means?, 67th IFLA Council and General Conference, August 16–25, 2001*. 096-152a-E. The Hague: IFLA. Last accessed 24 March 2008. *http://www.ifla.org/IV/ifla67/papers/096-152ae.pdf*
6. Vitali, Stefano. *The Second Edition of ISAAR (CPF) and Authority Control in Systems for Archival Descriptive Systems*. Florence: International Conference Authority Control: Definition and International Experiences, 10–12 February 2003. Last accessed 24 March 2008. *http://www.sba.unifi.it/ac/relazioni/vitali_eng.pdf*

7. *Ad Hoc* EAC Working Group. *Encoded Archival Context Beta*. Charlottesville, VA: University of Virginia, Institute for Advanced Technology in the Humanities. Revised 29 November 2004. Last accessed 24 March 2008. *http://www.iath.virginia.edu/eac/*
8. Schaffner, Jennifer. 'SAA EAC Working Group Receives Funding to Develop EAC Standard Version 1.' *RLG-Announce* [email list]. Dublin, OH: OCLC, 6 March 2008.
9. Vellucci, Sherry L. (2001) 'Music metadata and authority control in an international context'. *Notes* 57(3): 544.
10. LEAF Project Consortium. *LEAF (Home Page)*. Berlin: Staatsbibliothek zu Berlin, c2001–2004. Last accessed 24 March 2008. *http://www.crxnet.com/leaf/index.html*
11. Hickey, Thom, *et al. Virtual International Authority File* [presentation]. Dublin, OH: OCLC, c2008. Last accessed 24 March 2008. *http://www.oclc.org/research/projects/viaf/*
12. Library of Congress Program for Cooperative Cataloging. *NACO, Name Authority Cooperative Program of the PCC*. Last revised 28 February 2008. Last accessed 24 March 2008. *http://www.loc.gov/catdir/pcc/naco/naco.html*
13. Hickey, Thomas B. *(2007)* 'WorldCat identities: another view of the catalog'. *NextSpace, the OCLC Newsletter* 6. Last accessed 24 March 2008. *http://www.oclc.org/nextspace/006/research.htm*
14. Mimas. *The Names Project (home Page)*. Manchester: University of Manchester. Last revised 8 April 2008. Last accessed 11 May 2008. *http://names.mimas.ac.uk/*
15. Computerworld. (2008) *Quick Study: Authentication*. Framingham, MA: Computerworld. Last accessed 24 March 2008. *http://www.computerworld.com/action/article.do?command=viewArticleBasic&articleId=44257*
16. Bolten, Joshua B. (2003) 'Attachment A: E-Authentication Guidance for Federal Agencies' *Memorandum to the Heads of All Departments and Agencies*. Washington, DC: Office of Management and Budget. Last accessed 24 March 2008. *http://www.whitehouse.gov/omb/memoranda/fy04/m04-04.pdf*
17. Wikipedia. *Password Strength*. St. Petersburg, FL: Wikimedia Foundation, Inc. Last modified 19 March 2008. Last accessed 24 March 2008. *http://en.wikipedia.org/wiki/Password_strength*

18. Cooper, D., Santesson, S., Farrell, S., Boeyen, S., Housley, R. and Polk, W. (2008) *Internet X.509 Public Key Infrastructure Certificate and Certificate Revocation List (CRL) Profile, Request for Comments 5280*. Sterling, VA: Network Working Group, IETF, May 2008. Last accessed 18 May 2008. *http://www.ietf.org/rfc/rfc5280.txt*
19. *Kerberos: the Network Authentication Protocol*. Cambridge, MA: MIT. Last accessed 24 March 2008. *http://web.mit. edu/Kerberos/*
20. NISO MetaSearch Initiative, Standards Committee BA (Task Group 1) (2005) Access Management. *Ranking of Authentication and Access Methods Available to the Metasearch Environment, A Recommended Practice of the National Information Standards Organization*. Bethesda, MD: NISO. Last accessed 12 May 2008. *http://www.niso.org/publications/rp/RP-2005-01.pdf*
21. UW Technology Services. *Pubcookie: Open Source Software for Intra-institutional Web Authentication*. Seattle, WA: University of Washington Computing & Communications. Last modified 12 September 2007. Last accessed 24 March 2008. *http://www.pubcookie.org/*
22. Donnelly, Michael. (2000) *An Introduction to LDAP*. Ashland, OR: Ldapman.org. Last accessed 24 March 2008. *http://www.ldapman.org/articles/intro_to_ldap.html*
23. Yeong, W., *et al.* (1995) *Lightweight Directory Access Protocol. Request for Comments 1777*. Reston, VA: Network Working Group, IETF. Last accessed 24 March 2008. *http://www.ietf.org/rfc/rfc1777.txt*
24. Hazelton, Keith (ed.) 'eduPerson Object Class' *Net@edu., Leading Strategies for Networking in Higher Education*. Boulder, CO, US: Educause, c1999–2008. Last accessed 24 March 2008. *http://www.educause.edu/eduperson/*
25. Zeilenga, K. (ed.) (2006) *Lightweight Directory Access Protocol (LDAP): Technical Specification Road Map, RFC 4510*. Reston, VA: Network Working Group, IETF. Last accessed 24 March 2008. *http://tools.ietf.org/html/rfc4510*
26. Sermersheim, J. (ed.) (2006) *Lightweight Directory Access Protocol (LDAP): the Protocol, Request for Comments, 4511*. Reston, VA: Network Working Group, IETF. Last accessed 24 March 2008. *http://tools.ietf.org/html/rfc4511*

27. Schleiff, M. (2006) *LDAP Schema for eXtensible Resource Identifier (XRI) draft-schleiff-ldap-xri-01*. Reston, VA: Network Working Group, IETF. Last accessed 24 March 2008. *https://opends.dev.java.net/public/standards/draft-schleiff-ldap-xri.txt*
28. *OASIS* [home page]. Billerica, MA: OASIS, c1993–2008. Last accessed 24 March 2008. *http://www.oasis-open.org/home/index.php*
29. Cantor, Scott, *et al.* (eds) (2005) *Assertions and Protocols for the OASIS Security Assertion Markup Language (SAML) V2.0, OASIS Standard, saml-core-2.0-os.* Billerica, MA: OASIS. Last accessed 24 March 2008. *http://docs.oasis-open.org/security/saml/v2.0/saml-core-2.0-os.pdf*
30. Hughes, John, *et al.* (eds) (2005) *Profiles for the Security Assertion Markup Language (SAML) V2.0, OASIS Standard, saml-profiles-2.0-os.* Billerica, MA: OASIS. Last accessed 24 March 2008. *http://docs.oasis-open.org/security/saml/v2.0/saml-profiles-2.0-os.pdf*
31. Cover, Robin (ed.) 'Extensible Access Control Markup Language, XACML'. *OASIS Cover Pages Technology Reports.* Last modified 28 June 2007. Last accessed 24 March 2008. *http://xml.coverpages.org/xacml.html*
32. Griffin, Phil. (2004) *Introduction to XACML.* San Jose, CA: Dev2Dev, BEA Systems. Last accessed 24 March 2008. *http://dev2dev.bea.com/pub/a/2004/02/xacml.html*
33. Fedora Commons. *Fedora XACML Policy Writing Guide, with Reference Collection of Sample Policies for Fedora.* Ithaca, NY: Fedora. Last accessed 24 March 2008. *http://fedora.info/download/2.1b/userdocs/server/security/XACMLPolicyGuide.htm*
34. JA-SIG. 'CAS 1 Architecture' *Central Authentication Service: Single Sign-on for the Web.* JA-SIG, c2005–2006. Last accessed 24 March 2008. *http://www.ja-sig.org/products/cas/overview/cas1_architecture/index.html*
35. JA-SIG. 'CAS 2 Architecture' *Central Authentication Service: Single Sign-on for the Web.* JA-SIG, c2005–2006. Last accessed 24 March 2008. *http://www.ja-sig.org/products/cas/overview/cas2_architecture/index.html*
36. JA-SIG. *'Central Authentication Service: Single Sign-on for the Web.* JA-SIG, c2005–2006. Last accessed 24 March 2008. *http://www.ja-sig.org/products/cas/index.html*

37. University of Michigan Information Technology Central Services. *CoSign Collaborative Single Sign-On.* Ann Arbor, MI: Regents of the University of Michigan. Last updated 29 January 2008. Last accessed 24 March 2008. *http://www.umich.edu/~umweb/software/cosign/*
38. OpenID Foundation. 'What is OpenID?' *OpenID.net* [home page]. Last accessed 24 March 2008. *http://openid.net/what/*
39. OpenID Foundation. 'OpenID Authentication 2.0 – Final' *OpenID.net* [home page]. 5 December 2007. Last accessed 24 March 2008. *http://openid.net/specs/openid-authentication-2_0.html*
40. OpenID Foundation. 'OpenID Attribute Exchange 1.0 – Final' *OpenID.net* [home page] 5 December 2007. Last accessed 24 March 2008. *http://openid.net/specs/openid-attribute-exchange-1_0.html*
41. OpenID Foundation. 'Intellectual Property' *OpenID.net* [home page]. Last accessed 24 March 2008. *http://openid.net/foundation/intellectual-property/*
42. 'XRI and OpenID.' *Inames.* Last modified 11 May 2007. Last accessed 24 March 2008. *http://dev.inames.net/wiki/XRI_and_OpenID*
43. Internet2. *Shibboleth®*. Ann Arbor, MI: Internet2, c2007. Last accessed 24 March 2008. *http://shibboleth.internet2.edu/*
44. Cantor, Scott and Klingenstein, Nate. *Shibboleth Deployment Background.* Ann Arbor, MI: Internet2. Last edited 8 June 2007. Last accessed 24 March 2008. *https://spaces.internet2.edu/display/SHIB/DeploymentBackground*
45. SWITCH (The Swiss Education & Research Network). *Authentication and Authorization Infrastructure (AAI)* Zurich: SWITCH, c2008. Last accessed 24 March 2008. *http://www.switch.ch/aai/*
46. Muradora. *Welcome to DRAMA Wiki.* Sydney: Macquarie University, 14 February 2008. Last accessed 24 March 2008. *http://drama.ramp.org.au/cgi-bin/trac.cgi*
47. InCommon Federation (2008) VIVA Virginia!: Library Consortium Offers Access to PBS Video Resources through InCommon. Ann Arbor, MI: InCommon, 8 April 2008. Last accessed 14 May 2008. *http://www.incommonfederation.org/docs/eg/InC_CaseStudy_VIVA_2008.pdf*

48. Teets, Michael and Murray, Peter. 'Metasearch authentication and access management.' *D-Lib Magazine* v. 12, no. 6 (June 2006). Last accessed 3 July 2008. *http://www.dlib.org/dlib/june06/teets/06teets.html*

6

Digital rights metadata: describing rights and rights workflow

Overview

Metadata is 'data about data' – structured data that defines, describes and manages information. Metadata is a key enabling technology for DRM. Its importance is recognised in copyright treaty and law. As discussed in Chapter 2, the WCT and WPPT treaties require that signatory countries provide legal remedies against any party that knowingly removes or alters rights management information, where this information is defined as 'information which identifies the work, the author of the work, the owner of any right in the work, or information about the terms and conditions of use of the work, and any numbers or codes that represent such information, when any of these items of information is attached to a copy of a work or appears in connection with the communication of a work to the public.' (WIPO Copyright Treaty, art. 12).[1]

This chapter will examine rights metadata – a core enabling technology for rights expression and management. The chapter opens with a discussion of metadata terms, concepts and tools, followed by key concepts documented by rights metadata. The next section surveys the major rights metadata schemas currently in use, and the final section summarises the main issues associated with the implementation of rights metadata by libraries.

Rights metadata is expressed in XML (eXtensible Markup Language) and may serve three complementary but distinct purposes:

- *Rights description*, which includes the description of the copyright status of works, rights holder requirements for use of the resource, user attributes required for authorised use of a resource, and agreements between both parties for resource use. PREMIS rights metadata, <indecs>rdd (rights data dictionary) and METSRights are examples of *rights description*.
- *Rights licensing* is an emerging area of rights management within the library environment, which addresses the issuing and management of licenses – for library-owned or managed resources and for commercially licensed resources. Rights licensing is a niche area focused on the development and exchange of license information for resources. The Creative Commons rights expression language, ccREL is an example of *rights licensing* metadata.
- *Rights workflow languages* support rights transactions between the rights holder and the user. They are designed to be actionable within a suite of standards and protocols to manage the digital workflow of rights management, where workflow includes the authorisation of users, enforcement of rights agreements, control of resource access and tracking of resource use. Rights workflow generally incorporates documentation of licenses but goes beyond simple license messaging to providing an end-to-end actionable platform for managing agreements between parties. Rights workflow expressions include a complete syntax for expressing interchanges between two

parties and may incorporate messaging protocols and applications to enable rights transactions. XrML (eXtensible Rights Markup Language), the core technology within the MPEG-21 rights expression language, ODRL (Open Digital Rights Language) and XACML (eXtensible Access Control Markup Language) are examples of *rights workflow languages*.

These broad roles for rights metadata correspond quite closely to the roles identified by Karen Coyle in her 2004 overview of rights expression languages for the Library of Congress:

1. 'the statement of legal copyright
2. the expression of contractual language
3. the implementation of controls' (Coyle, p. 10).[2]

Rights metadata ranges from basic metadata schemas that are simply data elements and values to a complete syntax – a *rights expression language*, with nouns and verbs – which can describe and manage agreements, licenses and enforcement of rights. Rights metadata and rights expression languages are often used interchangeably but simple data elements with values lack the syntactical richness to be considered a rights expression *language*. In this chapter, *rights expression language* applies only to rights metadata schemas with syntactical expressions that enable rights workflow (e.g. MPEG-21/5, ODRL and XACML).

Metadata overview

Metadata consists very simply of data elements, which are structured fields populated by unique information, known as 'values', according to rules intended to structure metadata

Figure 6.1 **Metadata basics**

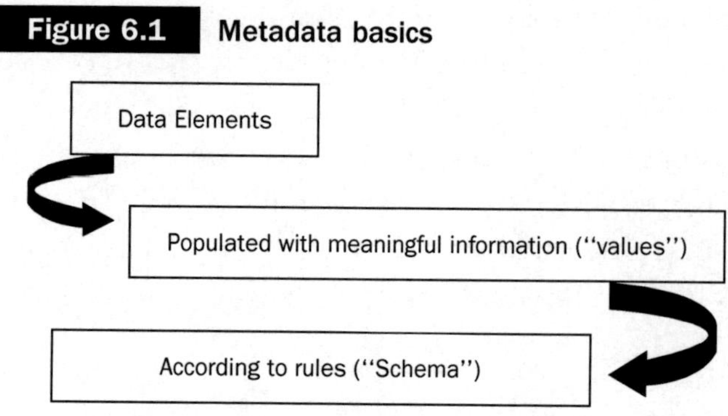
Data Elements
Populated with meaningful information ("values")
According to rules ("Schema")

Rules:

- **Data element (e.g. controlled vocabulary; formatting; prescribed value list or formatting rule)**
- **Record structure: data element constraints: (mandatory, recommended, optional) (repeatable) (order of elements)**

into a standardised format (Figure 6.1). These data elements, values and rules are collectively known as the 'metadata schema'. MODS (Metadata Object Description Schema) is an example of a metadata schema.

Metadata core concepts and technologies

Metadata, by its very nature, is intended to describe many entities, whether resources, people, events, concepts or all of the above. Consistency in design and application is thus critical for the creation of unambiguous and meaningful metadata. A well-constructed metadata strategy will generally incorporate the following core elements.

Data model

The data model provides the conceptual framework for metadata design. It identifies the entities that are described or managed by the metadata, as well as the relationships that exist among those entities. Data models can be expressed through a simple graphic or through standard modeling notations such as the Entity-Relationship (ER) model or the UML (Unified Modeling Language) syntax. The University of Texas, in its excellent overview of ER models, defines the entity as 'the principal data object about which information is to be collected. Entities are usually recognizable concepts, either concrete or abstract, such as person, places, things, or events ...'.[3] Entities relate to other entities. Metadata is about relationships and the way in which people use information to create relationships between disparate pieces of information. As an example, Newton related the apple's weight to its falling to discover gravity. A model formalises relationships, including:

- *Degree of relationship*. This refers to the number of entities involved in a relationship. The most common is *binary* – two entities that relate to one another, such as a resource creator authoring a resource. A more complex degree of relationship is recursive, when an entity relates to itself. A metadata instance, or record, may document multiple physical manifestations of the resource being described within the overall metadata instance. This is a recursive relationship for the metadata instance.
- *Connectivity and cardinality*. Connectivity and cardinality are also important aspects of relationship. Connectivity indicates whether the relationship is 'one' or 'many' and cardinality addresses the actual number of relationships that occur between each entity. An entity may relate to another entity in a one-to-one relationship. For example, each resource will have one, and only one, instance of metadata. A relationship may be one to many (1:*N*). For entity A, there is only one instance of entity B, but for entity B, there may be one or many instances of

entity A. For example, a resource (entity A) will have only one identifier but an identifier (entity B) may identify a single resource or a collection of two or more resources. A many-to-many relationship states that for each instance of entity A, there are one or many instances of entity B and for each instance of entity B, there are one or many instances of entity A. A resource may have one or many permissions associated with its use (display, copy, print, etc.). Each permission may apply to one or many resources.

- *Obligation.* Use of an entity within a metadata instance may be optional or mandatory. A resource may have zero, one or many subject headings, where subject heading is an optional entity involved in a many-to-many relationship with one or many resources.
- *Direction* is the final core attribute of an entity relationship. A relationship emanates from the parent entity in a relationship to the child entity. For example, a creator makes a resource available for use. The relationship originates with the creator (parent) to the resource (child).

A good metadata schema will begin with a data model, which conceptualises the entities and relationships that the metadata schema will make concrete. When evaluating a metadata schema, particularly for rights metadata, an excellent place to begin is by studying the data model, which is, to be hoped, provided early in the metadata documentation. This book, which is in the broadest sense 'metadata' about DRM, is organised around a simple data model, provided in Figure 1.1 and here in Figure 6.2.

Data dictionary/metadata registry

A data dictionary defines the data elements within a metadata schema. Data elements describe the entities

Figure 6.2 DRM book model

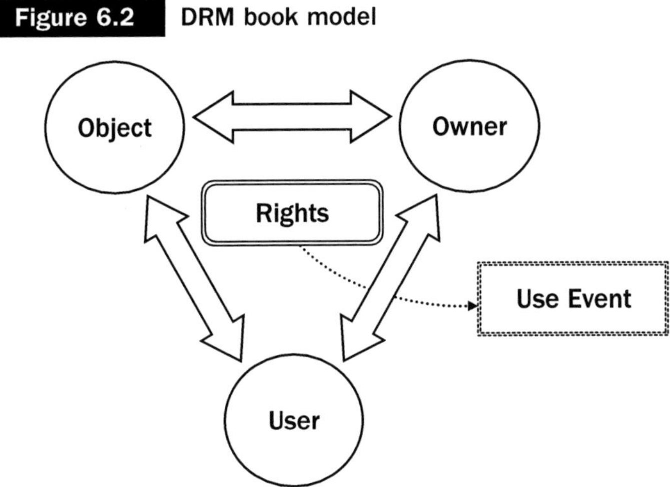

(people, places, things, dates, concepts) that the metadata schema as a whole will define. Examples of data elements include <creator>, <copyrightStatus> and <copyrightDate>. A data dictionary provides the following information for the data elements used within a metadata schema:

- *Identification.* The data dictionary identifies all the data elements used within the metadata, although the schema may provide for extensions to enable users to include additional data elements. A data dictionary will assign a name and often a label (the generally understandable name for the resource). A data dictionary may assign a unique identifier in addition to a name for each data element.
- *Definition.* A data dictionary should provide enough definition to enable unambiguous interpretation and use for each data element within the schema.
- *Repeatability.* The data dictionary indicates whether a data element can be repeated within a single instance of the metadata.

- *Obligation*. The data dictionary must indicate whether a data element is mandatory or optional within a single instance of the metadata. Optionally, the data dictionary may indicate that a data element is recommended for use.
- *Value formulation/constraints*. As previously noted, the value is the unique information contained within an instance of a data element. For example, 'Grace Agnew' is the value for the data element 'creator' in the metadata for this book. A data dictionary provides requirements for populating a data element, including controlled vocabularies and formatting principles [e.g. the use of ISO 8601 (YYYY-MM-DD) to formulate date values].
- *Relationship*. The data dictionary will indicate relationships between data elements, such as parent–child or sibling relationships.
- *Context and examples*. The data dictionary provides the context in which the data element is used and examples to enable users to implement each data element appropriately.

Data dictionaries address consistency – ensuring that each data element has both consistent meaning and representation and that each data element is used contextually with other data elements to create a meaningful and consistent metadata instance. Data dictionaries also ensure that metadata is unambiguous and can be interpreted by any type of user – a software application or a human user – in a consistent and accurate manner. For rights, metadata that is consistent and unambiguous is critical for presenting the rights of both parties in a legal agreement for use of a resource.

A data dictionary, as a component of a rights metadata implementation, is a very useful tool. ERMI (Electronic Resource Management Initiative), MPEG-21 rights metadata and ODRL (Open Digital Rights Language) are examples of rights metadata with data dictionaries. A data dictionary may be expressed in numerous ways, from a simple spreadsheet or other eye-readable representation to a software-interpretable representation. The Resource Description Framework (RDF), an XML syntax that expresses relationships between entities, is frequently used to document data dictionaries. An international standard, ISO/IEC 11179, provides guidelines for registering, identifying and defining data elements in a manner that provides unambiguous interpretation and reuse of data elements across different communities. Part 3, in particular, provides a metamodel for registering data elements and their basic attributes, such as repeatability or obligation.[4]

Schema

The metadata schema is the final core concept in the evaluation of rights metadata. Metadata designed by an organisation or community is variously referred to as a 'metadata standard', a 'metadata schema' or simply as a 'metadata format'. Although there are no hard and fast rules of nomenclature for metadata, it is useful to apply the same rules of nomenclature to metadata that are applied to other computer applications. The term 'standard' should refer to metadata that is managed by a standards body, committed to such principles as broad availability for the standard, documentation and training tools, versioning of the standard and encouraging public comment on proposed standards and versions, to ensure accountability to the community of users. Standards bodies should ideally have a national or international community role and should include representation from current and potential user groups. Examples of metadata standards bodies include the Dublin

Core Metadata Initiative, the National Information Standards Institute (NISO), the Moving Picture Experts Group (MPEG) and the Library of Congress. MPEG-21 rights and ODRL are two examples of rights metadata schemas that are maintained as international standards.

A metadata schema is documented in an XML schema that provides an actionable methodology for documenting and validating data element definition and use, including relationships among data elements within the schema. The schema will enforce formatting, data element population, data element obligation (which data elements are mandatory), etc. Each metadata instance should express the underlying data model of entity relationships to provide a complete expression of the metadata and a complete representation of the entity or entities it defines and describes. Metadata schemas are documented in XML as the XML schema language supports the rules required to enforce consistency and integrity within the metadata and provides a means of validating each metadata instance against those rules. A metadata schema thus will document the data elements and the rules governing those data elements. It will also provide a methodology for validating metadata instances against the schema.

Core rights concepts

Rights metadata may address any or all of the important rights concepts that are necessary for understanding the rights status of a resource and for accessing and using a rights-protected resource. In order to evaluate the usefulness of rights metadata schemas for supporting rights workflow in libraries, several important concepts that may be documented within rights metadata should be defined. These are enumerated below.

Provenance

Provenance is defined as the origin and ownership of a resource. Ideally, provenance should demonstrate an unbroken chain of ownership, particularly in a museum or archival setting, where the chain of ownership of a rare resource can demonstrate the legitimacy of the current ownership. Provenance in the digital space can document that a digital resource is unchanged from its ingest, or that any changes have been documented and justified in the metadata. Provenance was discussed at length in Chapter 4. In rights metadata, provenance is most important for documenting the attributes of a resource that are critical for identifying the copyright status and identifying the rights holder, which can enable end users to obtain further permissions for resource use.

Dates associated with a resource are essential as copyright is an intentionally limited term of protection, intended to balance benefit to the creator, who wants to exploit the resource economically, against the societal value of widespread and open access to the resource. Date of creation and date of publication are both important provenance dates to document. In countries such as the United States, the copyright law in force and in effect at the time of publication or creation applies to the work for determining both copyright status and copyright term. Date of publication is also important because copyright terms may differ for published versus unpublished works. Some countries, notably the UK, offer a publication term of protection in addition to copyright. The death date of the resource creator is particularly critical, as copyright term in international treaty and national law is generally defined as a period beginning from the end of the year in which the creator dies. Tying copyright term to the life of the creator ensures that the creator and his/her heirs will have a sufficient timespan to exploit the resource commercially to serve as incentive for the creation of works that contribute to the cultural fabric.

Creators and other contributors to a work should be identified, along with their role in the creation, publication or distribution of a resource. This is critical as all contributors to a work are potentially rights holders. As discussed in Chapters 2 and 3, performers and producers of phonograms have rights in a performance-based resource that are protected by international treaty as well as national law. Composers of musical works used within an audiovisual resource, such as the score of a feature film, retain their copyright unless it has been explicitly transferred. Publicity rights may also apply, for an individual or group of individuals appearing on or in a resource. Publishers, distributors, performers and individuals contributing to the intellectual content of a resource, such as the playwright and librettist, should be identified, together with the role or roles played in the creation, publication or distribution of the resource. If possible, any available licenses or permissions, such as publicity releases, should be attached to the relevant entities in a rights event. Rutgers University Library's RUcore rights metadata, discussed later in this chapter, provides this capability. Country of origin for the creator and country of publication are also critical for copyright, as copyright law differs by country. Karen Coyle also recommends a data element for publication status, with the values 'published, unpublished',[5] to which values the RUcore rights schema added 'publication pending', broadcast and 'unknown'.[6]

Rights holder

'Creator' and 'rights holder' are often not the same entity. Term of copyright outlasts the lifetime of the creator, so rights ownership will pass to the heir(s) of the creator, in the absence of any other explicit transfer of rights. The creator may transfer rights to a publisher or distributor of the resource or to a library or archive in a deed of gift. Whenever a rights holder is identified for a resource, contact information should be documented in metadata. Although this information can be viewed as ephemeral in this peripatetic age, contact information provides a starting point for researching rights for a resource or may represent the latest known information discovered by a rights researcher. Coyle also recommends documenting the rights researcher so it is clear how the information about the rights holder and the rights associated with the resource were obtained.[5] RUCore Rights includes a verification date for contact information so that contact information can be periodically assessed and re-verified, based on date of last verification. In addition, rights research can be documented as a rights event within RUCore Rights, with the rights researcher as an associated entity and his/her notes or comments as an associated object.[6]

Rights status

Coyle recommends documenting copyright status (copyrighted, public domain, unknown).[5] The documenting of copyright status is important for enabling users to select appropriate resources. Copyright status will assist an author searching for a public domain image to use in his or her resource. It will also enable the library to provide differential permissions for use, such as 'display' for copyright-protected images, and 'display' and 'download' for public domain images.

Rights data elements should remain durably tied to the resource. Although the rights holder may change, the rights holder is part of the evidentiary provenance chain and a critical component of the resource's life cycle. These elements are also important for resource discovery and identification. A change in publisher may also mean a change in the intellectual content, such as a different translation, different illustrations, or different accompanying critical notes. Most of these data elements are provided in some form by descriptive metadata, such as Dublin Core, MARC21 and MODS.

Many rights metadata schemas enable the integration of a descriptive metadata instance or descriptive metadata elements within the rights metadata. This is the strategy employed by Creative Commons, Open Digital Rights Language (ODRL) and MPEG-21 rights metadata. One issue with utilising descriptive metadata for rights description is that the provenance data elements used in descriptive metadata, such as publisher, creator and date of publication, were designed to enable resource owners (libraries) and users to identify the resource precisely, based on the metadata – the edition, the publisher, etc. The context of the data elements is descriptive rather than rights-oriented. For example, a creator's authoritative name in descriptive metadata may be based on his or her preferred form of the name rather than a legal name that might enable tracing the creator in a rights investigation.

Data elements such as 'rights holder' and 'copyright status' are generally not present in descriptive metadata.

Most rights metadata reflects the business model of the developer community, which is often to enable the management of resource access. The library business model involves managing a range of resources, from open-source to rights-protected, and either negotiating and managing licenses or enabling users to negotiate their own licenses for restricted resources. This ensures that everything in the library's collection – whether analog or digital – can be appropriately and effectively used. Any rights metadata schema used by a library must reflect this broad resource use agenda. The ability to incorporate rights data elements established by the library through an extension mechanism is thus an important component for a rights metadata schema that will be useful in a library or archival setting.

User and user roles

Beyond its purpose for describing rights status and provenance, rights metadata has been designed within many communities to enable rights workflow, particularly the documentation and description of an agreement or license between the creator or rights holder and the end user. As previously noted, an agreement can be explicit between the rights holder or his/her intermediary and a specific end user or it can be an open license with no identifiable end user, with no restrictions or one or more generally unenforceable restrictions, such as attribution or for educational use only. When an agreement is explicit between the licenser and one or more users, the user's role can be critical for authorised access to a resource. A user may need to demonstrate the attribute or role of 'student at university X', 'member of course Y at university X' or 'registered patron of public library Z'. An important role that is sometimes overlooked in rights workflow metadata is that of 'resource manager'. Another neglected role is that of the creator or rights owner, such as the university faculty member who needs ubiquitous access to his or her deposited resources for linking from his/her resume or website. The types of user roles or categories that are defined within rights metadata, as well as the ability to add user roles or categories by extension, is important for libraries and archives that tend to serve a broad range of users.

Rights or permissions

The terms 'rights' and 'permissions' are often used interchangeably in the DRM space. A 'right' within the DRM framework has been defined as a privilege or power granted by law that can be exercised on a resource. In some metadata, 'permission' has been more precisely defined as an approval that has been provided by the rights holder to do something to a resource. In other words, right and permission have sometimes been distinguished as the power or privilege granted by law to the creator or rights holder (right) versus the transfer or awarding of that right, often after one or more conditions are satisfied, to the end user (permission). Rights as defined in copyright are explicit in treaty and law as encompassing reproducing the work, making and authorising translations, adaptations, arrangements and other alterations, and the broadcasting or other public performance or communication of literary or artistic works. Permissions, by contrast, can encompass any aspect of access or reuse of a work, such as verifying the integrity of a digital file or deleting a resource from a repository file system.

Karen Coyle identifies four categories of rights: manage, including such rights as install and backup; re-use, defined as 'ways that all or part of a resource can be modified or incorporated into other resources' (Coyle, p. 27);[2] transfer, involving the transfer of rights from one agent to another; and use, which involves experiencing the resource in some manner, such as 'display' or 'print' (Coyle, pp. 27–28).[2] Rights metadata that is designed to support rights transactions must include a controlled vocabulary or values list for every type of right that a computer application might enable, such as print, download and copy, as an application cannot make judgments that an unspecified right is somehow allowable and thus actionable. In fact, a rights transaction or workflow expression language would forbid anything that is not explicitly stated within the expression. The rights that a metadata rights expression language incorporates can help the library discover the business model and scenarios of use that the metadata supports.

Constraints, requirements and conditions

The exercise of rights or permissions can be qualified or limited based on constraints, requirements or conditions. Constraints are limitations on the exercise of one or more permissions, such as a limitation on the 'print' permission to five pages of text. A constraint in the digital space may also be the limiting of access to a lower resolution/downsampled file or a visibly watermarked file. Constraints may be exercised when a requirement or condition for unlimited access is not met.

Conditions and requirements must generally be fulfilled before rights are authorised. Payment of a fee is a common condition. User attributes such as enrollment as a student in a course or membership in an organisation are common conditions. Requirements generally impose an obligation, often after the fact of resource access, upon the user. 'With attribution', 'non-commercial use' or 'educational use' are common requirements within the open access web environment. Requirements and conditions are also common within software licenses, where a user must check a 'terms and conditions of use' box and agree to broad legal parameters of use – e.g. no unauthorised copying – before first accessing a software application. These requirements and conditions are generally not enforceable within a software application but are legally binding. The action of checking a box and thus 'opting in' may be recorded in a digital audit trail that documents the user's understanding of, and intent to comply with, terms and conditions of use for a given resource. Within an institutional repository, the state of rights ownership for the deposited resource is a requirement for participating in the repository and is typically acknowledged through an 'opt-in' check box that can be maintained by the repository in a digital audit trail.

Agreement, contract or license

These three terms, in a DRM context, are defined and largely used synonymously. They are generally defined as a legal agreement between two or more parties to authorise resource use. Agreements, contracts and licenses may include conditions that must be satisfied, or constraints on the permissions for use that are offered with the agreement, such as a specific time period for use. Permissions for use may be exclusive to the receiving party or non-exclusive. While an agreement or contract is perforce an agreement between at least two parties, the offering party and the receiving party, a distinction may be made for licenses, which may be an offer by the rights holder to unidentified receiving parties, or to broad classes of receiving parties. ODRL defines this broadly available access as an *offer* from the rights owner to a broad class of users or to any potential user, who may be obligated by restrictions, such as attribution or not-for-profit use, that are generally not enforceable but may be nonetheless legally binding. Creative Commons licenses fall within this category.

Rights description

Rights metadata can support a range of objectives, from copyright expression to enforceable rights and agreements. This section provides an overview of broadly available rights metadata description schemas and evaluates their usefulness in a library or archival setting.

California Digital Library copyrightMD Schema

The California Digital Library (CDL) has developed an end-to-end rights framework in five steps: planning, rights evaluation, determining rights status for materials, recording rights and delivering digital resources to users.[7] A metadata schema to document copyright information has been developed with the assistance of consultant Karen Coyle to document copyright status information, as well as to provenance information relevant to determining the copyright status of a work. It is documented as an XML schema and can be used as a stand-alone schema or as rights metadata, within the administrative metadata section of a METS (Metadata Encoding and Transmission Standard) document.

The CDL copyrightMD schema documents copyright and publication status plus information about the creation (e.g. year and place of publication, creator); publication (e.g. publication status, publisher, date published, country of publication); rights holder (e.g. rights holder, contact information for rights holder); information specific to copyright (e.g. date of copyright, date of renewal, copyright notice from the work); a general note and a services element, for documenting services that might be offered with respect to the resource, such as copying.[8]

Library use of the CDL copyrightMD schema

This is a very simple and useful schema that can be incorporated into many library metadata implementations. The provenance and rights-specific data elements and values are largely jurisdiction-independent, with some exceptions, such as the value for copyright status of 'Public Domain, U.S. Federal document' and year of copyright renewal.

Generally, this is a very simple and elegant copyright expression schema that reflects the core concepts behind copyright: the date and country of creation for the work, the publication status of a work, the creator and date of death for the creator, the rights holder (who may not be the creator), and the copyright notice incorporated within or on the work. This schema could be incorporated by extension into the metadata schema or platform already in use by a library or could be used as the rights component of the administrative metadata section of a METS document. MARBI, the Machine Readable Bibliographic Information Committee, has published a discussion paper on adding rights data elements to the MARC21 (Machine Readable Cataloging) schema, based on the CDL rights schema.[9]

RUCore Rights schema

The Rutgers University Libraries has developed a rights metadata implementation, RUCore Rights, expressed in XML as the rights component of the administrative metadata section of a METS document. RUCore Rights builds upon, and thus includes, many of the data elements included in the CDL copyrightMD schema, particularly with respect to creation, publication, rights holder and copyright status. In addition, the schema includes availability status and the reason for availability, with a controlled value list based on the availability of a deed of gift, license or US copyright law (fair use, library copying exceptions in Section 108 of the copyright code, etc.). The most significant difference between CDL copyrightMD and RUCore Rights metadata is the rights event, a subschema for documenting rights events, including permission requests, permission responses, rights transfer and rights holder research. The rights event element includes associated entities involved in a rights event, such as the publisher, rights holder, donor and rights researcher, together with associated objects, including deeds of gift, rights request correspondence and research notes. The rights event is intended, among other purposes, to create an audit trail to demonstrate a reasonable effort to identify and obtain rights from rights holders, in the event that an orphan works law is passed, and ultimately to enable the automation of permission requests, similar to the claiming that occurs for serial issues. The event is also intended to co-locate written documentation in digital form, such as research notes and deeds of gift, with the relevant resource. In addition, the event data element functions to enable the automation of some rights events. Although the research to identify contact information for a rights holder may be labor-intensive, it should be possible to batch and automate the issuing of permission requests and the logging of responses.[6]

Library use of the RUCore Rights schema

The RUcore Rights schema is published as an open source document on the Rutgers Community Repository (RUcore) website. Libraries are welcome to download and customise it to their needs.. RUCore Rights can be incorporated by extension into a library's metadata implementation and used within a METS metadata implementation as the rights component of the administrative metadata section. The Rutgers University Libraries have developed a METS bibliographic utility, the Workflow Management System (WMS), for use with its Fedora-based institutional repository, RUcore. The bibliographic utility component of the WMS, which is repository-independent, will be available for open source download and use by any library or archive in August 2008. The RUcore bibliographic utility includes a full METS metadata implementation, with support for multiple analog and digital manifestations of a work and complete provenance metadata. It supports an event-based data model with contextual events in every METS section (descriptive, source, administrative, etc.).[10]

METSRights

A draft METS rights schema in XML, defined as a 'minimal administrative metadata about the intellectual rights associated with a digital object or its parts'[11] provides a broad rights declaration and identification of the rights holder. METSRights differs from other basic rights metadata such as CDL and RUCore Rights by providing the ability to create multiple contexts of use, which can be associated with different rights holders and categories of user. Context specifically documents the permissions and constraints associated with each context of use, which are identified by contextID. Rights holders, identified through a rights holder ID, and context class representing a class of user, can be associated within each context of use.[11] Context could be made actionable by associating one or more behaviors within METS with each context, as identified by contextID. The METSRights schema was issued as a draft for public comment in 2004. As of this writing, a rights schema to serve as a default or reference rights implementation with METS has not been provided in final form.[12]

Library use of METSRights

The METSRights schema is a straightforward schema that provides both a broad rights declaration to provide eye-readable guidance to the end user, identification of the rights holder including contact information, and a context sub-schema that enables the library to associate permissions and constraints on the resource, based on contextual elements, such as user category or group. Like the CDL copyrightMD and RUcore Rights metadata schemas, METSRights can be easily incorporated within an XML-based metadata schema or a library's METS profile. The context sub-schema could potentially be made actionable, particularly within METS, through the use of associated behaviors (which are procedures or software applications).

PREMIS Rights

As discussed in Chapter 4, PREMIS (Preservation Metadata Implementation Strategies) is a metadata architecture intended to document and enable the preservation of digital resources. The developers identified rights as a key entity for the preservation of digital resources. Many of the activities required to preserve a resource, such as reproducing the resource or transcoding it to another format, are actions that are reserved to the rights holder by copyright law, so that resources cannot be preserved by a repository unless permission has been granted by the rights holder, or the copyright law of the relevant country provides an exemption. The rights entity and associated metadata schema in PREMIS is a simple and straightforward schema with a predominant focus on enabling a 'preservation repository to determine whether it has the right to perform a certain action in an automated fashion, with some documentation of the basis for the assertion.' (PREMIS Editorial Committee, p. 11).[13]

PREMIS rights was recently revised as part of the PREMIS version 2.0 release in March 2008. The revision was based on Karen Coyle's excellent review of rights metadata for PREMIS. Coyle examined the activities involved in the preservation of digital materials and identified four broad categories of activity for digital preservation. Each broad category involves specific actions that must be permitted for digital preservation: copying, access or use, migration and transformation (Coyle, p. 14).[14] Coyle recommended that rights metadata within PREMIS should accommodate legal rights, including copyright status and the legal justification for use, particularly the exceptions for libraries enacted into copyright law, and permissions that the library uses to justify its preservation activities. She recommended extending the permissions statements within the rights entity to encompass the permitting license and/or permitting statute that provides legal justification for the action, including its jurisdiction and citation (Coyle, p. 28).[14] PREMIS rights metadata in the PREMIS 2.0 data dictionary has replaced the data element 'permissionStatement' with the top-level data element, rightsStatement'. Within 'rightsStatement' are the data elements 'rightsStatementIdentifier', 'rightsBasis', 'copyrightInformation', 'licenseInformation', 'statute Information', 'rightsGranted', linkingObjectIdentifier', 'linkingAgentIdentifer' and 'rightsExtension', as well as subelements below each of these data elements. (PREMIS Editorial Committee, pp. 157–158).[13]

Library use of PREMIS rights

PREMIS has become the *de facto* standard for the provenance and preservation metadata needed to support digital preservation of repository resources. The PREMIS rights schema is a simple, extensible schema for documenting the rights of the repository to manage digital resources for their long-term preservation. Additional rights metadata that provide information to users and that document an audit trail for attempts to identify and contact rights holders for permission to preserve or re-use a resource require additional metadata, some of which is related to preservation and can be documented in the PREMIS 'rightsExtension' data element.

Rights expression within standard metadata schemas

Copyright and rights for access and use have been acknowledged in every metadata schema as important information about the resource. Most metadata schemas include data elements to document copyright information, permissions for use and constraints on permissions for use, even if only a simple note field documenting that a resource is copyright protected and that reproduction or reuse of the work requires the permission of the copyright holder. Libraries that are providing collections with straightforward rights, such as public domain resources or open collections with few or no restrictions on use, may find a general-purpose rights note to be adequate. However, these libraries will want to ensure that other metadata elements in the schema are adequate to document the rights holder, the copyright status and the publication status of the resource, at a minimum.

Rights licensing expression languages

Licensing represents a critical and emerging niche area for libraries. Libraries license many resources on behalf of their users and, as digital resource creators, are increasingly interested in licensing their resources, either on behalf of their members who own copyright for the work they deposit with the library or as a revenue stream for the library itself. Licensing metadata schemas of interest to libraries include Creative Commons, the Digital Library Federation's ERMI, the ONIX-PL publications licensing and the PLUS Picture Licensing Universal System for digital images.

Creative Commons

The Creative Commons first emerged in 2001 with a mission to develop a methodology for assigning licenses to web-based resources to enable informed, responsible use of copyright-protected resources within the 'creative commons'. 'Creative commons' is conceptualised as a communal information space in which resources are made openly available to promote creativity, innovation and the exchange of ideas in a wide-ranging digital conversation. As noted on its website, 'Creative Commons provides free tools that let authors, scientists, artists, and educators easily mark their creative work with the freedoms they want it to carry. You can use CC to change your copyright terms from "All Rights Reserved" to "Some Rights Reserved".'[15]

Creative Commons provides open licenses that are offered to unspecified users by creators who want to reserve some or no rights for the reuse of their works. A creator selects a Creative Commons license based on specified core conditions for reuse of a resource. Applying the license involves downloading HTML code that embeds a Creative Commons license within the web page for the resource. Options also currently exist to place the Creative Commons license link, known as the verification link, within MP3 and XMP (eXtensible Metadata Platform) file headers to a license terms page controlled by the creator. XMP, which is explained later in more detail, is a metadata platform first developed by Adobe that enables the embedding of metadata in document formats (particularly PDF and HTML). and digital image formats.[16] In addition to the license, Creative Commons applies metadata, provided by the creator, which enables a potential user to discover the resource through a Creative Commons-enabled search engine. Creative Commons licenses can be applied to offline resources, through a notice that directs potential users to the relevant online license, or by applying in writing to Creative Commons for a copy of the license.

Creative Commons licenses are available in three formats: as a human-readable 'deed'; as legal code, which is a legal license that can be defended in a court of law; and as machine-interpretable metadata, expressed in RDFa (Resource Description Framework with attributes). Creative Commons licenses are non-exclusive, so that a creator could enter into a specific license with a user in addition to the Creative Commons license offered to any potential user. A common scenario is a Creative Commons license for non-commercial use and a specific license with a publisher for re-use of the resource in a commercial publication.

Creative Commons metadata is expressed in ccREL, an RDFa rights expression language that provides 'machine-readable expression of copyright licensing terms and related information' (Abelson *et al.*, p. 1).[17] ccREL addresses two classes of properties:

'1. Work properties describe aspects of specific works

2. License properties describe aspects of licenses.' (Abelson *et al.*, p. 6).[17]

Work properties are 'dc:title', 'cc:attributionName', 'cc:attributionURL' and 'dc:type', for type of work, 'dc:source' and 'cc:morePermissions'. License properties are 'cc:permits', 'cc:prohibits', 'cc:requires', 'cc:jurisdiction', 'cc:deprecatedOn' (identifying that the license is deprecated on a specific date) and 'cc:legalCode' (Abelson *et al.*, pp. 7–9).[17] Permitted values for license properties are also specified in the standard. ccREL is currently issued as version 1.0 (3 March 2008).

Creators wishing to apply a license to a work can complete a simple web form or select from a range of licenses, such as 'public domain', 'attribution, non-commercial, no derivatives' and other licenses. Licenses include *permissions*, which are rights governed by the license and include reproduction, distribution and derivative works; the *prohibition* on commercial use; and *requirements*, which are notice (requiring the inclusion of the copyright and license notices), attribution, share alike (requiring derivative works to provide the same license terms) and source code (requiring that source code be shared with others for derivative works). Other specialised licenses include sampling licenses and a public domain license to allow creators to enter works into the public domain by repudiating the creator's natural copyright. A creator can use one of six predetermined creative commons licenses based on standard combinations of permissions, prohibitions and requirements, or create his or her own combination.[18]

Creative Commons is intended to support a range of rights holders, from organisations, such as libraries that are presenting large digital collections or complex websites for use, to the individual creator who wishes to document ownership and permissions before placing his/her single digital creation on the web. Creative Commons licenses are intended to be assigned by the creator or rights holder.

As previously noted, Creative Commons metadata is documented in the RDFa, an XML schema intended to document relationships between entities. Creative Commons offers resource discovery through a Creative Commons-enabled search engine so that creators can discover resources based on conditions for reuse. For example, creators who are seeking resources that they can remix in a derivative work can evaluate resources based on license permissions to select resources with licenses that allow this re-use. As of this writing, Creative Commons licenses are offered for 46 jurisdictions, with nine jurisdictions in development.[19]

Library use of Creative Commons

Libraries can apply Creative Commons licenses to digital resources created by the library and made available to users. Creative Commons licenses are assigned by the rights holder and cannot be assigned by libraries for resources owned by others, including the collections typically found in a special collection or institutional repository. However, Creative Commons has taken a very expansive approach not only to licensing resources but also to sharing the tools and technologies that enable Creative Commons licenses so that libraries can enable the rights holders that they support to assign creative commons licenses to their works. Creative Commons web services can enable an academic library to integrate Creative Commons into an institutional repository and allow faculty to select and apply a Creative Commons license for their copyright-protected resources. A public library might integrate a Creative Commons web service into its portal to encourage its users to apply Creative Commons licenses to their personal photographs and memorabilia shared in a local history portal hosted by the public library.[20]

Digital Library Federation's ERMI

ERMI (Electronic Resource Management Initiative) is a two-phase project of the Digital Library Federation (DLF) intended to address a key workflow issue for libraries: the management of licensed electronic content. The ERMI initiative began in 2002. The Phase I report provided several key deliverables: functional requirements, workflow and entity-relationship (ER) diagrams, a data dictionary, and workflow diagrams to tie the ER diagrams and data dictionary together.[21] The needs of libraries in this area are many. Licensed electronic content is provided in many forms – as individual resources and as resource packages offered by content aggregators – and through many delivery methodologies, including the library's website, the provider's website and via the websites of consortia to which the library belongs. Access strategies include OpenURL access to full-text via commercial abstract and indexing services, search and retrieval at the aggregator website, and federated search and retrieval from multiple electronic resources. A licensed resource may be browsable as a single issue of a journal or may have article-level access only. Subscription time frames, embargo periods when access to online content is not available, access to back file archives, and availability for use in interlibrary loan or electronic course packs are only a few of the issues of interest to libraries and to their patrons. Also of importance are the access control methodologies to authenticate and authorise access to subscriptions, whether IP range, userID and password, Shibboleth®, etc. License issues are complex and have been increasing in complexity with emerging issues such as content archiving via LOCKSS (Lots of Copies Keep Stuff Safe) and Portico platforms, and micro-pricing strategies at the article and article component levels.

ERMI deliverables released in 2004 and 2005 were embraced by libraries and by vendors, particularly integrated library system vendors, who wanted to respond to the urgent needs articulated by their customers, for improved management of electronic resources.

The most extensive deliverable for the ERMI project in phase one is the data dictionary, which includes data elements intended to address the stages in electronic resource workflows:

new product identification and consideration; licensing negotiation and technical evaluation; implementation; and maintenance and review. The data dictionary is a largely complete product, encompassing more than 300 data elements (DLF ERM Initiative, Appendix D).[21] It has been implemented, in whole or in part, by commercial library system vendors and within open source library systems or modules. However, as the DLF acknowledges, without an architectural framework and reference implementations based on the framework, implementation is inconsistent with no assurance of interoperability for data sharing and system migration. Phase II is focusing on a review of the data dictionary, to add robustness, consistency and extensibility to systems that could utilise the data dictionary in an interoperable manner. Utilising the data dictionary for license expression is also an area of focus for ERMI Phase II.[22]

ERMI data elements that support DRM include data elements for identification of resources, jurisdiction of copyright law, and methodologies for authorisation and authentication of users. The data dictionary includes indicators, such as the all rights reserved indicator, and confidentiality of user information indicator. ERMI includes a thorough build-out of data elements for licensing terms and rights, including the rights for use in electronic course packs, course reserve, interlibrary loan, digital archiving, fair use and other rights negotiated within electronic materials licenses. Licensing terms and conditions include subscription term, license termination rights and cure period for breach of contract (DLF ERM Initiative, Appendix D).[21]

Library use of ERMI

ERMI provides a substantial data dictionary to serve a critical niche area for library DRM – the acquisition, management and delivery of commercially licensed resources. ERMI was developed in response to a critical need and was rapidly adopted within both commercial and open source library management systems, as well as by vendors of stand-alone or modular ERM systems that can interoperate with library management systems.

ERMI lacks a schema that relates data elements to each other in a durable and consistent manner and lacks guidance for mandatory or recommended core data elements. The Phase II work of the DLF ERMI is intended to address issues of consistency and robustness of application for ERMI tools. An important 'next step' for any library implementing ERM should be to identify commonalities across the library's ERM implementation and its other resources, to provide seamless information access to users. This entails developing transparency across the ERMI and other resource rights management initiatives, through data element mapping and common access strategies, such as federated searching and single sign-on authentication and authorisation, across all digital collections. Given that library users are predominantly interested in the content of the information package rather than its format or source, transparency across licensed resources and library-owned digital resources is a critical goal for libraries. Although licensed resources remain the 'gold standard' for information resources that advance research and learning, a library's institutional repository, in particular, can provide highly complementary resources through the preprint and postprint collections of its faculty. Libraries should seek to provide integrated access across all digital resources – to integrate fully the locally owned resources digitised by the library with its commercial journal collections and other licensed or purchased resources.

One of the significant developments that resulted in part from the DLF ERMI was the formulation of a NISO

License Expression Working Group, under the auspices of the NISO, DLF, EDItEUR and Publishers Licensing Society. NISO sponsored a Digital Rights Expression Workflow meeting in 2005 that identified standardised and coordinated digital licensing rights expression as a critical need. The three consortia are collaborating to recommend standards for electronic resources and license expression and to engage actively in the development of the ONIX license messaging specification. Two significant deliverables, the *ONIX-PL ERMI Encoding Format*[23] and the *Mapping ONIX-PL to ERMI*[27] were both released in 2007. EDItEUR has used the ERMI requirements to develop its ONIX for Licensing proof-of-concept model, discussed further below. As EditEUR notes, 'ONIX-PL adds depth in the specific areas of expressing license terms and conditions' to the breadth of the ERMI data dictionary, which covers every phase of the electronic resource management life cycle.[24]

ONIX-PL- (ONIX for Licensing Terms, Publications License)

The ONIX standard emerged from the commercial book publishing world to support the exchange of product information among participants in the publishing supply chain – publishers, wholesalers, distributors, etc. ONIX is managed by EDItEUR, the International Group for Electronic Commerce in the Book and Serials Sectors. ONIX, which began as an acronym for ONline Information eXchange, originally focused on interoperable data transmission for published book product information but has broadened its focus to incorporate the range of published resources. An important focus for ONIX is to build 'standards for the communication of licensing terms',[25] building on the DLF ERMI. ONIX-PL, the ONIX for Publications Licenses, currently in draft 0.9.26 (2 March 2007), is intended to build upon the work of ERMI to support the exchange of standardised licensing information. The ONIX-PL license utilises a message format with a header and a body containing the publications license expression. The header identifies the sender, the receiver, date of message and other control information. The publications license expression comprises license detail, which includes license identification, definitions of license terms, including agent, resource, time point, place and document, supply terms, usage terms, payment terms and general terms of the license.[26] The *ONIX-PL ERMI Encoding Format* was undertaken to 'look at the implications of using a version of ONIX-PL to communicate ERMI license encodings from one library's ERMS to another or from an intermediary that offers an ERMI encoding service to a customer library.' (EdItEUR, p. [1]).[23] The investigation concluded that the ONIX-PL and ERMI did not explicitly map but that a 'subset of ONIX-PL structural conventions' could carry an ERMI licensing instance. The report further cautions that 'it should not be perceived as an implementation of ONIX for Licensing Terms.' (EdItEUR, p. 2).[23] Essentially, the ERMI licensing metadata instance, <ERMILicenseEncoding>, is placed within the <ONIXPublicationsLicenseMessage>, replacing the ONIX-PL <PublicationsLicenseExpression>. The report notes a need for more consistency and standardisation of ERMI data elements with respect to both usage and expression (EdItEUR, p. 2).[23]

The *Mapping ONIX-PL to ERMI* report, released on 19 November 2007, provides an interim assessment of the mapping required to load ONIX-PL licenses into a library's ERM system that employs the ERMI data model. Terms are extracted and mapped from the ONIX-PL license for mapping to an ERM system. A reverse or round-trip mapping back to an ONIX-PL license was not deemed possible. Data element mapping is provided in three broad areas: supply terms, usage terms and general terms.[27]

Library use of ONIX-PL

Although ONIX-PL is still a draft standard, interoperability with ERMI makes it a very interesting licensing standard for libraries, particularly to automate not only the licensing but also the metadata documentation about terms and conditions of licenses, for resources with ONIX-PL digital licenses.

PLUS (Picture Licensing Universal System)

PLUS has emerged from the commercial image community to provide an end-to-end solution for licensing and tracking images, based on standardised metadata and protocols for issuing and tracking licenses. PLUS consists of three parts:

1. A 'picture licensing glossary' or data dictionary of the terminology needed for image licensing. The glossary currently provides more than 1000 terms, including acronyms and abbreviations. Terms and definitions can be searched or alphabetically browsed at the PLUS website.[28]
2. The PLUS License Data Format (LDF), currently in version 1.2.0, offers an ordered group of fields within an XML schema to provide an image license summary within digital files, such as within the XMP area of an image or document header. Fields include licensor and licensee information, media information such as duration, size and language, the number of versions that

can be reproduced, the quantity of times the file can be reused, and the term of license.[29]

3. The Media Matrix offers a uniquely streamlined approach to generating licenses to cover every possible image use within the PLUS system. The PLUS Media Matrix is an international licensing standard that allows you to describe a particular matrix of use, beginning with the 'media category' (editorial, motion picture, TV, etc.), the 'media type' (book, website, etc.), the 'media detail' (retail book, coffee table book, etc.), the placement of the image (e.g. single placement on any pages), the characteristics of the image, and usage characteristics (country, duration, etc.). The +MSC (PLUS Media Summary Code) is an alphanumeric code assigned to an image based on any combination of usage codes from the Media Matrix. As the PLUS website notes, 'Designed to allow image makers, image distributors and image users to easily and accurately communicate the specific image use desired or offered under a license, a single +MSC can describe more than two billion combinations of media and media options.' The Media Selector is a web menu tool intended to help image licensors select the appropriate +MSC. The +MSC is a generic license subset of the PLUS Universal License Statement, a PLUS license that draws from the glossary and media matrix to create a customised license particular to a specific image and licensee.[30]
4. The PLUS Packs offer streamlined licenses specific to particular industries and usages, in standardised, numbered packages. Examples of PLUS Packs are 'Display Advertising (PADA)' and 'Book Cover, One Edition, Printed (PBCP)'.[31]

The PLUS toolset includes a license generator that uses a web form to guide the licensor through the generation of a PLUS license. The PLUS decoder transforms a +MSC code or PLUS Matrix ID into an eye-readable text description.

Library use of PLUS

The PLUS Coalition is open to membership at the individual or organisational level and includes international members from the image industry, image and photography trade organisations, and consortia of museums, educational institutions and libraries. As libraries purchase more commercial image databases for use by their patrons, they will probably begin to discover PLUS licenses in image headers. PLUS does open the opportunity for library users to purchase individual images for use in scholarly publications, such as an art history dissertation. Libraries should become familiar with the PLUS suite of licensing standards and tools and encourage the interoperability of commercial licensing standards across the e-journal, e-books and digital multimedia communities.

Library use of licensing metadata

Licensing metadata is a critical niche area of rights management for libraries, with the potential for tremendous impact on the current business model for library acquisitions and subscriptions management. Libraries spend increasing amounts of their materials budgets on licensed digital resources, yet the technologies and services available within library management systems have not kept pace with the libraries' increasing digital workflow. Library management systems still reflect the concept of the one-time analog purchase of resources, rather than the ongoing management of digital resources. In contrast to analog resources, digital resources are a renewing resource that includes the potential for brokered re-use, where libraries might serve as intermediaries for users to request permission to re-use part of a licensed digital resource. Examples include use of an excerpt from a commercial music file in a musicology article or use of a commercially licensed image within a student term paper or dissertation. In addition, publishers and commercial information aggregators are increasingly viewing libraries as a source of digital resources, particularly of unique resources from library special collections and archives that might be repackaged and made available for a licensing fee or purchase cost.

Libraries are facing the dilemma that authors of scholarly research have always faced – the repackaging of their not-for-profit efforts into commercially licensed resources available to others for a fee. They must weigh the competing interests of support for the freely available information commons versus the potential for a steady revenue stream based on the license or sale of digital reproductions of unique library resources. Libraries choosing to charge a fee for use must decide whether to charge a one-time fee that allows any subsequent use or to develop a strategy to track downstream use of digital resources in a web environment and to enforce any constraints on downstream use. For example, a library may charge a fee for a single use of a digital resource and yet the purchaser may then elect to share the resource freely with others for further re-use on the web. Libraries must also decide whether to license their digital resources to third-party resellers, such as 'print on demand' book publishers or image licensing agencies. Decisions that libraries must make in negotiating these licenses include whether the third-party reseller has a non-exclusive license, so that the library can openly offer the digital resource to its users, or, in the event of an exclusive license, whether the term of exclusive license is fixed or unlimited. An important first step is for a library to develop policies for the re-use of its unique open space collections, perhaps as an extension to the organisational copyright policy, discussed in Chapter 2. Libraries emerged as a societal means for broadening access to resources to advance the research and learning objectives of their user communities. Repackaging of public domain resources represents a seismic shift in the library's underlying societal role and should not be adopted, even on a limited case-by-case basis, without a policy on the commercial licensing of library resources to guide decision-making.

Emerging licensing frameworks are developing on a parallel track rather than an integrated track with other metadata schemas intended to facilitate discovery, access and preservation of resources. This is a critical area of concern for libraries. The digital arena should provide greater opportunities for seamlessly integrating digital content, regardless of container or packaging, rather than the development of stovepipes that focus almost exclusively on the business models of their developers. Libraries should familiarise themselves with licensing standards, evaluate ERM systems based on their support for different licensing standards, and work for the harmonisation of discovery and access metadata and methodologies. This includes harmonising the rights description metadata incorporated in licensing standards with the library's metadata framework for building its digital collections as well as its ERM implementation, to enable a digital workflow for libraries that takes full advantage of digital technologies for streamlining workflow and providing seamless resource access to users, rather than a fragmented environment that requires different workflows, standards and technologies for the various resource-publishing sectors.

Emerging licensing standards have the potential to exert a huge impact on libraries, in terms of acquisitions and resource management workflow, which remain heavily focused on the one-time purchase and annual subscription workflow of the analog resource library. Three critical issues are important for libraries to consider in the emerging world of digital licensing and license tracking:

1. Digital technologies, such as messaging and the ability to integrate actionable metadata within digital files through standards such as XMP, which is discussed later in this chapter, have made it possible to automate and track licensing and the use of licensed resources as never before. Publishers' groups are focused on their own end-to-end business model and not on the impact they may have on the library's acquisitions and resource management workflow, particularly in the area of license compliance. Libraries, who are intermediaries for access to large amounts of licensed resources from many different publishing communities, may find themselves juggling competing technologies for licensing resources and responding to contract compliance issues at the single user, single resource level, as publishers develop methodologies to track compliance use across the web and hold libraries, as the licensee of record, responsible for resource misuse. Libraries will need to examine their licensing practises, resource documentation, management platforms and copyright policies to prepare for a future of microlicensing and resource tracking that will emerge in the digital publishing domain over the next decade.

2. Library technology, particularly as reflected in ERMs, is inconsistent and still reflects a primarily analog business model of the one-time purchase or at least of annual subscription management for continuing resources. ERM does not reflect or support microlicensing options, licensed resource use tracking, brokering individual licenses and all of the other capabilities for resource licensing that these emerging (and competing) technologies will support. Libraries need to accelerate the work of their standards bodies and digital library consortia to work in concert with the publishing community to develop interoperable digital resource management frameworks for the acquisition and management of licensed digital resources and not simply data dictionaries that provide a basic level of resource documentation and tracking.
3. Libraries are increasingly being viewed as providers of digital resources, particularly unique and rare resources from manuscript and special collections and library repositories. Many of these resources are in the public domain and are of considerable interest for digitising and packaging to enable further exploitation by commercial entities. The Google Books digitisation project was the beginning of an emerging marketing strategy to engage libraries by offering mass digitisation of resources in exchange for the opportunity to exploit the resources, sometimes through profit sharing with libraries. Libraries need to develop policies concerning the exploitation of public domain or library-owned resources before they respond piecemeal to these offers, which are currently a trickle but will probably become a flood as technologies make it commercially attractive to digitise and repackage these 'niche market' resources.

Rights workflow languages

ODRL

ODRL was begun by IPR Systems in Australia under the leadership of Renato Iannella and is currently managed by the ODRL International Advisory Board. The ODRL rights expression language schema is currently issued in version 1.1, with version 2.0 under active development. ODRL combines a data dictionary and a rights expression language, expressed as the two main sub-schemas within the ODRL schema. Data dictionary elements are prefaced with 'o-dd' and rights expressions with 'o-ex'.

The ODRL foundation data model consists of three primary entities: *assets* (physical or digital resources), *rights* (permissions, which can be limited by constraints, requirements and conditions) and *parties* (rights holders and users). The core of the data model is the expression of *rights*, which are made available to users through *offers* or *agreements*. As the ODRL v. 1.1 schema notes, 'the representation of Offers and Agreements is [an] important core aspect of ODRL.' (Iannella, p. 5).[32]

Offers are made by rights holders for rights over assets. Offers are very flexible and can be combined, linked in a hierarchy, provided to a class of users or based on a broad context, such as educational use. The ODRL v. 1.1 schema defines Agreements as 'the transformation of an Offer into a license for rights over an asset by parties.' (Iannella, p. 5).[32] An Agreement does not require a prior offer by a rights holder but can instead document rights and conditions over an asset after the fact.

As the ODRL version 1.1 Foundation Model in Figure 6.3 demonstrates, rights are at the heart of the ODRL schema. Rights include permissions, which are the

Figure 6.3 ODRL foundation model. ©2002 IPR Systems. Open Digital Rights Language (ODRL) Version 1.1 W3C Note 19 September 2002 *http://www.w3.org/TR/odrl/*. Note, this model is significantly changed in version 2.0, currently in development. From: *http://www.w3.org/TR/odrl/* Open Digital Rights Language (ODRL) Version 1.1 cIPR Systems 2002

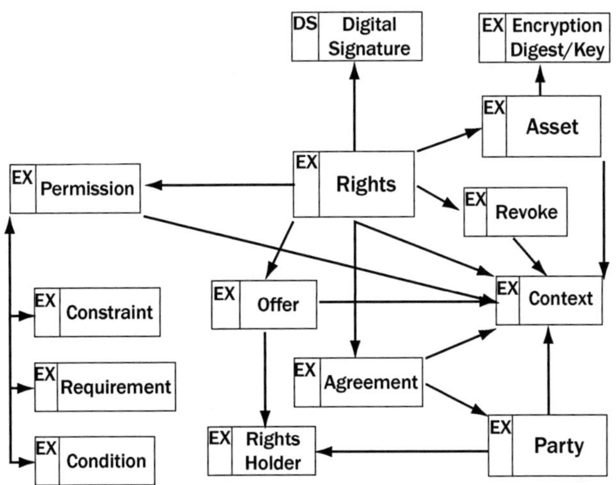

actual uses permitted over the assets, via an offer or a license. Permissions can be modified by constraints, which limit the exercise of permissions, such as a number (e.g. limit printing to five pages) or time (e.g. limit access to the asset to 24 hours) or by requirements, which are conditions that must be met before the permission is exercised (e.g. payment of a fee).

'Context' is an important entity in the ODRL model. Context can apply to any other entity in the model and can provide information about the entity or about relationships between entities. A context for Party may specify role, e.g. 'student enrolled in course X at University Y'. A context for an Offer may specify the country in which the Offer is valid.

Context always includes a unique identifier from a standard identification scheme to identify the entity to which it applies. This enables context to relate one entity to another, using the unique identifiers. This somewhat resembles the use of context in METSRights, discussed previously, except that context in ODRL is more fully developed as befits a complex rights expression language intended to enable the full expression of offers and agreements.

ODRL supports a broad range of business models, including the business model behind Creative Commons licenses, by which a creator or rights holder may wish to place some core conditions on the use of his/her works without identifying the potential users and without any expectation of active enforcement of these conditions, except perhaps serendipitously, for unauthorised uses discovered after the fact. A simple offer to play an asset for educational purposes only is expressed in this manner:

```
<o-ex rights>
 <o-ex offer>
  <o-ex permission>
   <o-dd display>
     <o-ex constraint>
       <o-dd:purpose o-ex:type="sectors:educational"/>
     </o-ex constraint>
   </o-dd display>
  </o-ex permission>
 </o-ex offer>
</o-ex rights>
```

ODRL supports secure rights expression through digital signatures and through encryption of assets. Profiles of the W3C XML Signature and W3C XML Encryption support a secured wrapping of the entire rights expression for an asset, which may include information about the encryption of the asset (Iannella, pp. 24–28).[32]

ODRL was designed to be readily integrated into a DRM framework, without specifying the framework or its component technologies. It can be implemented within a trusted system environment, a peer-to-peer environment or an open license environment, where a license is offered to unknown potential users. ODRL has no requirements for mandatory elements or mandatory expressions of offers, agreements, rights, agents or assets. It supports application profiles to customise ODRL to specific contexts and also supports extensions to the core data dictionary for community use. ODRL explicitly supports the modular implementation of other schemas, or data elements from those schemas, such as MPEG-7, MPEG-21 and MARC21. ODRL was selected as the basis for the rights expression language within the Open Mobile Alliance for use in the management and control of assets exchanged within a mobile network environment. ODRL is also a supporter of open digital rights management implementations, such as OpenIPMP, which is discussed in Chapter 7, as well as Creative Commons licenses.[33] A profile for geospatial data, intended to conform to the recently released GeoDRM reference model, is under development. A reference application for the Dublin Core Metadata Initiative, to be referenced by the Dublin Core 'rights' data element, is also under development.[33]

Library use of ODRL

ODRL is a mature, extensible rights expression language that supports both commercial and library/archival use of resources. Open licenses ('offers') supporting a broad context of use and individual licenses are equally supported. ODRL is a complex schema, supporting both a data dictionary and full rights expression. A library or a consortium planning an end-to-end rights implementation should give

ODRL serious consideration. Although its learning curve is steep, its ultimate value may lie in its ability to integrate both commercial resource licensing, institutional repositories and repositories of primary source materials, such as library special collections. The DLF ERMI found gaps in ODRL for commercial licensing, particularly for the management aspects of licensed resources (DLF ERM Initiative, Appendix F),[21] but ODRL remains the most functional and flexible expression language for the broad range of rights management issues facing libraries. Adopting ODRL and extending it to support the complex library business model for resource management would be a daunting task for an individual library but could be seriously explored by digital library consortia and organisations collaborating on an end-to-end DRM implementation.

MPEG-21

MPEG-21 is the over-arching designation for a suite of protocols and specifications that comprise a multimedia framework, defined in the *MPEG-21 Overview* as 'a normative open framework for multimedia consumption and use by all the players in the delivery and consumption chain ... MPEG-21 is based on two essential concepts: the definition of a fundamental unit of distribution and transaction (the Digital Item) and the concept of Users interacting with Digital Items.'[34] MPEG-21 emerged from the digital multimedia engineering industry, specifically the Moving Picture Experts Group, but MPEG-21 is designed to provide an end-to-end framework, from creation to distribution, for digital resources in any format. MPEG-21 consists of nine parts. In Chapter 4, I examined part 2, specifically the digital item declaration model. This chapter addresses part 5 (rights expression language) and part 6 (rights data dictionary).

In 2002, XrML was selected as the basis of MPEG-21/5, the rights expression language component of the MPEG-21 standard. The <indecs>2rdd data dictionary was selected as the basis for part 6 of the MPEG-21 standard. MPEG-21 parts 5 and 6 together provide a framework for the unambiguous expression of rights licenses. XrML, formerly an independent rights expression syntax, was frozen at version 2.0. Future versions of the schema, including version 2.1 currently in draft, will be issued by the Moving Picture Experts Group as part of the MPEG-21 framework.

The heart of the MPEG-21 rights expression language (REL) is the core schema. The top-level entity, and most important concept in the REL, is the *license*. The license is a container for one or more *grants* that convey to a *principal* the permission to exercise one or more *rights* against a *resource*, subject to one or more *conditions* that must be fulfilled. In addition to grants, the license may contain an issuer that conveys authorisation for rights to the user via the license.

MPEG-21/5 is designed to provide an end-to-end technical framework for automating and enforcing licenses. MPEG-21/5 utilises a 'sentence-like' syntax with subject (principal), verb (right), adverb (condition) and predicate (resource). XrML, the basis for MPEG-21/5, was explicitly designed to support a 'trusted systems' approach to rights management. With the focus on the establishment and enforcement of licenses, MPEG-21/5 would not explicitly support the scenario of an open license for an educational user to play a resource. MPEG-21/5 licenses are designed for enforcement. A close approximation for the open license might be an MPEG-21/5 license to members of Rutgers

University to play a resource. Portions of the license would be expressed in the following manner:

```
<license...>
 <grant>
  <forAll varName="RutgersUniversityMember">
  <everyone>
   <sx:propertyURI
    definition="urn:rutgers.edu:Rutgers
    UniversityMember"/>
   <trustedIssuer>
    <keyholder licensePartID="Rutgers">
     <info>
     <dsig:KeyValue>
     <dsig:RSAKeyValue>
       <dsig:Modulus>iuk MaZ==</dsig:Modulus>
       <dsig:Exponent>AQABAA==</dsig:Exponent>
     </dsig:RSAKeyValue>
    </dsig:KeyValue>
   </trustedIssuer>
   </everyone>
  </forAll>
 <grant>
 <principal varRef="RutgersUniversityMember"/>
  <mx:play/>
 </grant>
 </grant>
</license>
```

Several things occur in this example. The 'forAll' data element is used to create a group of principals to which licenses can be issued by the trusted issuer. The 'trustedIssuer' data element documents an RSA (popular algorithm for public key encryption) digital signature to validate the Issuer in a trusted environment. The trustedIssuer will validate that every principal possesses the value, 'Rutgers University member', in order to play the resource.

As the example makes clear, MPEG-21/5 is intended to support both expression and enforcement of licenses and of grants within licenses.

MPEG-21/5 can be used within a trusted system, where devices communicate directly with other devices in a resource management chain. The XrML REL, as utilised within MPEG-21/5, was selected as the basis for the Open eBook rights expression language by its Rights and Rules Working Group. As Coyle notes, 'A valid MPEG-21/5 license is intended to be unambiguous, with the goal that different systems will implement the license with the same results even if they approach the processing of the license differently.' (Coyle, p. 21).[2] As discussed in Chapter 3, use of XrML may involve negotiating a license for its use.

In addition to the rights expression language, based on XrML, MPEG-21 section 6 consists of a data dictionary to ensure unambiguous definition for the data elements in the rights expression language. <indecs>2rdd was selected as the base technology for MPEG-21/6. The goal for <indecs>rdd was defined as the 'development of standard rights terms to enable the exchange of key information between content industries for eCommerce trading of intellectual property rights.' (<indecs>rdd Consortium, p. 2).[35] <indecs>rdd was designed by Rightscom as a highly structured, relational data dictionary. Every term has a unique identifier and a 'genealogy' that defines how the term relates to other terms within the dictionary. <indecs>2rdd readily supports the mapping and incorporation of terms from other schemas to support interoperability with other rights implementations. As noted in Chapter 4, <indecs>dd forms the basis of DOI (digital object identifier) metadata, which also readily maps and incorporates terms from other data dictionaries and schemas to enable interoperability. <indecs>2rdd is legally neutral and does not define any legal terms, so that it can be used in any country and can support licenses that represent legal agreements and less formal licenses. <indecs>rdd is described by its consortium as being 'business model neutral' so that '<indecs>rdd terms can be used to describe any situation in which any kind of rights are owned, managed, protected, or used, at any point in the life of content from origination to "end use" or archiving.' (<indecs>rdd Consortium, pp. 5–6).[35]

Library use of MPEG-21/5-6

The MPEG-21 REL and data dictionary are highly functional within a commercial license framework. The MPEG-21 REL is not readily extensible to every context of resource use within a library environment. In particular, the ability to explicitly offer a broad open license to unknown users is an important scenario of use within the library resource environment. MPEG-21 is an important framework for multimedia management. The business model and impetus for development for MPEG-21/5 arose from the commercial multimedia community. With its emphasis on enforceable licenses within a trusted environment, MPEG-21/5 is probably not applicable to most libraries. However, libraries may license commercial resources, particularly e-books or moving images, for which third-party access is provided via an MPEG-21 content delivery system. MPEG-21/6, as part of the broader <indecs>rdd, is a very rich and functional approach to interoperability through data element mapping. As noted in Chapter 4, the indecs Data Dictionary, <indecs>dd or iDD, which includes the rights data dictionary, or rdd, provides the metadata platform for the DOI framework. Any library utilising DOI, or DOI-managed resources, will probably interact with the iDD.

XACML

XACML was discussed in detail in Chapter 5 but deserves mention in this chapter as an actionable rights expression language specific to the control of access to resources. XACML provides an XML schema for the 'expression of authorization policies in XML against objects that are themselves identified in XML.'[36] XACML describes policies that apply to targets, which may be resources, subjects ('users') or actions. A policy within XACML is a set of rules, an identifier for the rule-combining algorithm that combines decisions from multiple rules, such as separate applicable policies in a policy set, and optionally obligations that must be met to satisfy rules. XACML provides 'many-to-many' policy statements. An XACML policy statement may apply to classes or collections of resources, subjects or actions, or to a single target. Multiple XACML policy statements may be concatenated to a single target. Distributed policy statements may reference a shared target, perhaps under different scenarios of use.

XACML fits within a framework for authorising use of resources based upon XACML policies. A user's access request within the XACML framework is sent to the Policy Enforcement Point (PEP), which formulates attributes describing the user from attributes at the Policy Information Point. These attributes are provided to the Policy Decision Point, which returns an authorisation decision, so that the PEP can return a response to the user. The PEP performs the access control by formulating the access requests and enforcing the access decision provided by the PDP (Policy Decision Point).[37] XACML includes a Context Handler, which converts decision requests from their native formats to canonical XACML requests and converts authorisation decisions in the canonical XACML format to the native format, to support cross-platform interoperability (OASIS, p. 8).[38] XACML also includes a privacy policy profile, 'which defines standard XACML Attribute identifiers for expressing the purpose for which data is collected and the purpose for which data is being accessed. It also defines a standard rule for requiring that the purpose for which data is collected must be consistent with the purpose for which data is being accessed.'[39] XACML attributes can be used to make requests that go beyond simple access to the action the requestor wishes to take on the resource, such as 'read' or 'copy'. However, XACML does not provide copyright expression and is not intended to document and enforce licenses fully. Its focus is enforceable access control to enable the authorised use of resources based on policies tied to the attributes of the requestor, the resource or the actions to be taken on the resource (e.g. 'read', 'copy').

Library use of XACML

XACML is proving to be a functional and efficient access control mechanism that can be employed in a variety of contexts. It can interoperate with Shibboleth, as both utilise SAML messaging. XACML can be used within a repository framework to formulate access decisions based upon policies, which are based upon attributes of users, resources, actions or combinations of all three. The Fedora Commons open source repository architecture incorporates XACML for resource access control.

Domain-specific rights expression

The need for rights metadata to enable the expression and management of licensed content is emerging as an important issue in many arenas, including the publishing and commercial multimedia communities. Several standards and projects specific to a subject or usage domain are listed below. Readers are encouraged to explore other fields of interest for similar rights metadata developments.

PRISM (Publishing Requirements for Industry Standard Metadata)

PRISM is a product of the IDEAlliance (the International Digital Enterprise Alliance). PRISM 'defines an XML metadata vocabulary for managing, aggregating, post-processing, multi-purposing and aggregating magazine, news, catalog, book, and mainstream journal content.'[40] PRISM may be used within an XMP framework (described later in this chapter). PRISM integrates Dublin Core data elements for resource description with common rights data elements in the PRISM namespace and with a separate namespace for a PRISM rights language, <prl:>. Rights data elements in use within PRISM include <dc:rights>, <prism:copyright> and <prl:usage>.[41] Coyle notes, 'PRISM is used in a purely business-to-business environment where the parties have long-standing relationships, including contracts for syndication of their materials ... PRISM is a good example of an REL that was developed for a specific situation where a more general rights language was not necessary.' (Coyle, p. 13).[2] The current standard as of this writing is PRISM 2.0.

SMPTE DMS-1

SMPTE (Society of Motion Picture and Television Engineers) published the Material Exchange Format (MXF) in 2004 as a suite of standards, including the core standard, SMPTE

377M-2004, the MXF file format standard. MXF is a wrapper standard intended to promote transport and interoperability of content across the complex technical platforms needed to manage and display multimedia resources. MXF uses KLV (Key Length Value) coding for structuring files in a uniform manner for transport across disparate systems. The use of KLV in MXF allows compliant systems to ignore any content within the MXF wrapper that the system does not recognise or need. MXF is intended to support file interoperability between content creation devices, servers and workstations and to maintain the documentation chain for metadata about audiovisual essences throughout the resource life cycle – creation, broadcast, storage and re-use. A key component of MXF is metadata, which is intended to be captured, stored within the MXF container, and transported along the creation, management and display chain. The primary metadata implementation for MXF is SMPTE 380M-2004, DMS-1 (Descriptive Metadata Scheme-1), which is designed to capture and store information from creating devices, such as cameras, which can capture information such as GPS position, creator and date; management systems; and output systems, such as broadcasts or web services. MXF can carry metadata in the MXF header, generic container system item elements and specific areas of essence streams. MXF can utilise other metadata schemas in addition to its native metadata schema, DMS-1. These metadata schemas may be 'dark metadata' in that they may not be recognised by all MXF-compliant systems. DMS-1 utilises the SMPTE RP-210 Metadata Registry of Data Element Descriptions as its data dictionary. DMS-1 provides rights metadata and links to contract information at the production, scene and clip levels. The European Broadcasting Union issued a basic user recommendation for use of MXF metadata by its community in February 2007.[42]

IEEE LTSC

The IEEE Learning Technology Standards Committee develops 'internationally accredited technical standards, recommended practices, and guides for learning technology.'[43] On 14 September 2007, IEEE issued 1484.4-2007, *IEEE Trial-Use Recommended Practice for Digital Rights Expression Languages (DRELs) Suitable for eLearning Technologies*. IEEE 1484.4-2007 was based on an extensive examination of the needs of the learning technology community and a detailed evaluation and test of current rights expression languages by the IEEE LTSC Digital Rights Expression Language Workgroup (WG4).[44]

Open Geospatial Consortium GeoDRM RM

The Open Geospatial Consortium, Inc. has developed a Geospatial Digital Rights Management Reference Model (GeoDRM RM) (06-004r3), which 'defines the framework for web service mechanisms and rights languages to articulate, manage and protect the rights of all participants in the geographic information marketplace, including the owners of intellectual property and the users who wish to use it.'[45] The model, dated 28 February 2006, provides a conceptual model for rights workflow for geospatial information, a metadata model for rights expression and requirements for rights management systems to implement the metadata and workflow.[46]

Open Data Commons

The Open Data Commons has issued *Public Domain Dedication and License v.1.0.* open data license to enable broad use of data by enabling data producers to place their work in the public domain.[47]

Metadata-based rights tools

As metadata to express copyright and licensing emerges, tools that exploit this metadata to enable libraries to manage resources more effectively are also being developed. These tools enable organisations to implement, use and interpret rights metadata. Two useful examples are XMP and Rightsphere™.

XMP

The XMP is an open framework for creating and using metadata for digital file management, particularly for embedding and interpreting metadata in the file headers of images, documents and other formats. XMP was developed by Adobe Systems, which provides tools within the Adobe Creative Suite to combine metadata from EXIF (Exchangeable Image File Format), embedded in the file headers of images created by digital cameras, with descriptive metadata in any schema but particularly the IPTC (International Press Telecommunications Council) Information Interchange Model (IIM). XMP can embed metadata in digital file headers and also provide digital file management through cross-application creation and use of metadata for XMP-enabled application suites, such as the Adobe Creative Suite. Metadata for XMP is written in RDF. A number of partner organisations have implemented XMP, including PLUS, discussed earlier in this chapter. Many digital image encoding and editing systems can embed XMP metadata in image file headers.[48] XMP tools, such as the XMP Ifilter for indexing and searching XMP,[49] as well as open source XMP creation and management tools on the SourceForge download site, are becoming available.

Rightsphere™

From the US-based Copyright Clearance Center, Rightsphere™ is a 'rights advisory and management tool' that enables libraries and users to answer the question, 'what am I allowed to do with this content?'[50] Rightsphere™ consists of a database that can be populated by libraries with information about license agreements. Once the data is entered, differential rights to content can be assigned by location (including country), department or workgroup and content can be managed at the agreement, collection or title level. The user interface resides at the browser level. As a user discovers content, clicking on the Rightsphere icon in the browser toolbar provides information about the permissions for re-use available to the user. Rightsphere also enables the collection of data about secondary use of licensed resources. Rightsphere utilises the Microsoft ASP.NET development framework and is maximised for use within the Microsoft Internet Explorer and Mozilla Firefox browsers.[50]

Conclusion

Rights are generally bounded within context – the role of the user, the time frame of use, etc. At a minimum, rights associated with a resource are never permanent, as copyright itself is not permanent. Rights are, by law, provided to the creator and any subsequent rights holders for a specific period of time. Rights are best expressed not as absolutes but as events, that may be associated with a user or user category, with other resources, with place, and always with time. There is a natural tension between the desire to create metadata that will not need revision over time, and the contextual, time-bound nature of resource rights. There is also a natural tension between the description of the rights associated with a resource and the application of those rights. Actionable rights metadata may include data elements, such as the identification of the creator, or the current rights holder, that may outlast the technologies bundled within a general rights technology framework intended to implement the rights. Automating usage controls via a rights expression language also requires that any uses be explicitly identified within the associated rights metadata document. As Coyle notes, 'if a license is written that allows printing but fails to include that on-screen display is permitted, the rendering software should be defined to refuse to allow such display.' (Coyle, pp. 20–21).[2] Usage is frequently a series of sequential steps. For example, permission to modify a resource requires that the resource rights include the right to download and the right to copy.

A means to separate durable information from actionable usage statements and technologies is important. Technologies are often device- or transmission-dependent, while metadata, at least in theory, can exist independently of the technologies used to express or transmit the metadata. Workflow or transaction-based metadata schemas should be able to import more durable metadata that identifies the resource, its provenance and its rights status, from standard schemas, such as MODS, Dublin Core, MPEG-7, and rights description schemas into the rights expression framework. Conversely, metadata that identifies and describes permissions and constraints on resource use should be abstractable and indexable from the actionable rights workflow framework, to support discovery and selection of resources, based on criteria such as whether the work is copyright protected or associated with restrictions such as payment of a fee for access, which might have equal weight for a user with other selection criteria such as content currency and subject relevance.

At a minimum, libraries should implement metadata to document copyright status and resource provenance relevant to rights status and resource use and then explore how, and when, to interoperate with the emerging actionable rights systems that may impact library workflow at point of purchase and licensing or at point of specific resource use, such as resource use within DRM-enabled learning content management systems. The next chapter looks at DRM technologies and systems to manage digital rights management events directly – from resource identification and access control, to downstream usage tracking and control.

Notes and references

1. *WIPO Copyright Treaty, adopted in Geneva on December 20, 1996*. Geneva: World Intellectual Property Organization. Last accessed 24 March 2008. *http://www.wipo.int/treaties/en/ip/wct/trtdocs_wo033.html#P66_786\5*
2. Coyle, Karen. (2004) *Rights Expression Languages: A Report for the Library of Congress*. Washington, DC: Library of Congress. Last accessed 24 March 2008. *http://www.loc.gov/standards/Coylereport_final1single.pdf*
3. The University of Texas at Austin Information Technology Services. 'The Entity-Relationship Model' *Introduction to Data Modeing*. Austin, TX: University of Texas at Austin, c2004-2007. Last updated 29 February 2004. Last accessed 25 March 2008. *http://www.utexas.edu/its-archive/windows/database/datamodeling/dm/erintro.html*
4. ISO/IEC JTC1 SC32 WG2. 'ISO /IEC 11179, Information Technology Metadata Registries (MDR)' *ISO/IEC JTC1 SC32 WG2 Development/Maintenance*. Washington, DC: ISO/IEC JTC1 SC32. Last updated 30 December 2007. Last accessed 24 March 2008. *http://metadata-stds.org/11179/*

5. Coyle, Karen. (2005) 'Descriptive metadata for copyright status.' *First Monday* 10(10). Last accessed 24 March 2008. *http://www.firstmonday.org/issues/issue10_10/coyle/index.html*
6. Rutgers University Libraries. (2006) 'RUCore Rights Metadata Schema' *RUcore, Rutgers Community Repository Reference Materials*. New Brunswick, NJ: Rutgers University Libraries. Last accessed 24 March 2008. *http://rucore.libraries.rutgers.edu/collab/ref/doc_mwg_rulib_rights_md_v2.0.pdf*
7. CDL Rights Management Group. 'CDL Rights Management Framework' *Inside CDL*. Oakland, CA: California Digital Library. Last reviewed 28 June 2005. Last accessed 24 March 2008. *http://www.cdlib.org/inside/projects/rights/*
8. CDL Rights Management Group. 'CopyrightMD Schema, Version 0.9' *Inside CDL*. Oakland, CA: California Digital Library. Last reviewed 24 March 2006. Last accessed 24 March 2008. *http://www.cdlib.org/inside/projects/rights/schema/*
9. Machine Readable Bibliographic Information (MARBI) Committee. (2007) 'MARC Discussion Paper No. 2007-DP05.' *Library of Congress MARC Development Discussion Paper List*. Washington, DC: Library of Congress. Last accessed 24 March 2008. *http://www.loc.gov/marc/marbi/2007/2007-dp05.html*
10. Agnew, Grace and Yu, Yang. (2007) 'The Rutgers Workflow Management System: Migrating a Digital Object Management Utility to Open Source.' *Code4Lib Journal* 1(1). Last accessed 24 March 2008. *http://journal.code4lib.org/articles/25*
11. Hoebelheinrich, Nancy J., ed. (20045) *METSRights*. Washington, DC: Library of Congress. Last accessed 24 March 2008. *http://www.loc.gov/standards/rights/METSRights.xsd*
12. Library of Congress. (2006) 'Draft Rights Declaration Schema is Ready for Review' *METS Encoding & Transmission Standard* (METS News and Announcements). Washington, DC: Library of Congress. Last accessed 24 March 2008. *http://www.loc.gov/standards/mets/news080503.html*
13. PREMIS Editorial Committee. (2008) *PREMIS Data Dictionary for Preservation Metadata v 2.0.*. Washington, DC: Library of Congress, March 2008. Last accessed 14 May 2008 *http://www.loc.gov/standards/premis/v2/premis-2-0.pdf*

14. Coyle, Karen. (2006) *Rights in the PREMIS Data Model, A Report for the Library of Congress*. Washington, DC: Library of Congress. Last accessed 25 March 2008. *http://www.loc.gov/standards/premis/Rights-in-the-PREMIS-Data-Model.pdf*
15. *Creative Commons* [home page]. San Francisco, CA: Creative Commons. Last updated 23 March 2008. Last accessed 24 March 2008. *http://creativecommons.org/*
16. Creative Commons, 'Embedded Metadata' *Creative Commons* [home page]. San Francisco, CA: Creative Commons. Last modified 15 February 2008. Last accessed 24 March 2008. *http://wiki.creativecommons.org/Embedded_Metadata*
17. Abelson, Hal, Adida, Ben, Linksvayer, Mike, and Yergler, Nathan. (2008) *cc:REL: the Creative Commons Rights Expression Language*. San Francisco, CA: Creative Commons, 3 March 2008. Last accessed 15 May 2008. *http://wiki.creativecommons.org/images/d/d6/Ccrel-1.0.pdf*
18. Creative Commons. 'Creative Commons Licenses' *Creative Commons* [home page]. San Francisco, CA: Creative Commons. Last accessed 23 March 2008. *http://creativecommons.org/about/licenses/meet-the-licenses*
19. Creative Commons. 'International' *Creative Commons* [home page]. San Francisco, CA: Creative Commons. Last accessed 15 May 2008. *http://creativecommons.org/international*
20. Creative Commons. 'Web Services' *Creative Commons* [home page]. San Francisco, CA: Creative Commons. Last modified 24 March 2008. Last accessed 15 May 2008. *http://wiki.creativecommons.org/Creative_Commons_Web_Services*
21. DLF ERM Initiative. (2004) *Electronic Resource Management: Report of the DLF ERM Initiative*. Washington, DC: Digital Library Federation. Last accessed 25 March 2008. *http://www.diglib.org/pubs/dlf102/ERMFINAL.pdf*
22. Digital Library Federation. 'DLF Electronic Resource Management, Phase II' *Digital Library Federation* [home page]. Last updated 12 July 2006. Last accessed 25 March 2008. *http://www.diglib.org/standards/dlf-erm05.htm*
23. EDItEUR. (2007) *ONIX-PL ERMI Encoding Format, Draft 2*. Baltimore, MD: NISO. 29 July 2007 Last accessed 15 May 2008. *http://www.niso.org/workrooms/lewg/071119ONIX_ERMIencodingformat.pdf*

24. National Information Standards Organization. (2008) *License Expression Working Group*. Baltimore, MD: NISO. Last accessed 15 May 2008. *http://www.niso.org/workrooms/lewg*
25. EDItEUR. 'ONIX for Licensing Terms' *EDItEUR* [home page]. London: EDItEUR. Last accessed 25 March 2008. *http://www.editeur.org/*
26. EDItEUR. (2007) *ONIX for Licensing Terms Publications License Message Format, Draft 0.9.26*. London: EDItEUR. Last accessed 25 March 2008. Available at: *http://www.editeur.org/*
27. EDItEUR. (2007) *Mapping ONIX-PL to ERM, Draft 2*. Baltimore, MD: NISO, 19 November 2007. Last accessed 15 May 2008. *http://www.niso.org/workrooms/lewg/071119 ONIX_ERMImapping.pdf*
28. PLUS Coalition. (2007) 'The PLUS Glossary of Media Licensing' *PLUS, Picture Licensing Universal System* [home page] Pasadena, CA: PLUS Coalition. Last accessed 25 March 2008. *http://www.useplus.com/useplus/glossary.asp*
29. PLUS Coalition. (2007) 'PLUS Technical Specification' *PLUS Standards Library*. Pasadena, CA: PLUS Coalition. Last accessed 25 March 2008. Available at: *http://www.useplus.com/useplus/standards.asp*
30. PLUS Coalition. (2006) 'Media Selector' *PLUS, Picture Licensing Universal System* [home page]. Pasadena, CA: PLUS Coalition. Last accessed 25 March 2008. *http://www.useplus.com/plusmediaselector/License/LicenseGenerator.aspx?AspxAutoDetectCookieSupport=1*
31. PLUS Coalition. (2007) 'PLUS Packs' *PLUS, Picture Licensing Universal System* [home page]. Pasadena, CA: PLUS Coalition. Last accessed 25 March 2008. *http://www.useplus.com/useplus/pluspacks.asp*
32. Iannella, Renato, ed. (2002) *Open Digital Rights Language (ODRL) version 1.1*. IPR Systems Pty Ltd. Last accessed 25 March 2008. *http://odrl.net/1.1/ODRL-11.pdf*
33. *The ODRL Initiative* [home page]. Sydney, Australia: NICTA. Last updated 27 September 2007. Last accessed 25 March 2008. *http://odrl.net/*
34. Bormans, Jan and Hill, Keith, eds. (2002) *MPEG-21 Overview v.5*. Shanghai: Organisation Internationale de Normalisation, ISO/IEC JTC1/SC29/WG11 Coding of Moving

Pictures and Audio. Last accessed 25 March 2008. *http://www.chiariglione.org/mpeg/standards/mpeg-21/mpeg-21.htm*

35. <indecs>rdd Consortium. (2002) *<indecs>rdd White Paper: a Standard Rights Data Dictionary.* Last accessed 25 March 2008. *http://www.doi.org/topics/indecs-rdd-white-paper-may02.pdf*
36. Cover, Robin, ed. 'Extensible Access Control Markup Language, XACML' *OASIS Cover Pages Technology Reports.* Last modified 2 March 2005. Last accessed 25 March 2008. *http://xml.coverpages.org/xacml.html*
37. Griffin, Phil. (2004) *Introduction to XACML.* San Jose, CA: Dev2Dev, BEA Systems. Last accessed 25 March 2008. *http://dev2dev.bea.com/pub/a/2004/02/xacml.html*
38. OASIS (2005) *eXtensible Access Control Markup Language (XACML) Version 2.0: OASIS Standard.* OASIS. Last accessed 25 March 2008. available as *XACML 2.0 Specification Set* at *http://www.oasis-open.org/committees/tc_home.php?wg_abbrev=xacml#technical*
39. Anderson, Anne, ed. (2006) *Sun Position Paper: W3C Workshop on Languages for Privacy Policy Negotiation and Semantics-Driven Enforcement.* Palo Alto, CA: Sun Microsystems, Inc. Last accessed 25 March 2008. *http://www.w3.org/2006/07/privacy-ws/papers/17-anderson-position/*
40. IDEAlliance, Inc. (2001–2008) 'About PRISM'. *PRISM, Publishing Requirements for Industry Standard Metadata.* Alexandria, VA: IDEAlliance. Last accessed 25 March 2008. *http://www.prismstandard.org/about/*
41. IDEAlliance, Inc. (2001–2008) 'Technical Overview'. *PRISM, Publishing Requirements for Industry Standard Metadata.* Alexandria, VA: IDEAlliance. Last accessed 25 March 2008. *http://www.prismstandard.org/about/technicaloverview.asp*
42. European Broadcasting Union. (2007) *Material Exchange Format: Basic User Metadata Implementation.* Geneva: EBU-UER. Last accessed 25 March 2008. *http://www.ebu.ch/CMSimages/en/tec_text_r121-2007_tcm6-50026.pdf*
43. IEEE Learning Technology Standards Committee. (2007) *LTSC Home Page* IEEE LTSC. Last accessed 25 March 2008. *http://www.ieeeltsc.org/*

44. IEEE. (2007) '1484.4-2007: IEEE Trial-Use Recommended Practice for Digital Rights Expression Languages (DRELs) Suitable for eLearning Technologies.' *IEEE Xplore Release 2.4.* New York, NY: IEEE. Last accessed 25 March 2008. *http://ieeexplore.ieee.org/xpl/freeabs_all.jsp?tp=&arnumber=4303011&isnumber=4303010*
45. Open Geospatial Consortium, Inc. *Geospatial Digital Rights Reference Model (GeoDRM RM).* Wayland, MA: OGC, Updated 27 April 2007. Last accessed 25 March 2008. *http://www.opengeospatial.org/standards/as/geodrmrm*
46. Vowles, Graham, ed. (2006) *Geospatial Digital Rights Management Reference Model (GeoDRM RM) Version 1.0.0.* Wayland, MA: OGC. Last accessed 25 March 2008. *http://portal.opengeospatial.org/files/?artifact_id=14085*
47. Hatcher, Jordan. (2008) *Public Domain Dedication and License.* Open Data Commons. Last accessed 25 March 2008. *http://www.opendatacommons.org/odc-public-domain-dedication-and-licence/*
48. Adobe Systems Incorporated. (2008) *Extensible Metadata Platform (XMP): Adding Intelligence to Media.* San Jose, CA: Adobe Systems Incorporated. Last accessed 25 March 2008. *http://www.adobe.com/products/xmp/*
49. Softpedia. *XMP Ifilter2.2* Last accessed 15 May 2008. http://www.softpedia.com/get/System/File-Management/XMP-IFilter.shtml
50. Copyright Clearance Center. *Rightsphere Product Overview.* Danvers, MA: Copyright Clearance Center. Last accessed 25 March 2008. *http://www.copyright.com/media/pdfs/Prod-Rightsphere.pdf*

7

The technology of digital rights management

Introduction and definition

DRM technologies are understandably distasteful to many people who must interact with them – customers who want to use content as simply and intuitively as reading a book or listening to a record album; libraries, who find that their role as information intermediaries is hindered or even threatened by DRM; even content producers, who want the widest possible impact for their intellectual efforts. The early development of DRM emerged from a single compelling business model: protecting the content that represents the primary profit of a creator or an industry from unauthorised use. The creation of the 'perfect copy' that could be easily disseminated to an unlimited number of downstream users, thus destroying any financial reward for the rights holder, was perceived as not only possible but extremely likely.

The early days of DRM were marked by a high level of perceived threat combined with emerging technologies which were clumsy and inflexible and which reduced the entire life cycle of information from creation through consumption to a single yes-or-no question: can I have the resource or not? As Karen Coyle rightly noted, 'DRM is not a single technology and it is not even a single philosophy ... DRM is potentially a nearly absolute protection of works.'[1]

DRM has been called everything from 'digital restrictions management'[2] to a 'drive by shooting'.[3] Although opinions differ widely on the need for DRM, most would agree that current DRM systems do not effectively meet their core purpose of controlling access to content, except perhaps within a very well-defined delivery model, such as the Apple music delivery system, iTunes.

Do DRM technologies serve any purpose in the library or archives, if only as a trend that should be opposed? Have advances in digital technologies improved the performance of DRM such that the access to information can be seamless and efficient, without compromising the privacy of all entities in a rights transaction? This chapter will look at the complex world of DRM technologies, beginning with an overview of core concepts and technologies, followed by current DRM standards and commercial implementations, and then looking at emerging DRM technologies and standards. The chapter will conclude by examining the relevance of DRM technologies to libraries and offering practical suggestions for navigating the DRM technology space.

DRM concepts

I will begin by looking at the core concepts that underlie most DRM systems and technologies. John Manferdelli of Microsoft Corporation defines rights management very simply as 'a way to have rights persist with the thing they are trying to protect'.[4] As the previous chapters have shown, DRM technologies are designed to manage and protect more than resources and rights. Broadly speaking, DRM technologies enable the digital management of entities in a rights transaction – the resource (information or service), the agent (e.g. the content owner or user) or another component (e.g. a device or license). The focus of DRM is on the resource: protecting the integrity of the resource and managing its accessibility. The Information Technology Security Evaluation Criteria (ITSEC) identified three major criteria that must be supported by information security systems that will work equally well as core criteria for DRM:

1. '*Confidentiality* – prevention of the unauthorised disclosure of information
2. *Integrity* – prevention of the unauthorised modification of information
3. *Availability* – prevention of the unauthorised withholding of information or resources.'[5]

DRM technologies are designed to protect against threats to content and rights transaction entities through three broad strategies: deterrence, prevention and detection:

- *Deterrence* is usually defined in terms of the nuisance factor, where the effort to make inappropriate use of a resource is so difficult and time consuming that it is not worth the effort to circumvent DRM protections. Deterrence works best when the costs associated with authorised access, in terms of money, time and effort, are perceived as reasonable and a fair trade for the resource. Deterrence was the primary rights protection method in the analog space. Photocopying a book was time consuming and produced a copy that was unwieldy and of poor quality compared with an authorised copy, which could be purchased from any bookstore for a reasonable sum.
- *Prevention*, specifically the prevention of unauthorised access, use or damage to protected resources, represents the traditional function of DRM systems, particularly those that have been generally designated as 'access control' or 'copy control' systems.

- *Detection* is often referred to as forensic technology because it addresses unauthorised use of content after its distribution. Detection technologies are emerging as a very important strategy for content owners to exercise control over their resources, for two reasons. First, the use of the Internet for shared personal expression has exploded, with content creators freely integrating copyright-protected resources into their websites or remixed creations. Second, content providers are beginning to recognise that not all content users are focused on creating and distributing 'the perfect copy' to other unauthorised users, thus destroying all potential profits for the rights holder. As the perceived risk has declined, the inconvenience and expense of DRM have risen as a concern for digital media distributors. A cost-effective strategy might be to allow unprotected distribution, and then detecting unapproved content use through forensic technologies, particularly for content that is likely to be reused on the Web. Forensic technologies often involve the use of a watermark that can be discovered and tracked. Another forensic technology involves pattern matching to discover copies of the content on the Web. As forensic technologies improve, content owners may find it more cost-effective to identify egregious misuse 'after the fact' and deal with that misuse accordingly, even in the case of high-value content. A niche detection area of particular interest to many libraries is plagiarism-detection software, given that the nuisance deterrent for plagiarising the work of others has completely disappeared. Plagiarism technologies will be discussed at length later in this chapter, as many libraries serve student researchers who are directly affected by plagiarism detection systems.

Basic tools and components

DRM systems usually comprise a suite of several technologies that enable a transaction or digital communication, resulting in the release of protected content to an authorised user. Many core technologies are involved in each part of the DRM value chain, which includes packaging content; authenticating and authorising the user; making the protected content available to the authorised user; and controlling any further use of the content, such as copying the content to another device. DRM systems often differ in the workflow for packaging and releasing content, but the core technologies remain the same. In this section we will look at common technologies that comprise DRM systems.

Encryption

A standard method to protect digital content from unauthorised use involves scrambling the content, thus rendering it unintelligible until a key is used to decrypt the content and make it usable by the key holder. The key is the most important component in an encryption system. Two possible encryption schemes are private key (symmetric) cryptography and public key (asymmetric) cryptography.

Symmetric encryption (also known as private key encryption) is the most secure and requires both parties to know a private key in order to engage in a secured message exchange or other transaction. Public key cryptography involves the use of a pair of keys – a public key and a private key. The public key may be widely distributed, even to unknown users, but the private key is known only to its owner. The public key and private key are related computationally, but the private key should not be derivable from the public key. A message may be encrypted by anyone possessing the public key but can only be decrypted by the private key. This enables the key owner to engage in transactions with a wide range of other users who may possess the public key, while still maintaining the confidentiality and security of the transaction through the use of the private key, which is presumably known only to its owner. Wikipedia provides the analogy of a locked mailbox with a slot. The mailbox address, which is publicly accessible, is analogous to the public key. Anyone can thus send mail to the mailbox. However, only the private key can unlock the mailbox and read the mail.[6] To increase security, a message may first be encrypted with a randomly generated secret key, which is itself encrypted by the public key. Asymmetric key techniques involve algorithms that are intended to be very difficult to crack and include Diffie-Hellman, DSS (Digital Signature Standard) and the RSA encryption algorithm, the first algorithm developed for both encryption and digital signature, in wide use today.

Public keys can be compromised through interception across public communication channels and also through brute-force attacks, in which repeated attempts are made to break the key, until an attempt is finally successful. Brute-force attacks include the side-channel attack, which measures the amount of time it takes known hardware to encrypt plain text, which then simplifies the search for a decryption key, based on level of effort needed for encryption. The amount of effort required to break a key is called the 'work factor'. The more effort required, the less likely that an attacker will succeed in breaking the key. For this reason, larger key encryptions, such as 128-bit encryption, are preferred over shorter keys. A common interception attack is the 'man-in-the-middle' attack, where a third party intercepts and modifies a public key. This enables the attacker to intercept messages, which are then decrypted and re-encrypted.

A key is generally bound to a certificate that attests to the key's validity. Keys are generally assigned by trusted third parties, who are responsible for certifying the security of keys, so that all parties trust the keys, and for assigning keys to specific users and uses. The Certificate Authority (CA) is the third party that is trusted by all participants in a secured transaction. The CA maintains the integrity of the certificates it issues by verifying the identity of the certificate holder before issuing the certificate and also by promptly revoking any compromised certificates. Certificate revocation is an important means of guarding against corrupted public keys, as the public key is validated before acceptance by the presence of a valid certificate. If compromised certificates are not revoked or if the revocation is not published in a manner that can be easily discovered, a compromised key will appear to be valid. Key management is a common and critical point of failure for cryptographic systems.

Keys are so critical to the security of content and processes that an infrastructure consisting of policy, technology and practise has developed, known as the public key infrastructure, or PKI. Key management includes tasks performed by the CA such as key assignment; key escrow, in which keys are maintained until point of need; and key revocation, in which keys that are compromised are invalidated in key revocation lists. Secure processes will check relevant key revocation lists to ensure that a key has not been revoked, before the key is accepted to initiate a transaction. Assigning a key to a user involves binding the key to the user identity. The CA usually binds the key owner's identity to the key through the issuance of a certificate, which identifies the key owner, certifies that the key owner possesses the identity and other attributes documented in the certificate, and binds the private key uniquely to the identity documented in the certificate. Key distribution schemes need to be *obscure* so that they cannot be intercepted, *diverse* so that successful interception or attack on one key does not compromise the entire system, and *renewable* so that a PKI can recover from successful attacks without needing complete replacement.

The CA stores the user identity, public key, key binding, validity condition and attributes in a secure manner for each key holder. PKI exists to enable key holders in a public network to encrypt messages or transactions with each other, even in cases where the key holders do not know each other. There are many issues with PKI, the most important of which are the longevity and trustworthiness of the key system and the certificate authority. Keys must be closely bound to owners, and the integrity of keys must be protected as long as they are useful. Copyright protection, and inherent market value, for content may extend beyond the existence of the CA responsible for managing the keys used to encrypt and decrypt the content. Lightweight 'Web of trust' (WOT) schemes have been developed in which key owners create 'self-sign' certificates combined with third-party attestations of the certificates to provide a reliable encryption methodology sufficient for low-risk transactions. The most common example is PGP (Pretty Good Privacy), which is available in both commercial and open source implementations. Another lightweight system is the Simple Public Key Infrastructure (SPKI), in which the key is not bound to a person but is itself the principal. SPKI enables encrypted communications, but without the notion that the identity of either party to the communication can be verified and therefore trusted. SPKI does not use a trusted third party, as the key issuer is also the verifier of the key's authenticity.[7]

Although public and private key encryption are generally described for transactions between two parties, another common methodology is broadcast encryption, in which encrypted content is broadcast to a large number of parties via public telecommunications channels. Encryption is performed based on a secret session encrypting key (SEK). Key encrypting keys then encrypt the SEK and deliver the encrypted SEK only to valid group members, who must decrypt the SEK in order to access the content (Miodrag, pp. 258–259).[8] Broadcasting content to a large number of users poses inherent risks as every user may not be trustworthy. One method to increase security is to create time-bound keys with specific activation and expiration times to ensure that the encrypted content is only available within the constraints of the transaction. Time-bound keys are common in pay-per-view transactions, for example (Miodrag, p. 259).[8]

A common method of encryption in widespread use for digital media is CSS, Content Scrambling System, a proprietary encryption method developed by Matsushita and Toshiba, which is used to encrypt DVD content. CSS has been compromised many times, and CSS decryption applications for duplicating or 'ripping' DVDs are widely available on the Web. Encryption can add considerable overhead to the transmission and processing of content. In some cases, particularly for large multimedia files, parts of the file will be selectively encrypted to provide more efficient delivery, particularly across pubic networking channels.

Digital certificates

Digital certificates, which were discussed at length in Chapter 5, are an important component of a successful public key infrastructure system. According to the X.509 Version 3 Certificate standard, 'users of a public key shall be confident that the associated private key is owned by the correct remote subject (person or system) ... This confidence is obtained through the use of public key certificates, which are data structures that bind public key values to subjects.' (Cooper *et al.*, p. [8]).[9] Digital certificates are digitally signed by a CA, which asserts that the owner of the certificate possesses the identity documented in the certificate, based on some trusted level of proof. Certificates have a valid period of existence. When a certificate expires or is otherwise compromised, it is revoked, and the revocation is published in a manner that should ensure that no further communications that rely on the certificate can occur. Certificates include digital signatures of issuer and owner, validity period, unique identifiers for issuer and subject, and extensions that can include further attributes of the subject, or owner. The PKI digital certificate standard is ITU-T X.509, first released in 1988 as part of the X.500 directory recommendations and is currently in version 3 (Cooper *et al.*, p. [9]).[9]

Watermarking (including forensic watermarking)

Watermarks insert information into content that can be used for many purposes, such as provenance (creation and ownership), copyright and conditions of use. Watermarks are inserted in areas of a digital file that do not affect content presentation, generally using a spread spectrum approach that adds imperceptible noise to the content. Spread spectrum techniques emerged from secure radio communication systems and involve repetition of the watermark information to be embedded and modulation of the repeated bit sequence with a pseudo-noise signal. The resulting watermark is embedded in an area that is imperceptible to the content user, but detectible with watermark recognition applications (Hartung and Ramme, p. 82).[10]

Watermarks are evaluated in terms of capacity and original signal fidelity. Watermark capacity refers to the amount of information that can be embedded in a watermark. For high-capacity watermarks, there are obvious trade-offs with imperceptibility and efficiency of content transmission and display. A fidelity measure function measures the distortion between the unmarked file (the cover signal) and the watermarked file (the stego signal). Clearly, distortion should be minimal and should never impact the user's experience with the resource, particularly when the user has paid a fee or met other conditions for resource use. An effective watermark will have the following characteristics:

- *Imperceptible* – A watermark will not alter the content or aesthetics of the content perceptibly. The user's experience of the content should not be affected by the presence of a watermark. Visible watermarks may be used intentionally, particularly when the rights holder wants ownership to be openly presented to potential users. Visible watermarks are commonly used for preview versions of commercial digital image collections, to enable potential purchasers to browse all images via the Web before selecting an image for purchase. The purchased image will have either an imperceptible watermark or no watermark, depending on the terms of purchase.
- *Robust* – A watermark should withstand signal processing operations, such as editing or compression, that users may apply to content, as well as deliberate attempts to alter or remove the watermark. By contrast,

fragile watermarks are lost when manipulations are applied to a file. Generally, robust watermarks are preferred, particularly to maintain the durability of ownership or provenance information, but there are reasons for applying fragile watermarks, particularly when copyright ownership is transferred and downstream use is thus not an issue.

- *Reversible* – A watermark should be removable by authorised parties so that the original unmarked file is completely restored.
- *Secure* – A watermark should only be applied, detected and removed by authorised parties. Techniques such as secret keys are generally used to restrict access to watermark information. The key may be a randomisation of the source noise pattern or other secret that must be known to the detecting software before it can read the watermark.[11]

Watermarking is often discussed with a related technology – steganography, or data hiding – in which secret information is embedded in a digital file. Watermarks that contain information, and not just a link or code that references information, are a form of data hiding. Steganography and watermarking differ primarily in the intent, or business model, behind the application. Wikipedia defines steganography as 'the art and science of writing hidden messages in such a way that no one apart from the sender and intended recipient ever realizes there *is* a hidden message.'[12] Steganographic messages use the open content as a means of transport between the sender and the intended recipient. The use of steganography is kept confidential from anyone who uses the content beyond the authorised recipient. Watermarks serve a purpose of identification and content use management, generally as part of a larger DRM system or strategy for safeguarding content. Although the use of a watermark in content is not itself hidden, but generally acknowledged to serve as a deterrent for content users, it is intended to be robust and imperceptible and will rarely be removed or compromised, except through intentional tampering. Watermarks are a key component of DRM systems and are intended to be recognised by DRM-enabled devices, which may require the presence of a watermark containing ownership information as a precondition for access or may act upon usage information contained in a watermark, such as 'do not copy' or 'copy once'.

Watermarks can be successfully attacked through collusion, where multiple copies of the original signal, or cover signal, are combined and analyzed for small noise variations, to develop a composite copy that most resembles the original, unmarked, data. Watermarks can also be attacked by obtaining and reverse engineering the watermark detection application to determine the type and location of the watermark signal that the application was designed to detect.

The most famous and successful watermark attack was the response by a team of researchers from Princeton and Rice universities, led by Edward Felten, to an open challenge by the developers of the Secure Digital Music Initiative (SDMI). On 6 September 2000, in an *Open Letter to the Digital Community*, SDMI invited anyone to crack proposed SDMI technologies including four watermark technologies. The team 'analyzed the clips watermarked with the four technologies, and successfully modified them so that the watermarks could no longer be detected, while maintaining a level of audio quality satisfactory to SDMI.'[13]

Although watermarks can be successfully compromised, they are an efficient means of communicating information about ownership and use to DRM-enabled devices and software applications, and they definitely meet the deterrence requirement for DRM technologies in that they are not easily broken without significant time, effort and technological sophistication.

Digital signatures, fingerprints and timestamps

Other important tools for verifying identity, for persons and objects, are digital signatures, digital fingerprints and digital timestamps.

Digital signatures are used to authenticate participants in a transaction, such as the content owner or content user. Digital signatures are also used to attest to the authenticity of content. A hash, or unique numeric value derived from digital content, can be created by calculating the length of the content to create the hash, such that any change to the content will also invalidate the hash. The hash can then be digitally signed by using the private key of either party to the transaction. The combination of hash and signature provides verification that the content is unchanged (the hash) and attests to the authenticity of the content (the signature). A digital signature can be verified at any point in the transaction when verification of the signature owner is required, such as when issuing or obtaining a license to use a resource. The public key is used to validate the signature generated from the private key.

XML signature (IETF RFC 3275) is a standard schema for assigning signatures in XML to any content, to ensure integrity of the content or to authenticate the signer of the content. An enveloped XML signature is included within XML content. Detached signatures are assigned to any type of external data. Signatures are related to their assigned content via URIs.[14]

Digital fingerprints are data introduced into digital content to track content use, particularly to determine whether or not content has been redistributed in an unauthorised manner. There are three kinds of fingerprints – symmetric, asymmetric and anonymous asymmetric. In symmetric fingerprint schemes, a unique fingerprint is assigned to each distributed copy of the digital content. Symmetric fingerprinting enables the owner to tie unauthorised reuse or redistribution of content directly to the individual customer, but its use poses serious risks to the privacy of the customer and to the confidentiality of information use. Asymmetric fingerprinting is an interactive protocol in which a customer's own unique information is used to fingerprint the copy. The protocol enables the customer to know the fingerprinted copy, while the owner knows the customer's identity. In anonymous asymmetric fingerprinting, the customer's anonymity is maintained until the merchant has a need to identify an unauthorised copy. The merchant must apply to a registration authority to learn the identity of the customer (Yong and Lee, p. 193).[15]

Digital fingerprinting, sometimes known as forensic watermarking or individualised watermarking, is increasingly used for digital video content on the Web. Google has introduced video fingerprinting technology for YouTube videos. There are many commercial fingerprinting applications available, such as Audible Magic, Gracenote and Philips. Bill Rosenblatt has suggested in his online publication, *DRM Watch*, that file fingerprinting be part of copyright registration for content owners.[16]

Digital timestamps were first described in Chapter 4. Digital timestamps guarantee the integrity of a document through cryptographic information that guarantees the minimum and maximum age of a document. Digital objects are timestamped in a batch, and the timestamp is published in a manner that cannot be repudiated, such as in a dated newspaper issue. The entire batch of timestamped documents are also used to provide group support for the validity of content dating. The timestamp of a questioned document can be compared with other documents in the batch. If all dates contained within the batch are identical, this serves to validate the questioned document, as tampering with all documents is statistically improbable (Maniatis, p. 3).[17]

Simple marks

Simple marks, such as the broadcast flag, provide simple conditions to which a device or software application can respond. The broadcast flag, which was enacted in the United States through regulations of the Federal Communications Commission, was struck down in a US federal circuit court in 2005 and remains an unresolved and controversial DRM application. The broadcast flag has been defined as a 'series of binary data bits that manifest as an "on/off" switch in the data stream of digital TV programming to indicate whether it can be recorded and whether any other restrictions on usage should apply.' (Kirkman, p. 9).[18] Region codes, which are simple codes included within the CSS encryption application for DVD and Blu-ray discs, limit playback to the region or regions encoded on the content copy. Simple marks can be fairly easily compromised, and just as CSS has been cracked, DVD region codes have been cracked, with applications to override region codes available via the Web.

Licenses

Licenses, sometimes also called end-user license agreements (EULAs), are a core component of DRM systems. A license may be defined as 'an act of communication between two or more parties'.[19] The two parties are most often the distributor or rights holder for the content, who is imposing conditions for use on that content, and the user, who is the recipient of the license. Licenses document and control the permissions provided to end users to access and use the protected content. A license may be explicit, with an opt-in for the user, or hidden in encrypted content, such as a watermark. A license usually communicates directly with a device to allow access to content. The terms of the contract may be known to the user or known only to the compliant device. Even when the terms are known, the license is often encrypted or hidden and thus imperceptible to the user. A DRM system may bind a license with content to create DRM-protected content, or it may provide the license separately from the content as part of a DRM transaction. Licenses, which were discussed in more detail in Chapter 6, are often expressed in actionable rights expression languages that document permissions and constraints on permissions. Licenses store permissions that govern access and use and often store the key(s) that can make the content accessible.

Trusted system

A trusted system provides end-to-end support for a DRM system or transaction. In a trusted system, each node in the DRM process can be relied upon to enforce or obey the rules of the system. This ensures that content is protected throughout the DRM workflow, from content creation and packaging, through purchase and delivery, through any downstream uses beyond the initial access. In the early days of DRM, trusted systems tethered content to a single user device. With the advent of ubiquitous computing, where every user owns multiple appliances capable of accessing the

Web and playing back content, DRM systems are evolving to address the natural consumer desire to transfer content seamlessly across all the devices the consumer owns, from desktop computers to digital playback equipment to mobile devices, such as cell phones and portable music players. Trusted systems now incorporate the concept of the personal network or authorised domain, which can involve tethering the content to the person, using a secret key that is presumably known only to the consumer, or enabling the registration of multiple devices that are authorised to play the content on the consumer's personal or family network.

Secured hardware

In recent years, hardware components with embedded DRM support and other security features have emerged to provide native support for DRM-controlled content, as part of a trusted system. Recent examples of secured hardware include the SD memory card and the TPM (Trusted Platform Module) microcontroller.

The *SD memory card* was introduced in 2003 as a 'smart bridge' technology that enables different kinds of digital equipment to communicate and interoperate without requiring a PC to enable connectivity. The SD memory card includes integrated CPRM (Content Protection for Recorded Media), a mechanism for controlling the copying, playback, transfer and deletion of digital media. CPRM is described more fully in a later section. The SD memory card also has built-in key revocation and copy-counting technology to restrict the number of copies from an SD memory card to a PC.[20]

TPM (Trusted Platform Module) is a recent technology developed by the Trusted Computing Group (TCG), an industry consortium of computer and microprocessor companies (AMD, Hewlett-Packard, IBM, etc.) and intended to store keys, passwords and digital certificates in a robust and secure manner. It is generally affixed to a PC motherboard but can be used in any device that needs to store the information required for identity management and authorised access to protected content. TPM uses the secure TCG subsystem to secure sensitive information from external attack and physical theft. TPM provides hashing, random number generation, asymmetric key generation and asymmetric encryption/decryption. Each individual TPM on each individual computer system has a unique signature initialised during the silicon manufacturing process that enables it to be trusted in any DRM transaction. TPM maintains confidentiality of communications between the TPM microcontroller and external software and includes a tick counter for time-related transaction sequencing. TPM does not control the software that provides secure authentication and authorisation or secure messaging but instead acts as a 'slave' to higher-level applications. The TCG subsystem is platform-independent and currently runs on PCs, PDAs and cell phones. Microsoft's BitLocker Drive Encryption utilises TPM version 1.2 to protect critical system files and user data and to ensure that the Microsoft Vista software is not compromised.[21] The TPM specification is currently in version 1.2, revision 103.[22]

SVP (Secure Video Processor) is a DRM-enabled video-processing chip. Any video-processing chip can be SVP-enabled with additional circuitry. The chip can be embedded in any consumer electronics device. Each SVP has a unique, secure device certificate. The SVP-enabled chip permits decryption, decompression and playback only within the chip itself, subject to any rules imposed on the content by any DRM system. Content on an SVP chip might be governed by multiple certificates offering different rights for different networks and devices. All decompression, decoding and rendering are supported by an embedded tamper-resistant license, such that no unauthorised access is permitted or technically feasible for SVP-enabled devices.[23]

Secured transmission protocols

In addition to secure devices and the content protection standards and specifications discussed later in this chapter, it is important in an end-to-end DRM system to protect the communications between trusted devices. Several protocols have been developed to secure the transport of protected content between devices and across networks.

SSL (Secure Sockets Layer)/TLS (Transport Layer Security) are protocols for cryptographic communications over the Internet. SSLv.3 is still widely used but is being replaced by TLS, which is sometimes referred to as SSLv3.1. Both provide secure encrypted messaging across the Internet through three processes: algorithm negotiation, key exchange and authentication, and symmetric encryption and message authentication. TLS is used for many Internet communications including email and FTP.[24]

HDCP (High-bandwidth Digital Content Protection) protects content which travels across cables using high-definition interfaces, such as DVI (Digital Visual Interface), HDMI (High-Definition Multimedia Interface) and UDI (Unified Display Interface). HDCP is a proprietary specification that is licensed by Digital Content Protection, LLC, a subsidiary of Intel. HDCP protects transmission of content from a source device to a destination device, such as a TV set top, using authentication, encryption and key revocation.[25]

DTCP (Digital Transmission Content Protection) and *DTCP-IP (DTCP over IP)* protect transmission over the cable and interface components between two communicating devices, such as USB and FireWire. DTCP includes a device authentication and key exchange protocol (AKE) to verify connections, content control information, content encryption and renewability. DTCP also supports device revocation for compromised devices. DTCP was defined by the 5C group (Hitachi, Intel, Matsushita, Sony and Toshiba) and is licensed by the 5C/Digital Transmission Licensing Administrator, LLC. DTCP-IP extends DTCP to support transmission over IP networks, using 128-bit encryption. DTCP is designed to interoperate with other DRM protocols. CPRM (discussed below) and HDCP are DTCP compliant.[26]

The DRM system

DRM systems make use of the tools and technologies listed in the previous section to create an end-to-end secured packaging and distribution system for protected content. They have generally been developed to support the commercial distribution of copyright-protected content. DRM systems are designed to ensure the integrity of the object, so that the object is not tampered with or intercepted before delivery, and to ensure the security of the entire distribution chain, so that objects are delivered only to authorised consumers and devices. DRM systems generally include at a minimum:

- *Identification of the content.* Watermarks and identifiers are used to identify the content uniquely. This identification can also be used for downstream tracing of the content to ensure that the content is only used in an authorised manner.
- *Encryption* of all or part of the content, to ensure that only consumers with appropriate keys can access the

content and to ensure that the content is unchanged throughout the distribution and access process.

- *Key(s) and key management* to manage the encryption and decryption of the content by authorised entities in the content value chain.
- *License* containing usage rules to determine what conditions must be met for access and how the resource can be used by the consumer (e.g. copy once).

DRM involves packaging the content to provide security and integrity and to bind the license – which governs usage – to the content. The package generally consists of the content, encrypted for security, the key or keys required for content decryption and entity authentication, and often the license. A license may be combined with the content into a single package or distributed separately from the content, with key pairs used to bind content to license. The core DRM process is shown in Figure 7.1.

Figure 7.1 **Basic DRM system enabling access to content**

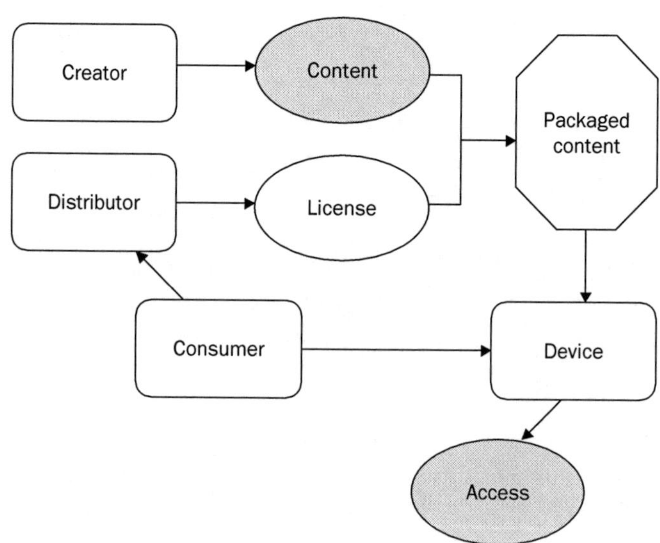

A user, also known as the consumer, generally initiates the transaction by discovering and requesting content. In order to control receipt of the package, however, the DRM-enabled, or packaged, content is delivered to a device that is able to interact with the DRM system, generally through a DRM client. The DRM client must be able to identify itself to the DRM system, through a unique identifier or device key; communicate securely with the content and license servers; receive, store and interpret the digital license; act upon the usage rules contained in the license; and store and manage the keys used to decrypt the content. Some DRM systems will interact directly with the user, who can apply a unique password to access content from any device. In most cases, however, the user will be identified via the authorised device. The user may be identified by a certificate that resides on an authorised device; the device may be pre-authorised at time of manufacture through a unique device key or digital identifier; or the user's device will be authorised at point of initial access, so that the content is explicitly tied to the unique device key or unique identifier. Content that is associated with a single authorised device is 'tethered' to that device because use of the content is restricted to that device.

Current DRM systems are designed to address several critical issues that impact either the consumer's experience or the security of the content.

Ubiquitous computing

Today's consumer is likely to have many devices capable of accessing resources, from PCs to mobile devices to digital set-top devices. This highly connected environment, where any device, from a cell phone to a portable device to a desktop computer, is capable of accessing any digital resource and enabling communication with other people or devices, is known as 'ubiquitous computing' – a term first promoted by Mark Weiser, a chief scientist at Xerox Parc, in 1988.[27] In the ubiquitous computing environment, the consumer wants to be able to transfer resources to any device in order to experience a resource in different environments, such as home, work and travels in between. Ubiquitous computing has also resulted in lower cost devices that can be readily replaced as compelling new functionalities are introduced, so that authorised access to a resource may last much longer than the authorised device itself. Many DRM systems have begun to accommodate user demands for untethered content by defining personal or family networks, where authorised users can register devices, which are then able to display the resource. Many DRM licenses allow copying to other devices, although the number of authorised copies and the types of devices that can receive these copies may be limited.

The 'analog hole'

DRM systems are designed to enable secure end-to-end transmission and delivery of protected resources in a digital environment. As noted in the previous section, digital resources can be easily controlled through encryption. Encryption keys can be compromised or broken, so that unauthorised users can decrypt and view content, but not without some level of effort and expertise. However, once a resource is decrypted and physically experienced through playback, it can be physically captured. A digital video may be captured with a video camera as it plays back on a television set or a computer monitor, for example. A digital sound file may be captured by a good microphone and re-recorded for further playback. This 'gap' in end-to-end protection for a resource is known as the 'analog hole'. Many DRM systems also include technologies to address the analog hole, such as watermarks that disrupt the appearance of an image during printing or video broadcast signals that incorporate visible distortions when recorded from the set-top display.

Device compliance

DRM systems depend upon compliant devices that can manage keys to decrypt content, interpret and enforce licenses, and read watermarks. Device manufacturers understandably find the concept of support for many different DRM systems daunting. In addition, DRM technologies can seriously interfere with efficient playback or device performance, particularly when the DRM technology may not have been optimised in advance for specific microprocessors and operating systems. Components optimised for DRM, such as the TPM discussed earlier in this chapter, are one way to modularise support for DRM technologies in an efficient manner that only requires the device to support the DRM hardware component rather requiring native device support for many proprietary DRM systems.

Renewability

Most DRM systems rely on the consumer's device to control access to the resource. When DRM technologies are compromised, such as when an encryption technology is cracked, the vendor can no longer trust that the DRM system will protect content. Upgrades to DRM are required to repair any security holes or to replace cryptographic algorithms or keys. Device vendors may also provide software or hardware upgrades, or produce new devices, that are incompatible with the DRM system. DRM systems must incorporate a strategy for upgrades to the DRM system to ensure ongoing system viability and compatibility with consumer devices. Many DRM systems automatically renew their software by providing updates to compliant tethered devices. This often occurs without the device owner's knowledge and may cause problems with device performance or with playback of content that is not compliant with the DRM system. Ideally, all renewability strategies should involve an informed 'opt in' by the consumer.

Transparency

As noted above, consumers should be informed of the components of a DRM system, particularly those that reside on the consumer's device, and should have the ability to 'opt in' to any DRM software installations at point of content purchase, as well as to any DRM system upgrades. Consumers choosing to opt out of a DRM installation or upgrade should be aware of the consequences, such as the inability to continue to experience licensed content that is protected by the DRM system. A trusted relationship between the content distributor and the content consumer is critical for the ongoing viability of DRM-protected content transactions. Unfortunately, most DRM vendors to date have focused on implementing a trusted relationship with the consumer's device, but not with the consumer, although as DRM technologies mature and as consumer awareness increases, this situation is slowly changing.

Standardisation

DRM technologies are cumbersome and can result in many content playback problems for consumers, including incompatibility with upgrades and patches for operating systems, incompatible hardware upgrades, such as sound or graphics cards, and collisions between the consumer's system and automatic upgrades from self-renewing DRM systems. DRM systems attempt to address these serious consumer concerns through DRM standards, which define an end-to-end process for content delivery and consumption, specify standardised technologies for each step of the DRM process, and provide a certification process for content providers and device manufacturers to prove compliance with the standard. Device manufacturers are the most obvious beneficiaries of widely adopted DRM standards, as they do not have to accommodate many proprietary technologies from many different content providers or DRM vendors. Content providers can benefit similarly by utilising standardised DRM technologies that can enable their content to be played on a wide range of devices, which increases the potential consumer base. Consumers also benefit from access to a wide range of content from many providers and from the transparency that published standards provide, such that the technologically savvy consumer can know what DRM hardware and software is resident on the playback devices they purchase.

What are the prevailing DRM standards, and how successful are these standards in providing efficient and effective delivery and playback for protected content? The next section looks at the common DRM standards in use today and their impact on digital resource use.

DRM standards

SDMI (Secure Digital Music Initiative)

The SDMI, a consortium of IT, consumer electronics, security technology, recording industry and Internet service provider organisations, was founded in 1998 to develop open technology specifications to enable the distribution, storage and playback of digital music in a secure but interoperable manner. SDMI issued its portable device specification pt 1, version 1.0 in 1999, which was intended to enable portable device manufacturers to develop compliant devices in time for the holiday season. The SDMI portable device specification consists of a set of principles and specifications governing applications, portable devices, media and licensed compliant modules that act as interfaces and translators between applications and portable devices/media.[28] SDMI has been inactive since 2001. As noted earlier in this chapter, a team of researchers from Princeton and Rice universities successfully cracked clips watermarked with the four SDMI technologies. The demise of SDMI can be attributed to many causes, including this much-publicised failure of encryption technologies to withstand cracking and the breakaway success of the competing Apple iTunes system, which combined a compelling device (iPod) with a lightweight and agile purchasing and playback technology to rapidly gain a commanding market share of the digital music download market.

CPSA (Content Protection System Architecture)

CPSA was developed by the 4C Entity, LLC, an organisation named after its four founding companies, IBM, Intel, Matsushita and Toshiba, in collaboration with the Copy Protection Technical Working Group, a DVD industry working group. CPSA is a content technology protection framework that encompasses a number of technologies designed primarily to protect content that is physically distributed through analog tapes or digital media such as DVD, but also for electronically distributed content. CPSA comprises 11 axioms that define how compliant devices handle copy management information, protected storage, protected playback, protected transmission and protected recording.[29] CPSA specifies technologies to protect content on personal computing and consumer electronic devices and to specify Content Management Information (CMI) to govern playback, recording and copy management for CPSA-compliant content. CPSA's three basic requirements are:

1. Protect content at its source (wherever it is stored and whenever it is copied).
2. Protect content as it is transmitted (between transmission points or between devices).
3. Protect content from unauthorised copying.

CPSA relies primarily on copy control information, watermarks and encryption. Key axioms include the access control axiom that specifies that compliant playback modules will not play back watermarked content that is not encrypted. Another axiom states that playback modules will encrypt their output to enforce the usage rules contained in a watermark. Simply put, CPSA ensures an enclosed system of protection from download to output for video and audio files that are intended to be protected for authorised use, based on usage rules. Copy management information dictates how a file should be used, watermarks carry the usage information and encryption is used to enforce usage rules, as the decryption key is only provided as usage rules dictate. CPSA is intended to protect analog and digital content, through a number of copy control technology standards that are CPSA compliant, including:

- *CSS* is an encryption technology first introduced in 1996 and is licensed primarily for encrypting content stored on DVD. CSS utilises a series of keys for encryption and decryption. Most DVD players incorporate a CSS decryption module, which can read the keys stored on the DVD in a special area that can be read by compliant drives. The keys are then passed to the decryption module via a secure handshake.[30] CSS was successfully cracked by three people, including a Norwegian teenager, Jon Johansen, who developed a program to unscramble DVD content encrypted with CSS. The decryption software, DeCSS, was first released in 1999 and is openly available via the Web in many different programming implementations for ripping protected DVD content.[31] CSS uses a multi-stage decryption process involving the title keys, disc key and player key.[32] In spite of these efforts, DVD ripping software is widely available over the Web. Content producers continue to use CSS to protect content primarily because of the vast amount of legacy DVDs that would be incompatible with a new encryption scheme. The industry tacitly acknowledges that the potential for consumer revolt, if large portions of their personal DVD libraries became unusable, was not worth the increased protection that a stronger, uncompromised encryption standard would produce. CSS for DVD proves the viability of the 'nuisance factor' axiom. DVDs are relatively inexpensive, such that the nuisance factor involved in downloading DVD ripping software and encoding decrypted video content is not worth the time and effort required, for many consumers.

- *CPPM (Content Protection for Pre-Recorded Media)* was developed for the newer DVD-Audio medium, in response to the compromised CSS. CPPM utilises a stronger encryption algorithm than CSS, key blocks, watermarking and revocation for compromised devices. However, CPPM was compromised in 2005 through audio ripping software that used a WinDVD patch to decrypt content and send the decrypted content to the hard drive rather than the sound card. The DVD-A ripping application was removed from the Rarewares site where it was first posted when legal action was threatened by the RIAA (Recording Industry Association of America).[33]

- *CGMS (Copy Generation Management System)* is information embedded in video signals, indicating whether the information can be copied, to prevent both initial and generational (copy of a copy) copying. CGMS-A, the analog standard, embeds information in NTSC line 20 or 21, which can be recognised by most digital camcorders and by some computer video capture cards, to plug the 'analog hole' by preventing recording from the physical screen of a playback device. CGMS is also implemented within DTCP and HDMI for digital transmission from source to sink devices, through transmission channels such as DVI, USB and FireWire.[30]
- *Macrovision ACP* protects analog video signals through automatic gain control and color stripe so that VCRs produce copies with color distortions, rolling stripes, dark and light cycling, and other methods for producing a severely degraded copy of analog video content that is protected against copying.[34]
- *CPRM* is a renewable copy protection format for DVD-R/RW and DVD-RAM discs. CPRM uses encryption and also ties the copy to the physical media to prevent further generational copying, through a unique media ID stored in an inaccessible area of the recordable disc. CPRM uses a block of data, the media key block, which is prerecorded on blank media. Each CPRM-compliant device reads the media key block and processes it to yield a media key unique to the device. If a circumvention device attempts to process the media to yield the same

key, it receives the wrong answer. The media key block is associated with a matrix of keys, called device keys that were generated by the CPRM licensing agency. The media key block is basically the media key encrypted over and over with licensed device keys. Each device has a different set of 16 device keys licensed for use with CPRM media keys. In this way, CPRM is able to tether CRPM-compliant media to CPRM-compliant devices without any involvement from the user or owner of the device (Lotspiech *et al.*, pp. 899–900).[35]

- *VCPS (Video Content Protection System)* provides copy-once protection for DVD+R and DVD+RW to enable direct digital recording of digital broadcasts from satellite and cable sources.[36]
- *HDCP* protects AV content from being copied over DVI and HDMI interfaces. It was developed by Intel and is licensed by Digital Content Protection, LLC.[25]
- *DTCP* protects digital content on high-performance digital interfaces such as FireWire and USB, using Hitachi's M6 encryption cipher. DTCP-IP extends DTCP to IP network connections, using the 128-bit Advanced Encryption Standard (AES). DTCP involves three keys: authentication key, exchange key and content key. DTCP will revoke a device certificate if the device's private key has been compromised or stolen. DTCP was developed by the 5C Entity and is licensed by the DTLA (Digital Transmission Licensing Administrator).[37]
- *Verance VCMS/AV Watermarking Technology* protects DVD audio, HD-DVD and Blu-ray audio content from being captured by either analog or digital recorders. The watermark is embedded transparently into the audio waveform. Multiple layers of watermarking data can be embedded, each of which can respond to a different decoder.[38]

- *AACS (Advanced Access Content System)* is a newer encryption standard for personal computing and consumer electronics devices that is intended to support high-definition content and to provide stronger protection for digital audiovisual content than the compromised CSS encryption technology provides. AACS uses 128-bit AES encryption, and a stronger key management system that involves media key block technology. AACS supports 'managed copy', allowing users to copy content from one AACS-protected medium on an AACS-compliant device to another, to support the personal, or home, networking requirements of the consumer. AACS is incorporated into the Blu-ray high-definition optical disc medium, which is emerging as the *de facto* standard for high-definition discs.[39] AACS has already been compromised, but newer versions of the standard have strengthened the encryption algorithm. AACS LA, the licensing authority, also has taken action to revoke compromised encryption keys in response to one circumvention application and begun what it terms 'proactive renewals' to 'renew and refresh' encryption keys and expire old encryption keys, thus enabling a more agile response to AACS encryption compromises.[40]

CPSA is a ubiquitous DRM framework that was particularly designed for the digital multimedia marketplace. Anyone using a DVD or Blu-ray disc is likely to experience CPSA content protection. CDs, by contrast, are largely DRM-free, in part because CD technology emerged before effective DRM strategies, and the risk of alienating consumers, with vast amounts of unprotected legacy content that would be incompatible with CD protection technologies, was too high. In fact, the commercial success of the CD distributed content is demonstrating that most consumers will pay for convenient access to resources, which is helping to convince content producers that DRM may not be the critical factor for ensuring profits from the sale or licensing of content.

There are many DRM standards in addition to the CPSA-compliant suite:

- *BD+* is an additional layer of content protection developed for Blu-ray discs. It is defined as a 'virtual machine-based content protection technology'.[41] BD+ is based on a technology called 'self-protecting digital content', which integrates content with security code such that the content becomes responsible for its own security, rather than the playback device.[42] Blu-ray also incorporates a ROM-Mark, a unique identifier embedded in Blu-ray discs that is required for disc playback but that can only be inserted on discs through equipment licensed to authorised BD-ROM manufacturers, thus preventing both casual copying and unauthorised mass copying.[43]
- *MPEG IPMP-X*. The Moving Picture Experts Group (MPEG) is responsible for a range of standards to encode and manage digital video and audio. IPMP-X (Intellectual Property Management and Protection Extension) is a DRM architecture based on principles of normative re-use of standard DRM technologies; mutual authentication to create an authenticated channel for secure communications; renewability through mutual authentication; and flexibility to select and apply any IPMP DRM tool to content at point of authorship or point of need. IPMP-X is available for MPEG-2 and MPEG-4 encoding standards. MPEG-2 is the high-bandwidth encoding standard used for DVD and high-definition content. MPEG-4 is a relatively recent encoding standard that supports multiple layers of digital information in any format (audio, video, image, text, etc.) within an encoding standard that supports a range of

transmission bandwidths, from Internet streaming to high definition. MPEG-4 Part 13 provides the IPMP-X specification for MPEG-4 systems. IPMP-X can implement any tool (watermark, encryption, authentication, etc.) as modules that perform IPMP functions. IPMP-X specifies an architecture to plug tools into an IPMP-X terminal, without specifying how these tools must perform.[44] ObjectLab, LLC offers an open source product, OpenIPMP, described as a 'content management and distribution framework for securing digital assets', for download via SourceForge.net.[45]

- *OMA DRM*. OMA DRM is a digital rights management system that emerged from the Open Mobile Alliance, a consortium of mobile system manufacturers, mobile phone manufacturers, mobile telecom providers and IT companies. OMA DRM provides specifications and test applications to ensure compliance with the specifications. Two versions of OMA DRM have been released. OMA DRM 1.0 was released in 2004 and specified three main DRM mechanisms: forward lock, which prevents downstream sharing of protected media from one mobile device to another; combined delivery of rights and media; and separate delivery of rights and metadata. OMA DRM 2.0 was released in 2006 and extends the DRM 1.0 separate delivery mechanism with a PKI infrastructure. Each device has an individual certificate with both public and private key. Each rights object is encrypted with the device public key and contains, in turn, the key to decrypt the media object. Delivery of rights objects requires registration with a Rights Issuer (RI), who also validates the device certificate against a device revocation list, using the Online Certificate Status Protocol (OCSP). This enables the exclusion of compromised devices.[46] OMA DRM v2.1 is, at the time of writing, in enabler release, defined as a release to solution providers to develop and test implementation and interoperability before the final, or approved, release. OMA DRM 2.1 enables content providers to define permissions for any type of format (ring tones, games, etc.) on any operating system or run-time environment. The encrypted content requires an associated rights object to enable playback.[47] OMA DRM includes a rights expression language that is an application profile of the Open Digital Rights Language.[48]

- *CMLA (Content Management Licensing Administrator)* 'is an LLC created by four companies – Intel, Nokia, MEI/Panasonic and Samsung – to implement a "trust model" for the Open Mobile Alliance ("OMA") Digital Rights Management ("DRM") technical specification version 2.0 standard. The CMLA trust model defines a compliant implementation of this specification for use with a wide variety of digital client devices and applications.'[49] CMLA provides the trust framework that underlies OMA DRM 2.0 implementations. CMLA licenses OMA DRM 2.0 technologies and enforces compliance with OMA DRM 2.0 requirements and in return supplies certificates and keys and attests to the trustworthiness of its licensees. CMLA has a membership consisting of organisations ranging from content providers to wireless carriers, in the categories of participant (content participant, service provider, client adopter), authorised reseller and developer.[49]

Commercial DRM systems

In addition to open standards that might be utilised by a range of commercial and non-commercial entities, there are many proprietary DRM systems that are in widespread use by virtue of the large market share that each vendor owns for part of the protected content delivery value chain. In this section, I look at several proprietary systems in widespread use.

Windows Media DRM

Windows Media DRM (WMDRM) is an end-to-end DRM system that can be applied by anyone in a Windows environment to provide secure delivery of digital media over an IP network. WMDRM includes software development toolkits to customise WMDRM components. WMDRM core components are:

- *Packaging.* WMDRM packaging encrypts the media file for secure distribution. The digital license is packaged separately from the media file. The decryption key for the encrypted media is stored in the separately encrypted license. A link to the license is included with the media file.
- *Distribution.* WMDRM supports both distribution and superdistribution (i.e. the sharing of encrypted content among different devices in a home, personal or family network).
- *License server.* A publisher chooses a license clearing-house to store specific rights and establishes a license server to authenticate the consumer's request for a license. Licenses and protected media are stored separately. Multiple license servers can be hosted by a WMDRM system, to ensure robustness for this critical WMDRM module.
- *License acquisition.* A consumer must acquire a license, which contains the decryption key and the usage rights, in order to play the encrypted content.

- *Content playback*. The playback device must support WMDRM to ensure that usage rules, such as duration and counted playbacks, are honored.

WMDRM makes each media player unique and binds the player to the host device, making it easier to identify, isolate and revoke compromised players. Digital certificates with a unique public key are issued to each client. Licenses can only be issued to authenticated clients with valid certificates. The digital media file key in the license is tied to the authenticated client to which it is issued, so that only that client can decrypt the media file key. Each license is thus 'tethered' to the device playing the content. WMDRM supports renewability and revocation for clients and third-party applications. Like most DRM implementations, WMDRM has been cracked. Renewability and revocation are used to recover from compromises without full system replacement. Another interesting feature of WMDRM is 'secure audio path' – a technology that secures the transfer of content from the media player to the sound card, so that a media file cannot be intercepted and diverted to an unprotected medium (e.g. a CD) after it is decrypted. Secure audio path is available for the Windows XP and Windows Millennium Edition operating systems.[50]

At time of writing (May 2008), WMDRM includes the following software components:

- Windows Media Rights Manager 10.1 SDK (software development kit) for content packaging and issuing licenses.
- Windows Media Format 11 SDK for building player applications.
- Windows Media DRM 10 for Portable Devices, for managing secured playback on portable devices.

- Windows Media DRM for 10 for Network Devices, for managing secured playback on networked devices.
- Microsoft Device Bridge for Windows Media DRM, for devices that transfer content to portable devices or stream content to receivers on a home network.
- Windows Media Data Session Toolkit, for the protection of content on physical media such as CD or DVD.[51]

Adobe Systems

Adobe has incorporated DRM into its digital creation applications, such as Adobe Acrobat Professional, which supports assigning digital signatures to verify a file's authenticity, file encryption, password protection for files, and role-based permissions for file access and use.[52] Adobe also offers enterprise-level DRM with its *LifeCycle ES Rights Management*, which enables secure collaboration and version control management across a network.[53] In 2007, Adobe began offering DRM for Flash videos in its Adobe Media Player, including encryption of the video stream, and tracking of content use through 'permission based analytics data'.[54]

Apple FairPlay

FairPlay is a DRM system integrated with QuickTime multimedia technology that provides DRM for protected digital files for the iPod, iTunes and iTunes Music Store applications. FairPlay utilises encrypted AAC files within an MP4 container and prevents their playback on unauthorised devices. FairPlay enables users to play their music on an unlimited number of iPods and on a limited number (five as of March 2008) of authorised computers at one time. The master key to decrypt the audio stream is encrypted within the MP4 container file. A user key is required to decrypt the master key to enable playback. When a user purchases a media file via iTunes, a new user key is generated, stored with the user's account information and stored in the encrypted key repository, where it is retrieved to decrypt the AAC audio stream. When a user authorises a new playback device, iTunes sends a unique machine identifier to the iTunes server, which manages all the user keys that are stored with the account information. This enables iTunes to ensure that all authorised devices can play the user's licensed content, and also enables iTunes to limit the number of devices by type that each customer can use to play back FairPlay-enabled content. FairPlay works smoothly within the iTunes system but is not compatible with most other DRM systems and playback devices. The iTunes server also sends the user key to the iPod, which the iPod also maintains in its encrypted key repository, to ensure that the iPod and iTunes are synchronised with regard to the protected files that can be played on the iPod.[55] iTunes has vigorously prevented competing platforms, such as RealNetworks' Harmony music platform, from converting music protected with Helix DRM to a FairPlay-compatible file that could play back on the iPod,[55] a strategy that Steve Jobs defended in a February 2007 essay titled 'Thoughts on Music'. Jobs states that the tightly controlled access provided by FairPlay DRM for the iTunes system was contractually required by music producers. He recommends that content owners distribute music without bundled DRM, noting that CDs provide DRM-free music and remain a very profitable and popular method for purchasing and listening to digital music.[56]

RealNetworks Helix Security Manager

The Helix Security Manager is a Java application that generates secure playback URLs that must be validated by the security adapter, on a Helix server or HTTP download server, before playback is authorised. Helix works on Microsoft Windows, Red Hat Enterprise Linux and Solaris platforms. Helix Security Manager supports playback to PCs and to mobile devices.[57] In 2004, RealNetworks announced plans to integrate Open Mobile Alliance DRM 2.0 into the Helix Security Manager.[58]

Emerging DRM strategies

DRM has evolved steadily from its beginnings almost a decade ago, when the focus was on securing content and devices according to very tightly defined usage rules, at great expense to user satisfaction. A significant emerging issue for DRM is interoperability, as DRM vendors acknowledge that users are ill served by completely closed distribution chains that tether the user to one system or device, such as the iPod. Interoperable DRM systems enable users to select the most appropriate content, regardless of the DRM system used to protect the content. Interoperable DRM enables users to purchase new devices without worrying about the playback of their legacy content. Interoperable DRM systems also enable vendors in any part of the content value chain to work together to offer competitive services to users.

Other developments in 'next-generation' DRM architectures include agile content delivery to a wide range of devices in the user's personal network, support for a range of business models in addition to licensed content delivery, as well as flexible support for many delivery options and platforms, including peer-to-peer, and mobile networks. OMA DRM 2.0, described in the previous section, is an example of an emerging framework, with an emphasis on flexibility and interoperability. This section looks at two other next-generation architectures: Coral Consortium's DRM architecture and Sun's Project DReaM.

Coral Consortium

The Coral Consortium is a group of organisations across the DRM value chain first organised in October 2004 to address the need for an interoperable DRM architecture. Founding members of the Coral Consortium include Hewlett Packard, InterTrust Technologies Corporation, Koninklijke Philips Electronics N.V., Panasonic (Matsushita), Samsung, Sony, and 20th Century Fox Film Corporation.[59] The Coral Consortium grew out of an interoperable architecture proposed by InterTrust called Networked Environment for Media Orchestration (NEMO).

Coral's interoperability is based upon a tiered infrastructure beginning with standardised communications using Web services; core roles that are common to most DRM transactions that can be assigned at the Coral Core Architecture applications layer; and the higher-level Coral Ecosystem, a context-based DRM implementation that might involve communities of trust across the entire supply chain. Coral ecosystems are DRM implementations specific to a business model, type of resource, type of organisation, etc., that rest at a higher-level applications layer on top of the trusted communications and core architecture layers. Web services are used to discover and invoke DRM applications to enable interoperability across independent DRM implementations.

To address interoperability, the Coral Consortium developed a set of specifications for trusted communications across different participants in the DRM value chain. These specifications define interfaces across standard components of a DRM value chain as well as an interoperability framework that enables DRM systems to coexist and to work together with minimal or no change to those systems.

The Coral DRM architecture (Figure 7.2) is a layered architecture providing for communications, core functionality and sophisticated collaborations.

- *The Coral Trusted Communications Layer* is a secure messaging service, which requires each participant to have a secure, certificate-based identity and roles associated with that identity. Each secure participant is a node. Nodes communicate using encrypted and digitally signed messages in a Web services architecture based on NEMO.
- *The Coral Core Architecture* establishes a set of core roles that appear in Coral interoperability transactions and standardises the messaging between the entities performing those roles in a Coral implementation.

Figure 7.2 **Coral DRM architecture**

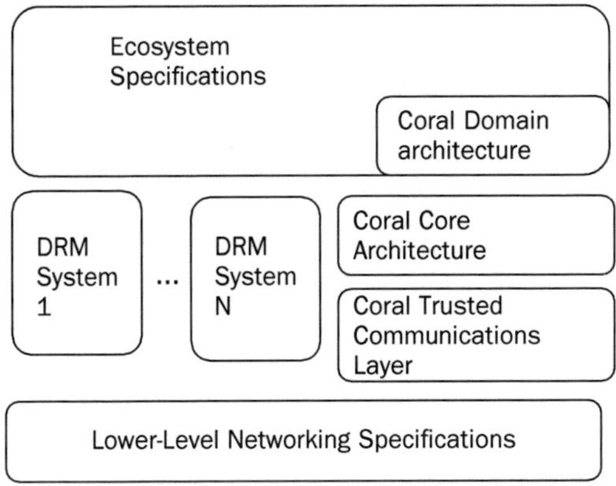

- *The Coral Domain Architecture* builds a domain, or specialised implementation, of the Coral Core Architecture to form the basis for building ecosystems among participants sharing a common business model and usage rules.
- *The Coral Ecosystem* is the digital community space in which stakeholders determine common usage models; identify DRM systems that can comply with, and enforce, these usage models; and establish a community of trust to interoperate across the DRM value chain.

One of the key concepts in the Coral architecture is that of 'license derivation' using rights tokens. A rights token is defined as a 'standardized policy artifact' (Coral Consortium, p. 5).[60] Rights tokens are not licenses and contain no keys for accessing or decrypting content but instead authorise the derivation of licenses. License derivation derives equivalent usage rules from licenses, which may be expressed in different syntaxes. Coral is premised on the concept that 'there needs to be a consistent way for various DRM licenses to be derived from a common policy artifact which is the rights token' (Coral Consortium, p. 9).[60] Much of the interoperability in the Coral architecture is based on fulfilling licenses. A license is requested through a standard interface to a Rights Mediator, which determines whether a rights token should be forwarded to the Rights Instantiator, which converts it to an appropriate license. The rights token serves in effect as a standardised 'avatar' for licenses that may be expressed in different syntaxes but that document equivalent usage policies that can be mapped and translated across DRM systems.[60]

Project DReaM

Project DReaM is a Sun Microsystems initiative to develop an open standards-based service-oriented DRM architecture that can interoperate with proprietary DRM products and technologies. DReaM decouples the DRM architecture from DRM services and technologies, such as authentication, licenses, PKI, etc., so that these become simply services available to be selected and utilised by the DReaM architecture, rather than tightly integrated components of the architecture. This approach to technology support is similar to the normative technology modules utilised in the MPEG IPMP-X framework.

DReaM separates usage rights and content protection. Usage rights contained in licenses are separately managed by license servers facilitated by DReaM, so that existing licensing strategies already in use in proprietary or open source DRM systems can be supported. DReaM supports a range of authentication services, so that DRM is not explicitly tied to a device but can be bound to users, through role-based identity management systems, such as the Liberty Alliance Project and Shibboleth. DReaM's role-based identity architecture is based upon the federated role-based identity work pioneered by the Liberty Alliance project. DReaM's development goal is transparency across content formats, devices, DRM technologies and DRM system implementations.

DReaM's focus is on disintermediation – separating service components in the authentication and content protection areas to enable multiple instances of DRM service components to coexist in an end-to-end implementation. A disintermediating agent component accepts a license request from a front-end service, directs the request to the conductor, which initiates a back-end service that conducts authentication and rights verification. The conductor then alerts the front-end service to provide a license.

DReaM is currently developing two specifications. CAS (Conditional Access System) is a 'DRM lite' specification intended to address limited conditional access scenarios. DReaM CAS will utilise open standard technologies such as

PKI, TLS and AES, to control access to resources and the conditions that govern that access. The two primary components of DReaM CAS are the DReaM Licensor, which manages the centralised components of the content control process (including the key management, protocols and interfaces), and the DReaM CAS client, which communicates with the DReaM Licensor through specified protocols and interfaces.

DReaM MMI (Mother May I) is an innovative approach to rights management that enables clients to negotiate for rights from a range of DRM systems through standardised protocols, rather than requesting a license that may be embedded with the protected content. In DReaM MMI, content keys are stored in a key and license server. Rights associated with content are stored in a rights repository (DReaM Contracts Manager). A DReaM MMI-compliant client can request protected content based on specified usage terms. The DReaM Licensor contacts the DReaM Contracts Manager to determine whether the usage terms comply with those stored in the rights repository for the content. If yes, then the terms are translated into a license for use and keys are released from the key and license server to the client. Keys, usage rights and content are all disambiguated, with a simple communication chain employed to manage the content request and access. The need for a complex rights expression language or a predefined license packaged with the content are thus avoided. DReaM MMI provides the possibility for seamlessly negotiating content from a range of content providers, without the need for compliant proprietary software clients or devices tethered to each content provider.[61]

Emerging DRM strategies and libraries

Coral and DReaM both offer opportunities for libraries to interact with DRM vendors and systems. The Coral ecosystem is designed to support a range of business models beyond the simple commercial purchase or lease of protected content. A federation of universities or libraries could establish a Coral ecosystem to support an end-to-end DRM system for high-value content that needs the protection that encryption and key management services can provide. An example might be shared courseware or student registration information. Similarly, DReaM addresses a range of content management needs, from enabling minimal resource protection to encryption and key management for high-value commercial content, such as databases and e-books. Sun has designed a DReaM MMI implementation that enables a user, identified via an Anonymising Agent based solely on the role attributes (e.g. 'student at university X'), to make fair use of a resource, as determined by the fair use exceptions in US copyright law, described in Chapter 2. The user has registered with the Anonymising Agent and completed a form indicating the fair use purpose or purposes, such as educational use, parody or review. The user thus asserts fair use through the request, which is then transmitted by the Anonymising Agent to the Service Provider. The Service Provider must grant the use, which may optionally involve applying a watermark to the content. The Service Provider may determine, through tracking the content usage via the watermark, that the use does not conform to the fair use purpose(s) asserted by the user. The Service Provider may then request the identity of the user, and if the conditions for the release of identity have been met, the Anomyising Agent will release the user identity to the Service Provider. The conditions for release of identity should have been mutually agreed upon by user and Service Provider in advance of any transaction.[62]

Both Coral and DReaM provide flexible architectures that can enable libraries to engage with commercial content distributors utilising a range of DRM implementations to provide library repositories with commercial content from a range of vendors and with the economies of scale resulting from a single resource infrastructure that supports differing usage rules and users. Although both architectures offer potential for libraries, they are emerging rather than mature strategies. Both require significant policy and business model developments in advance and considerable technical expertise to establish. As Coral and DReaM are premised on the integration of current DRM architectures and technologies, libraries collaborating with vendors for integrated access to resources may have to accept core 'ground rules' based on a commercial licensing business model that may be antithetical to the open access model preferred by libraries. Neither architecture precludes or requires current restrictive DRM technologies, but instead provides for seamless integration of these technologies as needed by the utilising organisation. The final chapter of this book, 'Putting the Pieces Together', suggests a more streamlined approach for integrating protected and open content in a repository that may be more congruent with the library and educational institution business model.

Plagiarism detection

Plagiarism detection is a niche DRM implementation that is gaining increasing traction in educational environments. Plagiarism detection software offers two plagiarism services: protecting the organisation's Web-based content from plagiarism by others and checking submitted content against known content to determine whether the submitted content is original to the author. Plagiarism software uses techniques such as forensic watermarking and pattern matching to search the Web for unauthorised use of protected content.

Plagiarism software that validates submitted documents for originality of expression through plagiarism algorithms looks for contiguous words forming phrases and sentences, using algorithms such as Rabin-Karp that seek for matching text strings or algorithms that perform distance calculations between words or phrases. An important concept for text-matching algorithms is 'nearest neighbor' search (NNS) or proximity search, where the closest point between the query to every other point in the database is calculated, in terms of physical proximity in metric space. An efficient NNS strategy is critical for efficient pattern matching, which may need to search millions of pages in order to declare authoritatively that a work does not contain plagiarised text.[63]

Techniques that increase the efficiency of plagiarism detection, which may involve matching against millions of documents, include 'shingling', in which contiguous terms, or shingles, are compared at the subdocument level. Hash values are created for sub-documents and compared, to reduce the number of comparisons the algorithm must perform, as hashes that are not identical presumably do not represent plagiarised content. Another technique involves clustering, in which documents are compared with each other and a similarity weight assigned in order to group potentially identical documents together for further, more fine-grained analysis. Both techniques involve creating hashes or unique tokens, for phrases or textual strings. Hashing provides a unique numerical value for each string that is hashed. Collisions between the submitted document and the stored hashes result in potential plagiarised content that requires further analysis, frequently by a human reading a report that highlights the matching text across the submitted document and the reference text.[64]

Plagiarism software may compare a submitted document, or a portion of a document, against a repository or database of documents. Documents submitted for testing may be added to the database, thus growing the reference database through use. Alternatively, the plagiarism application may search text strings within a submitted document or text against the Web to find documents against which more complete comparisons can be made. Some examples of plagiarism software in common use include:

- Wcopyfind, which compares documents by searching for, and reporting, matched phrases of a specified minimum length.
- Turnitin, a commercial Web-based application that compares submitted documents against billions of pages, both archived and 'in the clear'. The Turnitin archive includes documents from the Web and previously submitted student papers.
- Copyscape, a Web-based service available in free and premium versions. The free version provides a limited number of free searches, while the premium service provides an unlimited number of professional grade searches with broader coverage. An optional fee-based Copysentry service provides content scanning and matching on an automatic, ongoing basis.

Institutions should evaluate plagiarism detection applications and services with respect to copyright, privacy statutes and institutional policy. Students should understand how the application works and how their rights of authorship and identity will be safeguarded, even beyond the lifetime of the service. The service must safeguard the authors' exclusive rights to exploit their own creations throughout the term of copyright. Privacy safeguards must ensure that authorship of individual papers cannot be identified or inadvertently revealed. Before an institution implements plagiarism software, these issues of copyright and privacy must be considered and addressed. Although plagiarism is itself a serious act of copyright infringement, the compact of trust between an educational institution and its students is important for a good educational experience and for bonds of loyalty between the institution and its alumnae in the future. And of course copyright infringement and misuse of student identity have serious legal implications for the institution. As with many DRM implementations, the crimes of the few must be weighed against the ethical treatment of the many. At a minimum, the institution should ensure that the selected application does not violate the institution's published policies for copyright and identity protection. Libraries have long recognised awareness and avoidance of plagiarism as an important information literacy skill. A proactive response that a library can make to an institutional decision to utilise a plagiarism detection system is to capitalise on students' heightened interest in avoiding plagiarism with information and tutorials that assist students in understanding plagiarism and applying appropriate citation strategies for their resources.

Libraries and DRM technologies

Many commercially licensed resources are bundled with digital rights licenses or watermarks that may be imperceptible to the libraries as well as to the end users. As discussed in Chapter 2, the WIPO Copyright Treaty (WCT) and the WIPO Performances and Phonograms Treaty (WPPT), and conforming national copyright legislation, prohibit removal or tampering with copyright information and circumvention of technological protection measures (TPM) that restrict uses that are not permitted by the author or permitted under law (WIPO Copyright Treaty, art. 11).[65] Some national legislation allows circumvention by libraries in specific circumstances, such as the 2000, 2003 and 2006 rule-makings with respect to the Digital Millennium Copyright Act by the Librarian of Congress that permit circumvention of technological protection measures to enable non-infringing uses of TPM-protected resources during each 3-year interval since the law was enacted.[66] In most circumstances, libraries and their users are enjoined from tampering with either copyright information or technological protection measures, such as embedded digital licenses or watermarks that are embedded in content.

As we have seen in this chapter, licenses, watermarks and simple marks, such as region codes, are generally imperceptible to the consumer, so the library may loan a DVD or Blu-ray disc, for example, without knowledge of embedded DRM information. If a library patron attempts to circumvent a protected disc at a library computer or on their own computer, they risk revoking the device keys that enable these compliant devices to use protected media. Libraries collecting content on DRM-protected formats such as DVD, DVD-A and Blu-ray should be aware of the DRM technologies embedded in the content, as well as the DRM-compliant software and hardware applications embedded in the devices they purchase. Libraries can guard against unauthorised tampering by locking down library workstations with protection software that does not enable users to run applications.

Libraries may license resources, such as e-books, images and videos, which may require a DRM system such as Helix DRM or WMDRM to protect the files from copying or misuse. Evaluation of the DRM implementation with respect to issues such as copyright support, fair use or fair dealing protection, renewability, and degradation of transmission and playback performance should become a standard part of the resource evaluation process. In particular, for large files such as video and audio, the library should test streaming and playback performance for protected and unprotected files, as part of the trial period, to see if the DRM system requires unacceptable performance compromises for the user experience. Although there are emerging technologies with much promise for streamlined DRM implementations, the reality is that DRM technologies today are cumbersome and may require unacceptable trade-offs for a quality user experience. Another issue of concern to libraries is that DRM systems may unfairly disadvantage disabled users. Most countries provide exemptions from anti-circumvention provisions in law to support access to information for disabled users. Libraries should ensure that DRM bundled with licensed content either includes special provisions for the disabled or can be made accessible to disabled patrons in some manner, perhaps through special certificates or at designated library workstations. Needs of disabled patrons include access to captioning, the ability to enlarge file display size, and the ability to use text-to-speech and speech-to-text conversion applications.

Libraries that routinely purchase DRM-protected content may want to investigate the use of modular hardware components such as the TPM, to avoid collisions with operating systems and other applications whenever a DRM component is automatically renewed.

Increasingly, computer-intensive 'information commons' areas in libraries provide workstations dedicated to digital creation with multimedia encoding and editing software. It is important to provide copyright and plagiarism information for users that are updated to reflect the use of multimedia files in content remixing. Although students, in particular, have at least some knowledge about acceptable quotations from text, many are unaware that copyright laws also apply to digital multimedia.

Libraries have transactions that require increased protection, such as the paying of library fines with credit cards. Libraries that are part of larger organisations, such as a university or a local government, should investigate using the strategies employed by the larger institution for protecting user identity and high-value content, such as credit card information. If the institution does not have a strategy for protecting this information, the library should either negotiate for an institution-level strategy, develop its own, or wait to offer credit card payments when an acceptable DRM strategy can be developed. Hardened servers, encrypted messaging, certificates and other technologies are employed to protect credit card transactions and user identity information, such as US social security numbers. Without stringent protections, libraries can unwittingly compromise very sensitive user information and expose themselves to legal action from injured patrons. It is better to delegate the risk management for something as serious as identity theft to the library's parent organisation, rather than to attempt a solo risk management strategy within the library. In fact, many parent organisations will not permit any of its subordinate units to assume such a risk.

As this chapter demonstrates, there are hopeful signs that more agile and sophisticated DRM architectures are emerging. Currently, however, DRM remains that 'extra feature' that libraries are frequently purchasing with their hardware and resources that they would much rather not have. The best current strategy for dealing with embedded DRM is awareness – studying the system configuration and DRM specifications that vendors provide. Be aware that in many cases, this investigation is a two-step process, where you first identify the hardware or applications (e.g. Helix server) and then determine if any DRM is resident. The DRM components of any given product are marketed to the content rights holder, not to the user.

You then need to ask how your vendor is applying the DRM. Questions to ask include: what is deposited on library or user devices, if and how the content can be experienced by non-compliant devices, how the license or device key for a device that may be revoked in error or through patron misuse can be replaced or renewed, how renewability occurs and whether the library can choose to opt out, how patrons with disabilities can be accommodated, and any number of other issues specific to the content and its particular uses.

In this and the preceding chapters, I have examined every entity in the DRM model, ending with the technologies and DRM standards that provide the glue to bring all the entities in the model together in a secure digital conversation. The final chapter will look at the broader role for libraries as actors in the DRM development space.

Notes and references

1. Coyle, Karen. *The Technology of Rights: Digital Rights Management, Based on a Talk Originally Given at the Library of Congress, November 19, 2003*. Last accessed 25 March 2008. *http://www.kcoyle.net/drm_basics.pdf*
2. Free Software Foundation. *Digital Restrictions Management and Treacherous Computing*. Boston, MA: Free Software Foundation. Last modified 18 September 2006. Last accessed 25 March 2008. *http://www.fsf.org/campaigns/drm.html*
3. Demerjian, Charlie. (2006) 'DRM is a complete lie: opinion, it has never protected a single thing'. *The Inquirer: News, Reviews, Facts and Friction*. London: The Inquirer. Last accessed 25 March 2008. *http://www.theinquirer.net/en/inquirer/news/2006/01/23/drm-is-a-complete-lie*

4. Varian, Hal, Farber, David, Manferdelli, John, Green, Lucky, and Alben, Alex. (2003) 'Impacts of DRMs on innovation, competition & security'. *The Law & Technology of DRM Conference Transcrirptions*. Berkeley, CA: Berkeley Center for Law and Technology. Last accessed 25 March 2008. *http://www.law.berkeley.edu/institutes/bclt/drm/trans/drm-2-28-p2.htm*
5. European Commission. (1991) *Information Security Evaluation Criteria (TSEC): Provisional Harmonised Criteria, Version 1.2* Document COM(90) 314. Brussels: European Commission. Last accessed 25 March 2008. *http://www.ssi.gouv.fr/site_documents/ITSEC/ITSEC-uk.pdf*
6. Wikipedia. *Public-key Cryptography*. St. Petersburg, FL: Wikimedia Foundation, Inc. Last modified 18 May 2008. Last accessed 18 May 2008. *http://en.wikipedia.org/wiki/Public-key_cryptography*
7. Wikipedia. *Public Key Infrastructure*. St. Petersburg, FL: Wikimedia Foundation, Inc. Last modified 6 May 2008. Last accessed 18 May 2008. *http://en.wikipedia.org/wiki/Public_key_infrastructure*
8. Miodrag, J., *et al.* (2006) 'A novel broadcast encryption based on time-bound cryptographic keys'. Safavi-Naini, Reihaneh and Yung, Moti, eds. *Digital Rights Management: Technologies, Issues, Challenges and Systems, First International Conference, DRMTICS 2005, Sydney, Australia, October/November 2005, Revised Selected Papers*. Berlin, Germany: Springer-Verlag: 258–276.
9. Cooper, D., Santesson, S., Farrell, S., Boeyen, S., Housley, R. and Polk, W. (2008) *Internet X.509 Public Key Infrastructure Certificate and Certificate Revocation List (CRL) Profile, Request for Comments 5280*. Sterling, VA: Network Working Group, IETF, May 2008. Last accessed 18 May 2008. *http://www.ietf.org/rfc/rfc5280.txt*
10. Hartung, Frank and Ramme, Friedhelm. (2000) 'Digital rights management and watermarking of multimedia content for M-commerce applications'. *IEEE Communications Magazine*, 78–84.
11. Mintzer, Fred, Lotspiech, Jeffrey and Morimoto, Norishige. (1997) 'Safeguarding digital library contents and users: digital

watermarking'. *D-Lib Magazine*. Last accessed 18 May 2008. *http://www.dlib.org/dlib/december97/ibm/12lotspiech.html*

12. Wikipedia. *Steganography.* St. Petersburg, FL: Wikimedia Foundation, Inc. Last modified 13 May 2008. Last accessed 18 May 2008. *http://en.wikipedia.org/wiki/Steganograph*
13. Felten, Edward. (2000) *SDMI Challenge FAQ*. Princeton, NJ: Princeton University. Last accessed 25 March 2008. *http://www.cs.princeton.edu/sip/sdmi/faq.html*
14. Eastlake, Donald, Reagle, Joseph, and Solo, David, eds. (2002) *XML-Signature Syntax and Processing, W3C Recommendation 12 February 2002*. Sterling, VA: IETF W3C. Last accessed 18 May 2008. *http://www.w3.org/TR/xmldsig-core/*
15. Yong, Seunglin and Lee, Sang-Ho. (2006) 'An efficient fingerprinting scheme with secret sharing'. Safavi-Naini, Reihaneh and Yung, Moti, eds. *Digital Rights Management: Technologies, Issues, Challenges and Systems, First International Conference, DRMTICS 2005, Sydney, Australia, October/November 2005, Revised Selected Papers.* Berlin: Springer-Verlag: 192–202.
16. Rosenblatt, Bill. (2007) 'Thoughts on notice, takedown, fingerprints and filtering.' *DRM Watch*. Darien, CT: Jupitermedia, 15 March 2007. Last accessed 18 May 2008. *http://www.drmwatch.com/legal/article.php/3665921*
17. Maniatis, Petros, Giuli, T.J. and Baker, Mary. (2001) 'Enabling the long-term archival of signed documents through time stamping'. Stanford, CA: Stanford University. Last modified 1 February 2008. Last accessed 25 March 2008. *http://arxiv.org/PS_cache/cs/pdf/0106/0106058v1.pdf*
18. Kirkman, Catherine S. (2006) *Digital Rights Management: Law & Technology, 23rd Annual Institute on Computer and Internet Law, Practicing Law Institute, March 9–10, 2006.* Palo Alto, CA: Wilson, Sonsini, Goodrich, & Rosatti. Last accessed 26 March 2008. *http://www.svmedialaw.com/PLI%20DRM%20outline%2001-08-06.pdf*
19. Coyle, Karen. (2006) 'The automation of rights.' Preprint. *The Journal of Academic Librarianship* 32(2): 326–329. Last accessed 25 March 2008. *http://www.kcoyle.net/jal-32-3.html*

20. SD Card Association. (2008) *About the SD Memory Card.* San Ramon, CA: SD Card Association. Last accessed 25 March 2008. *http://www.sdcard.org/about/memory_card/*
21. Trusted Computing Group. (2008) *The Trusted Platform Module (TPM) FAQ.* Beaverton, OR: Trusted Computing Group. Last accessed 25 March 2008. *https://www.trustedcomputinggroup.org/faq/TPMFAQ/*
22. Trusted Computing Group. (2008) *The Trusted Platform Module (TPM) Specifications.* Beaverton, OR: Trusted Computing Group. Last accessed 25 March 2008. *https://www.trustedcomputinggroup.org/specs/TPM/*
23. SVP Alliance. *SVP Secure Video Processor, Digital Content Protection, Anytime, Anywhere!* Newport Beach, CA: SVP Alliance. Last accessed 25 March 2008. *http://www.svpalliance.org/docs/SVP_datasheet.pdf*
24. Wikipedia. *Transport Layer Security.* St. Petersburg, FL: Wikimedia Foundation, Inc. Last modified 17 May 2008. Last accessed 18 May 2008. *http://en.wikipedia.org/wiki/Transport_layer_security*
25. Digital Content Protection LLC. (2006) *High-bandwidth Digital Content Protection System, Revision 1.3.* Beaverton, OR: Digital Content Protection LLC. Last accessed 25 March 2008. *http://www.digital-cp.com/files/static_page_files/8006F925-129D-4C12-C87899B5A76EF5C3/HDCP_Specification%20Rev1_3.pdf*
26. Andre, Michael. *Digital Transmission Content Protection ('DTCP').* Morgan Hill, CA: Digital Transmission Licensing Administrator, LLC. Last accessed 25 March 2008. *http://www.uspto.gov/web/offices/dcom/olia/teachcomments/digitaltransmn.pdf*
27. Wikipedia. *Mark Weiser.* St. Peterburg, FL: Wikimedia Foundation, Inc. Last modified 23 January 2008. Last accessed 25 March 2008. *http://en.wikipedia.org/wiki/Mark_Weiser*
28. *Secure Digital Music Initiative.* (1995–2007) Copyright Website, LLC. Last accessed 25 March 2008. *http://www.benedict.com/Digital/Internet/SDMI.aspx#*
29. Intel Corporation, et al. (2000) *Content Protection System Architecture: a Comprehensive Framework for Content*

Protection, Revision 0.81. Morgan Hill, CA: 4C Entity, LLC. Last accessed 25 March 2008. *http://www.4centity.com/data/tech/cpsa/cpsa081.pdf*

30. Taylor, Jim. (2008) *DVD Frequently Asked Questions (And Answers)*. DVD Demystified. Last accessed 25 March 2008. *http://dvddemystified.com/dvdfaq.html*
31. Touretzky, David S. *Gallery of CSS Descramblers*. Pittsburgh, PA: Computer Science Department, Carnegie Mellon University. Last modified 13 February 2008. Last accessed 25 March 2008. *http://www.cs.cmu.edu/~dst/DeCSS/Gallery/*
32. Ziff-Davis Media (2002) 'CSS: Under the Hood'. *Protecting Digital Assets: Digital Content Protection, Part III*. New York: ExtremeTech, Ziff-Davis Media. Last accessed 25 March 2008. *http://www.extremetech.com/article2/0,1697,1231654,00.asp*
33. Robinson, Stuart M. (2005) 'DVD-audio copy protection defeated via WinDVD software hack'. *High Fidelity Review DVD Audio News Story*. Updated 7 September 2005. Last accessed 25 March 2008. *http://www.highfidelityreview.com/news/news.asp?newsnumber=14550899*
34. Macrovision Corporation. (2005) *Secure DVD Content in Today's Digital Home*. Santa Clara, CA: Macrovision Corporation. Last accessed 19 May 2008. *http://www.macrovision.com/webdocuments/PDF/acpdvd_brochure.pdf?link_id=productsResources*
35. Lotspiech, Jeffrey, Nusser, Stefan and Pestoni, Florian. (2004) 'Anonymous Trust: digital rights management using broadcast encryption'. *Proceedings of the IEEE* 92, no. 6: 898–909.
36. Philips Intellectual Property and Standards. (2004–2006) *Video Content Protection System, VCPS*. Eindhoven, The Netherlands: Koninklijke Philips Electronics NV. Last accessed 25 March 2008. *http://www.ip.philips.com/licensing/vcps*
37. Digital Transmission Licensing Administrator. *Digital Transmission Content Protection (DTCP): Technical and Licensing Overview*. Last accessed 25 March 2008. *http://www.dtcp.com/data/DTCP_Overview.pdf*

38. Verance. 'Verance Technology' *Verance* [home page]. San Diego, CA: Verance. Last accessed 19 May 2008. *http://www.verance.com/technology/index.php*
39. Intel Corporation, et al. (2006) *Advanced Access Content System (AACS): Introduction and Common Cryptographic Elements, Revision 0.91*. Beaverton, OR: AACS LA LLC. Last accessed 26 March 2008. *http://www.aacsla.com/specifications/specs091/AACS_Spec_Common_0.91.pdf*
40. AACS LA. (2007) *News: AACS LA Announces Security Updates*. Beaverton, OR: AACS LA. Last accessed 25 March 2008. *http://www.aacsla.com/news/*
41. BD+ Technologies, LLC. (2007) *BD+ Technologies Launches Content Protection Licensing Program*. Los Angeles: BD+ Technologies, LLC. Last accessed 26 March 2008. *http://www.bdplusllc.com/news*
42. Cryptography Research, Inc. *About SPDC*. San Francisco, CA: Cryptography Research, Inc. Last accessed 19 May 2008. *http://www.cryptography.com/technology/spdc/index.html*
43. Wikipedia. *ROM-Mark*. St. Petersburg, FL: Wikimedia Foundation, Inc. Last modified 28 March 2008. Last accessed 19 May 2008. *http://en.wikipedia.org/wiki/ROM-Mark*
44. Chiariglione, Leonardo. *MPEG-4 IPMP Extension*. Last accessed 26 March 2008. *http://www.chiariglione.org/mpeg/faq/mp4-sys/sys-faq-ipmp-x.htm*
45. Objectlab, LLC. (2001–2003) 'Key concepts.' *OpenIPMP: Open-source Rights Management*. New York: Objectlab, LLC. Last accessed 25 March 2008. *http://objectlab.com/clients/openipmp/id34.htm*
46. Wikipedia. *OMA DRM*. St. Petersburg, FL: Wikimedia Foundation, Inc. Last modified 14 January 2008. Last accessed 26 March 2008. *http://en.wikipedia.org/wiki/OMA_DRM*
47. Open Mobile Alliance. (2008) *OMA Digital Rights Management V2.1*. San Diego: Open Mobile Alliance. Last accessed 25 March 2008. *http://www.openmobilealliance.org/Technical/release_program/drm_v2_1.aspx*
48. *The ODRL Initiative* [home page]. Last updated 14 February 2008. Last accessed 25 March 2008. *http://odrl.net/*

49. Content Management License Administrator. *CMLA Overview and Answers*. Last accessed 26 March 2008. *http://www.cm-la.com/about/faq.aspx*
50. Microsoft Corporation. (2005) *Windows Media DRM FAQ*. Redmond, WA: Microsoft Corporation. Last accessed 25 March 2008. *http://www.microsoft.com/windows/windowsmedia/forpros/drm/faq.aspx*
51. Microsoft Corporation. (2008) *Platform Components of Windows Media DRM*. Redmond, WA: Microsoft Corporation. Last accessed 26 March 2008. *http://www.microsoft.com/windows/windowsmedia/forpros/drm/components.aspx*
52. Adobe Systems, Inc. (2008) *Protect Sensitive Information*. San Jose, CA: Adobe Systems, Inc. Last accessed 26 March 2008. *http://www.adobe.com/products/acrobat/solutions/detail/protect_info.html*
53. Adobe Systems, Inc. (2007) *Adobe Solutions for Digital Rights Management*. San Jose, CA: Adobe Systems, Inc. Last accessed 26 March 2008. *http://www.adobe.com/manufacturing/pdfs/drm_sb.pdf*
54. Adobe Systems, Inc. (2007) *Adobe Unveils Next Generation Internet Video Solution*. San Jose, CA: Adobe Systems, Inc. Last accessed 26 March 2008. *http://www.adobe.com/aboutadobe/pressroom/pressreleases/200704/041607AMP.html*
55. Wikipedia. *FairPlay*. St. Peterburg, FL: Wikimedia Foundation, Inc. Last modified 23 February 2008. Last accessed 26 March 2008. *http://en.wikipedia.org/wiki/FairPlay*
56. Jobs, Steve. (2007) *Thoughts on Music*. Cupertino, CA: Apple. Last accessed 26 March 2008. *http://www.apple.com/hotnews/thoughtsonmusic/*
57. RealNetworks, Inc. *Media Security*. Seattle, WA: RealNetworks, Inc. Last accessed 26 March 2008. *http://www.realnetworks.com/products/security/index.html*
58. RealNetworks, Inc. (2004) *RealNetworks to Expand Reach of the Helix Platform through Integration of OMA DRM 2.0*. Seattle, WA: RealNetworks, Inc. Last accessed 26 March 2008. *http://www.realnetworks.com/company/press/releases/2004/omadrm.html*

59. Coral Consortium. (2007) *Documents and FAQs*. Fremont, CA: Coral Consortium Corporation. Last accessed 26 March 2008. *http://www.coral-interop.org/main/faqs/faqs.html*
60. Coral Consortium. (2007) *Coral Core Architecture Specification*, CCAWC. Fremont, CA: Coral Consortium Corporation. Last accessed 26 March 2008. Available for download at: *http://www.coral-interop.org/main/specifications/Index_4.0.html*
61. Fernando, Gerard, Jacobs, Tom and Swaminathan, Vishy. (2005) *Project DReaM: An Architectural Overview, White Paper.* Santa Clara, CA: Sun Microsystems, Inc. Last accessed 26 March 2005. *http://openmediacommons.org/collateral/DReaM-Overview.pdf*
62. Sun Microsystems Laboratories. (2008) *Support for Fair Use with Project DReaM: Version 1.0* Santa Clara, CA: Sun Microsystems, Inc. Last accessed 26 March 2008. *http://www.openmediacommons.org/collateral/DReaM-MMI-Fair-Use-v1.0-CClicensed.pdf*
63. Wikipedia. *Nearest Neighbor Search*. St. Peterburg, FL: Wikimedia Foundation, Inc. Last modified 23 March 2008. Last accessed 26 March 2008. *http://en.wikipedia.org/wiki/Nearest_neighbor_search*
64. Wikipedia. *Near Duplicate Algorithms*. St. Peterburg, FL: Wikimedia Foundation, Inc. Last modified 23 March 2008. Last accessed 26 March 2008. *http://en.wikipedia.org/wiki/Near_Duplicate_Algorithms*
65. WIPO. *WIPO Copyright Treaty, adopted in Geneva on December 20, 1996*. Geneva: World Intellectual Property Organization. Last accessed 26 March 2008. *http://www.wipo.int/treaties/en/ip/wct/trtdocs_wo033.html#P66_786\5*
66. American Library Association. *DMCA Section 1201 Anti-Circumvention Rule Making*. Chicago, IL: American Library Association. Last updated 4 December 2006. Last accessed 26 March 2008. *http://www.ala.org/ala/washoff/woissues/copyrightb/federallegislation/dmca/section1201/sec1201.cfm*

8

Putting the pieces together

Now that you are at the end of this book, you should have a good understanding of all the components of a DRM strategy. This chapter will help you decide on the next steps to implement DRM on behalf of your patrons and the library profession. It also looks at emerging issues that are still to be resolved and makes recommendations for the next steps in DRM for libraries and their users.

Although the book, I hope, provides a good overview of the current legal and technical landscape, what should be clear is that DRM is a volatile area, with continuous developments in treaty, law and technology. However, the underlying concepts of good DRM policy and practise remain the same. This book was structured around a model placing equal attention on the object, the rights owner and the rights user.

This final chapter looks at recommendations for an effective digital rights management strategy for each entity of the model (Figure 8.1), as well as a research and advocacy agenda so that libraries can take their rightful place as key stakeholders and innovators in DRM.

The object

Authentic, readily available resources are at the heart of any effective DRM implementation. Content users have a basic

Figure 8.1 **Digital rights management model**

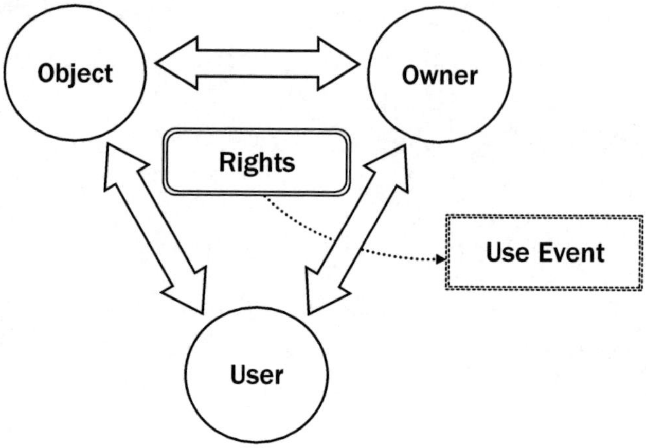

right to the resource that they expect, containing authentic information, whether the user has paid a fee for the access or not. One of the most critical decisions a library will make is the identification strategy for the digital objects it creates or collects. An important first step in developing an identification strategy is to decide on the nature of the object in your repository. As the review of information models in Chapter 4 demonstrates, this is not an easy task, particularly for complex objects such as a digital book or a website that may consist of many objects related either hierarchically or by intellectual content and related use. New technologies, such as the OAI-ORE model and protocol, are emerging to enable object managers and object users to build and document relationships among individual digital objects.

An identification strategy should be adopted that enables the library and the user to identify, select and retrieve digital objects within the library repository. This identification strategy should support both current and future assumptions about the nature of the information object and enable interoperability with other libraries and complementary digital initiatives. Taking the time to test, analyze and develop a position on identification of the digital object should be one of the first steps any library considering a digital collection or repository should take. The California Digital Library (CDL, a consortium of University of California system libraries) is a leader in the area of digital object identification. CDL, under the leadership of John Kunze, made a thorough analysis of the digital object identification landscape, particularly with regard to its own needs, before choosing to develop the ARK (Archival Resource Key) identifier system.[1] I do not recommend developing your own identifier system, unless you really feel your unique circumstances cannot be met by the many excellent identification standards that are readily available, but I do recommend taking the time to analyze your collections and their identification needs, and then basing your identification strategy on that analysis. Any identifier selected should be evaluated and tested before full adoption. Many identifier systems are actionable and require as a minimum a server, and in some cases a client-server implementation. A robust, interoperable identifier strategy should underpin a good object management strategy. Implementing a solid, extensible identifier strategy that will serve your library's object management needs for many years is worth the initial effort involved in selection, testing and implementation.

Provenance metadata is also critical for establishing the authenticity of an object. Provenance metadata should document all the circumstances surrounding the creation of the object, including the roles of the different actors involved in the creation and distribution of the object. As Chapter 3 explained, the copyrights and related rights surrounding works with multiple authorship are complex. Libraries do not really have a role to play in the adjudication of copyright and ownership among the various interested parties, but they do have a critical role to play in setting standards for the documentation of these agents and their roles. The Rutgers Community Repository (RUcore) bibliographic utility provides documentation for provenance events with documentation of all associated agents and their roles in a METS implementation, available as open source at the RUcore website. Figure 8.2 illustrates the metadata entry form for provenance event. Libraries can edit or replace the controlled vocabularies (ProvenanceEventType, AssociatedEntityRole) to accommodate any event type and any role that an agent can play. The RUcore bibliographic utility also provides rights

Figure 8.2 **Metadata entry form, RUcore open source bibliographic utility**

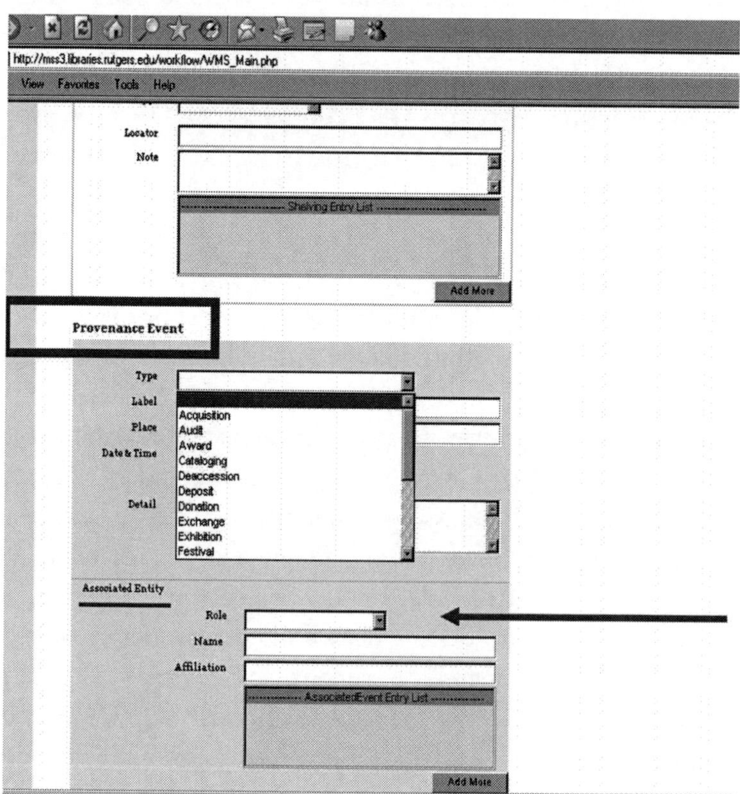

events for documenting licenses and deeds of gift as well as the documentation of multiple rights holders and their roles with contact information.[2]

In the digital space, articles and books can be corrected without the need for published errata. The distinction between continuing resources, such as newspapers and serials, and monographs, such as books, is blurring, as there is theoretically no need for any digital information object to be a completed, unchanging object. This book is almost certainly out of date with respect to some of the technologies and standards it describes, even as you are reading it. In the digital space, there is theoretically no need for a book such as this one to ever be out of date. I use the term 'theoretically' because the practical limits are on the ability of the author to continually refresh the content to reflect new information, rather than the technology for updating the digital text, which has an unlimited capability to provide a constantly updated information object.

There is a real need for new definitions to replace the print-based concept of 'edition'. New definitions and digital curation practises need to be developed to document versions and changes to digital objects and to identify the types of changes. Were errors corrected or was content replaced to reflect new developments in the object's topic? Is it sufficient to document all changes in digital provenance events that can be quickly scanned by a user or does a new version need to be declared that supersedes the previous version? Should the previous version be archived or abandoned? Once an object is part of the digital information space, it may be used by others to build forward on its conceptual and thematic content. It is important that previous versions of a work are archived in such a way that the evidentiary chain among digital objects that cite and build upon each other is maintained. Is the concept of the immutable digital object still valid in the digital information space, where currency of information, an often elusive goal, can potentially be achieved? Is the digital object no longer a marriage of durable structure and durable content but perhaps a relatively durable structure for continuously changing content, in which the structure provides both an organising construct, including navigation and tools for quickly identifying and reviewing changes to content, and in which authenticity resides in the documentation of change and archiving of superseded information rather than in the concept of authoritative, 'canonical' content? E-book publishers are beginning to explore the mutability of content and thus the disappearance of the distinction between monograph and continuing resource. The library, in its role as informed surrogate and advocate for the user, has an important role to play in discussions with publishers, distributors and creators, to develop and implement answers to these important questions about the competing needs of immutability and currency for authoritative information.

Although all libraries should develop an archiving strategy for their locally digitised resources, there are no similar requirements for commercial publishers. LOCKSS (Lots of Copies Keep Stuff Safe),[3] its companion project CLOCKSS (Controlled LOCKSS)[4] and Portico[5] are three initiatives to archive electronic journals, particularly those journals under the management of commercial vendors. Many journal publishers and distributors are now participating in Portico, LOCKSS and CLOCKSS. Libraries can exercise influence on journals without a preservation platform as part of the license negotiation process, by making an archiving strategy, either by the publisher or by the library, as a condition for subcription. Libraries can also advocate with the authors of the articles in these journals to consider a long-term archiving policy as one of the criteria, along with peer review and ranking within the subject domain, when selecting a publication for their work. The long-term availability of their articles is important for ensuring the durable impact of their creative work. Academic libraries can be strong advocates for the open access movement, encouraging their research faculty to actively support open access to the products of their research. The Harvard University Faculty of Arts and Sciences 'voted ... to give the University a worldwide license to make each faculty member's scholarly articles available and to exercise the copyright in the articles, provided that the articles are not sold for a profit.'[6] Other models can include requiring permanent archiving of scholarly articles in the institutional repository, as a condition for inclusion in the faculty member's tenure packet. These are momentous policy changes for research faculty and the library must do its part by providing a robust and flexible institutional repository that can support any open access policy that a university or a faculty might adopt. Many commercial publishers require embargoes, so that the publisher can exploit the intellectual content before it is made openly available. DRM strategies employed within the repository, such as XACML policies supporting delayed access, are an important strategy for enabling faculty to meet the conditions of journal publishers in order to make their articles openly accessible.

Rights holder/creator

One of the most critical roles that libraries can play with respect to the creator is that of *education*. Authors of scholarly works are increasingly aware of copyright issues with regard to their works. The SPARC *Author's Addendum*, provided on SPARC's *Resources for Authors* website, provides excellent guidance for creators of scholarly works in negotiating a publishing contract that enables archiving and reuse of the author's work.[7] However, any creative work that is fixed in a tangible medium is protected by copyright in every country with copyright laws. Digital technologies, particularly the Web, have made it extremely easy to share digital resources through personal networking sites such as YouTube, Facebook and Flickr, and through blogs, wikis and other information-sharing technologies. Even individuals who do not routinely share their family history on the Web are sharing photos and digital video clips via email or their mobile phones. Most creators are unaware that these are now copyrighted works and that copyright will persist for 50–70 years beyond their lifetimes.

The Creative Commons initiative is a true licensing success story that has more than lived up to its mission to add depth and richness to the open information space. Creative Commons has moved into licensing for data and for open source software applications and has also restructured its metadata into an RDF-based schema, ccREL, that is optimised for XMP delivery. Creative Commons makes open source licensing intelligible and simple to apply for the individual creator. Creative Commons also makes available its web services utilities for selecting and applying licenses.[8] Libraries creating digital collections of historical and cultural artifacts could implement Creative Commons licensing web services and encourage local residents to share their personal artifacts with current and future local history enthusiasts by uploading their artifacts into the library's portal and assigning a Creative Commons license, thus ensuring that today's artifacts become tomorrow's historical record. Libraries that are creating institutional repositories can encourage faculty to assign Creative Commons licenses to their research products, such as article preprints and postprints and research data in all formats, as long as they hold the rights to their works. The result will be research resources that are not only widely available for reading and citing via the institutional repository, but available in perpetuity for a broad range of reuse by other scholars.

Many people might be wary of sharing personal memorabilia with an unknown audience, but after the passage of several decades, as the subjects of photographs and correspondence grow up or pass on, issues of family privacy tend to fade, yet the term of copyright persists. By the time these artifacts can be made available for the historical and cultural record, the digital formats may be obsolete and no one may remember any details about the provenance and subjects of images, video, etc. Generally, even the creator is no longer known.

Libraries that are creating historical and cultural portals today that rely on artifacts of the past should think also about today's artifacts that are critical components of tomorrow's history. As noted earlier in this chapter, libraries can – and in fact are beginning to – encourage their patrons to contribute their own artifacts and memorabilia to local history portals. Implementing a Creative Commons licensing platform behind local history portals can enable long-term access to these copyrighted resources. In addition, libraries can encourage users to practice good documentation and management practises for their photo albums, scrapbooks, etc., by using archival quality supplies and including relevant and detailed information that can benefit future generations of their own family as well as tomorrow's historical researchers. The New Jersey Digital Highway, a statewide cultural heritage portal, provides guidance and a license for individual creators to use to preserve and document their personal memorabilia for future generations.[9]

A neglected area for educating creators of tangible works is to encourage copyright registration, in countries that offer this service. Copyright registration is generally inexpensive and frequently as simple as completing an online form. A copyright registration record can help to ensure that the creator can be contacted if a publisher or individual wishes to reuse the work in some manner that requires the creator's permission. Copyright registration can thus play an important role in the long-term impact of the work. Before registration, the creator must be certain that the terms of his/her contract with a publisher do not preclude copyright registration by the creator, as a contract may mean the transfer of rights to a publisher. Being aware of the benefits of copyright registration can encourage an author to look more carefully at any transfer of rights contained in a publisher's contract. Publishers can also be encouraged to register copyright on behalf of the author, or jointly with the author, as part of the publication process.

A critical area for leadership by libraries, archives and museums is in the documentation of the rights holder, to provide authoritative information about rights holders, to provide those who would reuse copyright-protected works with the ability to contact rights holders, while still protecting the privacy of rights holders, and to identify the roles of creators with respect to works of multiple authorship. Libraries are active advocates for copyright legislation that is less restrictive for resource users. A neglected area of advocacy is to encourage national agencies, such as a copyright registration authority or a national library, to provide coordination of national-level rights holder directories, with links to national-level authority records, and with processes to protect the privacy of rights holders. National agencies should be encouraged to coordinate the development of an online rights holder directory that enables individual creators to complete and update directory forms, and that provides simple methods for libraries, to batch-upload directory information. This directory should include all rights holders, from creators to publishers and distributors, to enable those who wish to reuse works to contact rights holders quickly and to obtain rights. Emerging creator directories[14] are an important first step but a more expansive international approach is needed.

Resource user

In the DRM arena, resource users are most impacted by terms and conditions within licenses that restrict their ability to use resources and by resource usage tracking technologies that may violate the user's right to make private use of information resources. Chapter 6 discusses the changing world of the user license. License standards such as PLUS and ONIX-PL, discussed at length, and tools such as the XMP standard for metadata contained within file headers, will make it fairly easy to market individual digital resources, with accompanying end user licenses, directly to users. They will also make it possible to track downstream use, particularly as digital rights information that is embedded in a resource cannot be changed or removed without infringing copyright treaty and law.

Libraries have always licensed resources for the benefit of their users, from the newspapers that were placed on wooden poles for public reading to complex e-journal aggregations. The important role of libraries in the digital licensing arena is reflected by the Digital Library Federation Electronic Resource Management Initiative (DLF ERMI) that forms the basis of most commercial ERM systems available today. Libraries continue to play an important role as an informed advocate for users, to ensure that digital licenses, particularly licenses for individual resources or components, are equitable, respect user privacy and lead to increased options for obtaining resources without increased cost to libraries and to users. The commercial license standards community has shown a willingness to work with the library community. PLUS Coalition membership is open to individuals and consortia and has involved library and museum consortia in its governance. EDItEUR is working with the DLF ERMI to develop interoperability practises between the ONIX-PL license framework and the ERMI data dictionary.[10] Libraries should build upon this interest to engage in opportunities to examine and evaluate new versions of digital license standards. Libraries should evaluate all licenses for issues such as user privacy and usage tracking, but also to ensure that as technologies have now made it practicable for licensing of resources to travel full circle from the individual resource to the aggregation of resources and back to the individual resource, the benefit accrued from a greater number of resources available to users and the increase in the user base does not outweigh any disadvantages such as complexity of access or the cost of the component parts being always greater than the cost for the original 'whole' resource.

New methods of licensing will also have a significant impact on library workflow, particularly for managing rights to digital resources. Libraries need to advocate with their integrated library system vendors, or with the developers of open library systems, to support new digital workflows, for resources with one or more embedded licenses, from ordering and invoicing to user access and interlibrary loan.

Libraries should also advocate with resource licensors to make works openly available for reuse in education, scholarship and personal research. ARTStor, the image database, together with the Metropolitan Museum of Art, has an innovative licensing program, *Images for Academic Publishing* (IAP) that makes nearly 1700 images available for reuse in articles, dissertations, etc. Users must agree to the 'terms and conditions of use', which grants a 'worldwide, royalty-free, non-exclusive, perpetual license to exercise the rights in the Images' for academic publishing, including publications with a print run of 2000 copies or fewer, an educational website that does not accept advertisements and other specified publishing venues.[11] Libraries can advocate for other publishers to follow suit, or at least to make resources more easily licensed for reuse. Currently, the effort for enabling reuse rests with the author, who must determine what rights he or she has to enable reuse and then, in some cases, to petition the publisher for reuse rights. Authors should ask that the policy and process for requesting reuse be included in the author's contract. Authors can use the *SHERPA/RoMEO Publisher Copyright Policies & Self-archiving* database, described in Chapter 2, to assist them in selecting a journal with appropriate policies for authors' rights for self-archiving and reuse.

Libraries and archives can serve rights holders and resource users through the development of community best practises, which can establish fair use or fair dealing practises, and develop 'best effort' strategies for locating and contacting creators of resources, so that if efforts to locate the creator fail, the work can be declared an 'orphan work'. In countries with orphan works legislation, libraries that are able to demonstrate a diligent effort to locate the rights holder that conforms to rigorous and published community best practice will be able to make works without an identifiable or locatable creator openly available for the public good. The Center for Social Media at American University in Washington, DC, produced a seminal community best practise, *Code of Best Practices in Fair Use for Online Video* in July 2008.[12] Part of the *Code*, the *Documentary Filmmakers' Statement*, has been successfully tested in the US courts and has already transformed the use of copyright-protected resource excerpts in documentaries. More recently, the Open Data Commons has released draft *ODC Community Norms* for the open sharing of data.[13] The

Figure 8.3 **RUcore rights event**

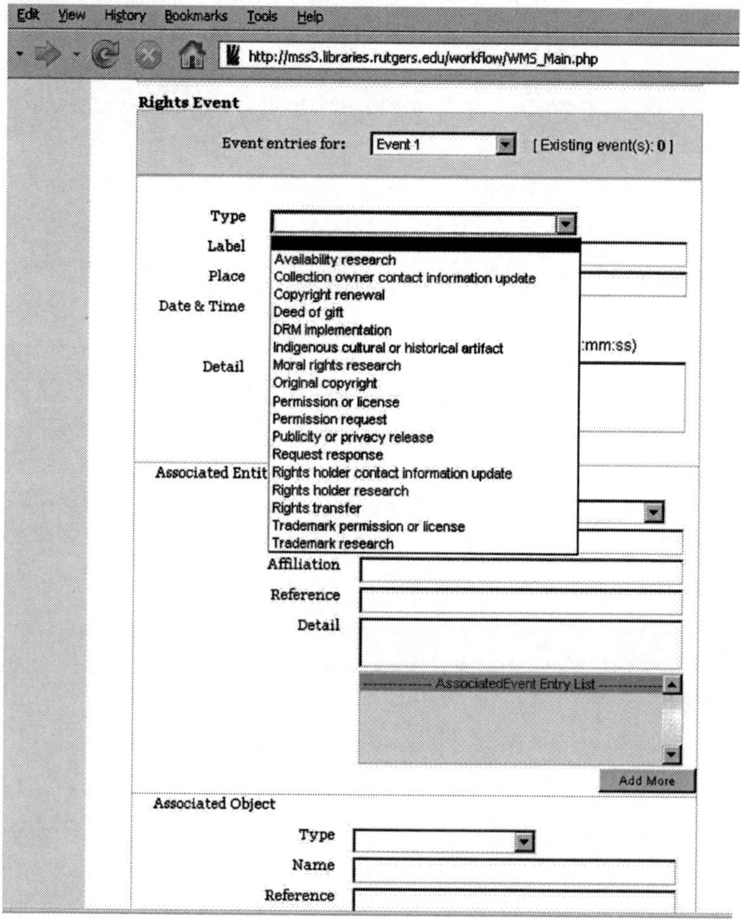

RUcore bibliographic utility, referenced earlier, provides a rights event subschema within its rights metadata schema that can be used to document rights holder research and correspondence with rights holders, to create an 'audit trail' that can demonstrate a good faith effort to locate and obtain permissions from rights holders. The rights event is displayed in Figure 8.3.[2]

DRM systems

DRM systems have also reached a stage of maturity and flexibility where libraries can actually consider their adoption in order to provide integrated access to all digital information – open source and copyright-protected. The DRM systems discussed in Chapter 7 represent three major stages of development, as illustrated in Figure 8.4.

Figure 8.4 **DRM systems: three stages of development**

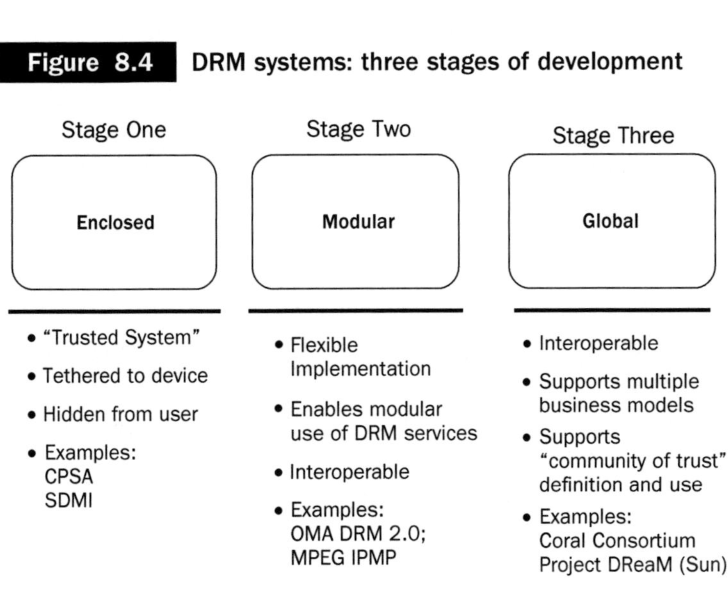
Stage One
Enclosed
• "Trusted System"
• Tethered to device
• Hidden from user
• Examples: CPSA SDMI
Stage Two
Modular
• Flexible Implementation
• Enables modular use of DRM services
• Interoperable
• Examples: OMA DRM 2.0; MPEG IPMP
Stage Three
Global
• Interoperable
• Supports multiple business models
• Supports "community of trust" definition and use
• Examples: Coral Consortium Project DReaM (Sun)

Stage three DRM systems, such as the Coral Consortium and Project DReaM from Sun Microsystems, can support library and educational initiatives with a need to secure resources, such as a learning objects repository, as well as consortia of libraries, educational institutions and commercial resource vendors. However, stage three DRM systems are not trivial to implement and still represent an underlying business model that places most control with the rights holder rather than balancing the needs of the rights holder and the resource user.

Stage four in the development of DRM systems should balance the needs of the rights holder and the resource user, as copyright law originally intended. Two possible approaches to DRM that take a more lightweight approach, with more reliance on the judgment of the resource user, are described below.

'Levels of trust' approach

In Chapter 5, the 'Levels of Assurance' (LoA) approach of the US federal government was described. Simply put, LoA assigns a level of assurance from one to four for identity providers and service providers, with the goal of matching level of security risk, to enable users to access low-risk services fairly easily, while requiring more trustworthy authentication methods for higher-risk services. The goal behind the US LoA initiative is to combine flexibility of access with increased security, where that security is applied only at point of need. Many DRM systems, particularly those governing digital media and broadcasting, remain in phase one development – hidden from end users, applying a high level of security for all services and resources, regardless of need, and with all trust residing in the DRM-enabled receiving devices. A novel approach to DRM for enclosed systems might be a 'Levels of Trust' approach, modeled on 'LoA' that assigns new users and their devices a high level of trust. As long as the user, or the user's device, never attempts an unauthorised use, the DRM remains dormant. The user is able make full use of the resource, as defined in the digital license, including the transfer of content to new devices, which are then registered to the user. If the user makes an unauthorised use of a resource, such as transferring the resource to the Web, the user's 'level of trust' would degrade, and full DRM protections would be applied to all subsequent resources acquired. A further attempt for unauthorised use could result in the lowest level of trust, which could include the penalty of license revocation. This strategy places responsibility for authorised use on the resource user, rather than the device, reposes trust in the user and provides at least one intermediate level of trust before license revocation. For 'levels of trust' to work, the resource user must obviously be fully cognizant of all license requirements, as responsibility for fulfilling the license now rests with the user rather than the device. The 'levels of trust' approach is more legally defensible than the current stage one 'trusted systems' approach, as the terms of a contract are between two legally recognized entities, and not between a resource provider and a device.

'OpenPeople' approach

Another approach, premised on the idea of interoperable, federated user authentication and authorisation directories, perhaps based on LDAP, is the concept I developed and named 'OpenPeople'. OpenPeople would leverage an identifier standard such as XRI (eXtensible Resource Identifier), described in Chapter 4, and would use an interchangeable cross-reference within the XRI identifier that would resolve to the directory of record for the user.

'OpenPeople' leverages a viral approach to information seeking, where the seekers are the discovered resources. Resources would carry licenses within their headers that defined the attributes required to obtain a resource. Each discovered resource would want to propagate, i.e. to attach itself to the discoverer, and would open the referenced directory record to see if the user possessed one or more of the attributes required for use of the resource. For open licenses, such as 'educational use only', the resource could respond to the user with a clickable 'opt-in' license. Otherwise, the resource would attempt to match to the user's attributes and, in the case of a match, populate the results list for the user's search. Where no match resulted, the resource could provide a link to the rights holder, for further options, such as payment of a fee. 'OpenPeople' is fairly lightweight in design, and as Figure 8.5 demonstrates, places the burden on the resource, as surrogate for the rights owner, rather than on the resource user. This represents a more efficient practise, as a resource

Figure 8.5 'OpenPeople' DRM concept

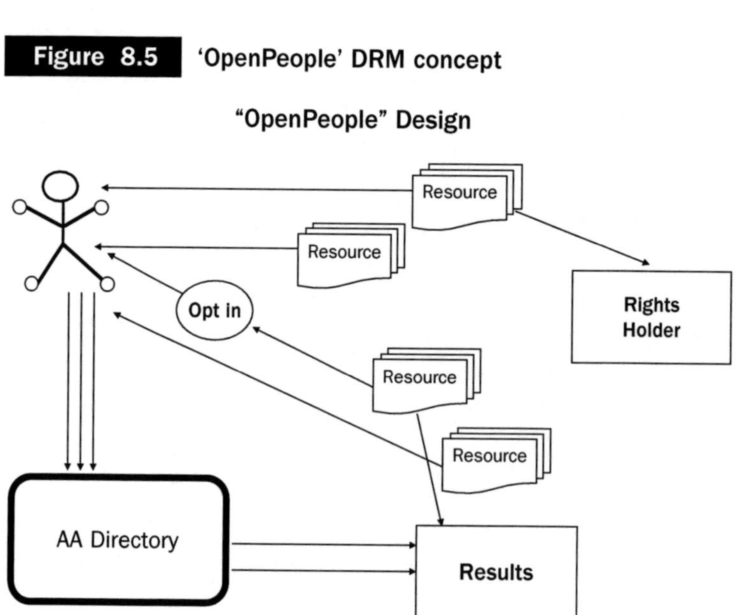

uscr might discover potentially thousands of relevant resources in an open environment where copyright-protected resources jostle against open access resources. To discover the rights for each resource would be extremely time consuming, even in a digital environment, whereas each resource has only to resolve one resource user, and in cases where discovered resources are part of an aggregation, one resource could discover that the user is authorised to use the resource and propagate that information to all other resources in the aggregation cohort. 'OpenPeople' is envisaged as a simple web service, much like the OAI protocols, but has considerable potential to enable efficient hybrid environments of open access, copyright-protected and commercial resources, where the emphasis can be placed on the usefulness of the information rather than the commercial status of the resource.

Legislative agenda

As Chapters 2 and 3 made clear, copyright is a legal construct, managed by treaty and national law. Library organisations are very diligent about responding to proposed treaties and legislation that may not represent the resource user's best interests, or a proper balance between the interests of the rights owner and the resource user. This chapter concludes by suggesting two additional legislative agendas. As previously noted, copyright is poorly understood by most creators. Given that term of copyright outlasts the lifetime of the creator, and generally outlasts the economic usefulness but not the societal and research impact of most resources, it is in the creator's best interests to enable the discovery and reuse of copyright-protected works and thus to have a lasting impact for the works of his/her creation. Two important areas where the needs of the creator and resource user intersect are in the need for orphan works legislation, where the creator can no longer be located, and often cannot be identified, and in documentation strategies, such as rights owner directories, perhaps as an adjunct to copyright registration. Orphan works exemptions meet the critical 'Berne three-step test' discussed in Chapter 2 and would release a tremendous amount of unclaimed but valuable resources to the information space. Safeguards for creators, in the form of published 'best practises' from the library and archives professions, for discovering and locating creators and for determining that no commercial copy is available for use at a reasonable cost, could make orphan works legislation more acceptable to commercial rights holders. In addition, the requirement to withdraw resources immediately from the digital information space if the creator asserts his or her rights would provide an additional safeguard for rights holders.

A resource owner directory that protects rights holder privacy, conforms to international standards and enables rights holders to change permissions at will, as economic viability fades or the rights holder's circumstances change, could greatly increase the amount of information in the digital information space. Owners of high-value resources continue to push the commercial limits of copyright legislation. The fact that most digital resources have no economic value, or at most limited economic value, has been largely overlooked in recent copyright legislation, to society's great detriment.

Conclusion

Copyright law and DRM technologies are continually evolving, but the critical role of libraries in leveraging copyright-protected resources to support the public good remains the same. Libraries have an important role to play in the DRM landscape, not just as reluctant consumers but also as the designers and implementers of the next generation of DRM that embraces the important concepts of privacy, user judgment and responsibility, and the seamless integration of commercial and open source resources to truly realise the concept of the 'one-stop-shop' for information. By paying equal attention to all entities in the DRM model, libraries can also bring balance back to copyright, particularly with regard to the competing but equally important needs of the rights holder and the user.

Notes and references

1. Kunze, John A. *Towards Electronic Persistence Using ARK Identifiers*. Oakland, CA: California Digital Library. Last accessed 23 March 2008. *www.cdlib.org/inside/diglib/ark/arkcdl.pdf*
2. Rutgers University Libraries. *RUcore, Rutgers Community Repository*. New Brunswick, NJ: Rutgers University Libraries. Last accessed 29 March 2008. *http://rucore.libraries.rutgers.edu*
3. *LOCKSS, Lots of Copies Keep Stuff Safe* [home page]. Palo Alto, CA: Stanford University Libraries. Last modified 26 March 2008. Last accessed 30 March 2008. *http://www.lockss.org/lockss/Home*
4. *CLOCKSS: Controlled LOCKSS, a Trusted Community Archive*. Palo Alto, CA: Stanford University Libraries. Last modified 12 March 2008. Last accessed 30 March 2008. *http://www.clockss.org/clockss/Home*
5. *Portico* [home page]. New York: Ithaka Harbors, Inc. Last accessed 30 March 2008. *http://www.portico.org/*
6. Mitchell, Robert. (2008) 'Harvard to collect, disseminate scholarly articles for faculty' *Harvard University Gazette Online*. Cambridge, MA: Harvard University, 13 February 2008. Last accessed 20 May 2008. *http://www.news.harvard.edu/gazette/2008/02.14/99-fasvote.html*
7. SPARC. (2007) 'Resources for authors'. *SPARC, the Scholarly Publishing & Academic Resources Coalition* [home

page]. Washington, DC: SPARC. Last accessed 21 March 2008. *http://www.arl.org/sparc/author/*

8. Creative Commons. 'Web services'. *Creative Commons* [home page]. San Francisco: Creative Commons. Last accessed 23 March 2008. *http://wiki.creativecommons.org/Creative_Commons_Web_Services*
9. New Jersey Digital Highway. *Your Personal Story: Document and Preserve Your Family History*. New Brunswick, NJ: Rutgers University Libraries. Last updated 19 January 2007. Last accessed 30 March 2008. *http://www.njdigitalhighway.org/personal_story_ever.php*
10. EDItEUR. (2007) *Mapping ONIX-PL to ERM, Draft 2*. Baltimore, MD: NISO, 19 November 2007. Last accessed 15 May 2008. *http://www.niso.org/workrooms/lewg/071119ONIX_ERMImapping.pdf*
11. ARTStor. *IAP-Metropolitan Terms & Conditions of Use*, available at *Images for Academic Publishing*. New York: ARTStor. Last accessed 30 March 2008. *http://www.artstor.org/what-is-artstor/w-html/services-publishing.shtml*
12. Center for Social Media. (2008) *Code of Best Practices in Fair Use for Online Video*. Washington, DC: School of Communication, American University. Last accessed 2 August 2008. *http://www.centerforsocialmedia.org/resources/publications/fair_use_in_online_video/*
13. Open Data Commons. 'ODC Community Norms'. *Open Data Commons: Legal Solutions for Data*. Edinburgh: Open Data Commons. Last accessed 30 March 2008. *http://www.opendatacommons.org/odc-community-norms/*
14. Emerging creator registries include the following: OCLC's initiative to prototype a cooperative "identities hub" as an outgrowth and extension of the LC/NACO authority file, *http://www.oclc.org/programs/ourwork/renovating/leveragevocab/idresource.htm*, ResearcherID, sponsored by Thomson, is an invitation-only "global, multi-disciplinary scholarly research community, which assigns a unique identifier to each researcher in the directory, *http://www.researcherid.com/*, and CrossReg, a contributor ID service in planning by CrossRef that would provide a directory of creators of works identified by a DOI identifier, *http://www.crossref.org/01company/newsletter/newsletter111207.pdf*

Bibliography

Chapter 2: Copyright

General works

Aufderheide, Patricia and Jaszi, Peter. (2008) *Code of Best Practices in Fair Use for Online Video*. Washington, DC: Center for Social Media, American University. June 2008. Last accessed 2 August 2008. *http://www.centerforsocialmedia.org/files/pdf/online_best_practices_in_fair_use.pdf*

Australian Copyright Council. (2008) *Special Case Exception: Education, Libraries, Collections*. Strawberry Hills, NSW: Australian Copyright Council.

Besek, June M. (2003) *Copyright Issues Relevant to the Creation of a Digital Archive: a Preliminary Assessment.* Washington, DC: Council on Library and Information Resources and Library of Congress. Last accessed 20 May 2008. *http://www.clir.org/pubs/reports/pub112/contents.html*

Bielefield, Arlene and Cheeseman, Lawrence. (2007) *Technology and Copyright Law: A Guidebook for the Library, Research and Teaching Professions*, 2nd edn. New York: Neal-Schuman.

British Academy. (2006) *Guidelines on Copyright and Academic Research, A Supplement to the British*

Academy's Review of Copyright and Research in the Humanities and the Social Sciences. London: The British Academy, September 2006. Last accessed 20 May 2008. *http://www.britac.ac.uk/reports/copyright/guidelines.pdf*

Bruwelheide, Janis H. and Reed, Mary Hutchings (1995) *The Copyright Primer for Librarians and Educators*, 2nd edn. Chicago: American Library Association and Washington, DC: National Education Association.

Crews, Kenneth D. with contributions by Dwayne K. Buttler, et al. (2005) *Copyright Law for Librarians and Educators: Creative Strategies and Practical Solutions*, 2nd edn. Chicago: American Library Association.

Gowers, Andrew. (2006) *Gowers Review of Intellectual Property.* Norwich, UK: Her Majesty's Stationery Office, December 2006. Last accessed 20 May 2008. *http://www.hm-treasury.gov.uk/media/6/E/pbr06_gowers_report_755.pdf*

Harper, Georgia. *Collectanea: Collected Perspectives on Copyright* [blog] University College, MD: Center for Intellectual Property, University of Maryland University College. Last accessed 20 May 2008. *http://chaucer.umuc.edu/blogcip/collectanea/*

Lessig, Lawrence. (2006) *Code: Version 2.0.* New York: Basic Books, c2006. Last accessed 20 May 2008. *http://pdf.codev2.cc/Lessig-Codev2.pdf*

Lipinski, Tomas A. (2006) *The Complete Copyright Liability Handbook for Librarians and Educators.* New York: Neal-Schuman.

Lipinski, Tomas, ed. (2002) *Libraries, Museums, and Archives: Legal Issues and Ethical Challenges in the New Information Era.* Lanham, MD: Scarecrow Press.

Lynch, Clifford A. (2006) 'Copyright Law, Intellectual Property Policy, and Academic Culture'. In Kimberly M. Bonner, ed. *The Center for Intellectual Property*

Handbook. New York: Neal-Schuman, pp. 153–174. Last accessed 20 May 2008 *http://www.cni.org/staff/cliffpubs/Lynchcopyrightlaw.pdf*

Minow, Mary and Lipinski, Tomas A. (2003) *The Library's Legal Answer Book*. Chicago: American Library Association.

Mitchell, Henry C., Jr (2005) *The Intellectual Commons: Toward an Ecology of Intellectual Property* (Lexington Studies in Social, Political and Legal Philosophy). Lanham, MD: Lexington Books.

Section 108 Study Group. (2008) *The Section 108 Study Group Report: An Independent Report Sponsored by the United States Copyright Office and the National Digital Information Infrastructure and Preservation Program of the Library of Congress*. Washington, DC: United States Copyright Office, March 2008. Last accessed 20 May 2008. *http://www.section108.gov/docs/Sec108StudyGroupReport.pdf*

Senftleben, Martin R.F. (2004) *Copyright Limitations and the Three-Step Test: an Analysis of the Three-Step Test in International and EC Copyright Law* (Information Law Series, 13). The Hague: Kluwer Law International, c2004.

Wherry, Timothy. (2007) *Intellectual Property: Everything the Digital-Age Librarian Needs to Know*. Chicago: American Library Association, c2007.

Creating a copyright policy

Copyright Clearance Center. (2005) 'Copyright Compliance: Compliance Policy'. In *The Campus Guide to Copyright Compliance*. Danvers, MA: Copyright Compliance Center, c2005. Last accessed 20 May 2008. *http://www.copyright.com/Services/copyrightoncampus/compliance/policy.html*

Friend, Frederick J. (2003) *Copyright Policies and Agreements: Implementing the Zwolle Principles.* Utrecht: SURF, May 2003. Last accessed 20 May 2008. *http://copyright.surf.nl/copyright/files/implem_Zwolle_principles.pdf*

Harper, Georgia. 'Copyright and the University Community: Developing a Comprehensive Copyright Policy: A Presentation for University Administrators'. In *Copyright Crash Course.* Austin, TX: University of Texas System, last updated 15 November 2004. Last accessed 20 May 2008. *http://www.utsystem.edu/OGC/intellectual Property/admin2.htm*

Intellectual Property Task Force, Association of American Universities. *Intellectual Property and New Media Technologies: A Framework for Policy Development at AAU Institutions.* Washington, DC: Association of American Universities. Last accessed 20 May 2008. *http://www.aau.edu/reports/IPReport.html*

Keogh, Patricia and Crowley, Rachel. (2008) *Copyright Policies: CLIP Note #39.* Chicago: American Library Association.

Zorich, Diane M. *Developing Intellectual Property Policies: A How-To Guide for Museums.* Ottawa, Canada: Canadian Heritage, last modified 6 February 2004. Last accessed 20 May 2008. *http://www.chin.gc.ca/English/Intellectual_Property/Developing_Policies/index.html*

Sample copyright policies

Columbia University. *Preamble to the Columbia University Copyright Policy.* New York: Columbia University. Last accessed 20 May 2008. *http://www.columbia.edu/cu/provost/docs/copyright.html*

Kelley, K., Bonner, K., McMichael, J.S., and Pomea, N. (2002) 'Intellectual Property, Ownership and Digital Course Materials: a Survey of Intellectual Property Policies at Two- and Four-Year Colleges and Universities.' *portal: Libraries and the Academy*, 2:2, pp. 255–266.

University of Oxford. *Intellectual Property Policy*. Oxford: University of Oxford, last modified 19 November 2007. Last accessed 20 May 2008. *http://www.admin.ox.ac.uk/rso/policy/ip.shtml*

University of North Carolina at Chapel Hill. *Copyright Policy of The University of North Carolina at Chapel Hill*. Chapel Hill, NC: Office of the Vice Chancellor and General Counsel, effective date, 1 August, 2001. Last accessed 20 May 2008. *http://www.unc.edu/campus/gpolicies/copyright.html*

University of Toronto, Office of the Governing Council. (2002) *Copyright Policy*. Toronto: University of Toronto, 3 June 2002, amended 30 May 2007. Last accessed 20 May 2008. *http://www.utoronto.ca/govcncl/pap/policies/copyright.html*

Identifying copyright holders

Australian Copyright Council. (2006) *Owners of Copyright: How to Find*. (Information sheet G51). Strawberry Hills, NSW: Australian Copyright Council, July 2006. Last accessed 21 May 2008. *www.copyright.org.au/publications/G051.pdf*

Canadian Authors Association. 'Seeking the Copyright Owner'. *Copyright*. Campbellford, Ontario: Updated 10 November 2007. Last accessed 21 May 2008. *http://www.canauthors.org/links/copyrite.html*

Canadian Intellectual Property Office. *Canadian Copyrights Database*. Gatineau, Quebec: Canadian Intellectual

Property Office. Last updated 19 May 2008. Last accessed 21 May 2008. *http://strategis.ic.gc.ca/app/cipo/copyrights/displaySearch.do?language=eng*

Copyright Board of Canada. *Copyright Collective Societies.* Ottawa, Ontario: Copyright Board of Canada, last updated 9 January 2008. *http://www.cb-cda.gc.ca/societies/index-e.html*

Dunning, Alastair. *Tracing Copyright Holders: How Two Digitization Projects Coped with Copyright for Historical Material.* London: Arts and Humanities Data Service, Last modified 13 March 2008. Last accessed 21 May 2008. *http://ahds.ac.uk/creating/case-studies/tracing-copyright/index.htm*

George, Carole A. (2002) *Exploring the Feasibility of Seeking Copyright Permissions.* Pittsburgh: Carnegie Mellon University: 31 January 2002. Last accessed 21 May 2008. *www.library.cmu.edu/Libraries/FeasibilityStudyFinalReport.pdf*

Harper, Georgia. 'Clearing Rights for Multimedia Works.' *Copyright Crash Course.* Austin, TX: University of Texas, last updated 31 October 2003. Last accessed 21 May 2008. *http://ww.utsystem.edu/ogc/intellectualproperty/multimed.htm*

Library Rights Committee, American Library Association. 'Locating U.S. Copyright Holders'. *WATCH, Writers, Authors and their Copyright Holders.* Austin, TX: Harry Ransom Center and University of Reading. Last accessed 21 May 2008. *http://tyler.hrc.utexas.edu/us.cfm*

Lesk, Michael. *U.S. Copyright Renewal Records* [database]. New Brunswick, NJ: School of Communication, Information and Library Studies. Last accessed 21 May 2008. *http://www.scils.rutgers.edu/~lesk/copyrenew.html*

Ministry of Economic Development (New Zealand). *Useful Intellectual Property-Related Websites.* Wellington, NZ:

Ministry of Economic Development, last reviewed 25 October 2005. Last accessed 21 May 2008. *http://www.med.govt.nz/templates/Page_1228.aspx*

'Online Copyright Resources' *WATCH, Writers, Authors and their Copyright Holders.* Austin, TX: Harry Ransom Center and University of Reading, Last modified 16 August 2005. *http://tyler.hrc.utexas.edu/resources.cfm* Last accessed 21 May 2008.

Pritcher, Lynn. (2000) 'Ad*Access: Seeking Copyright Permissions for a Digital Age'. *D-Lib Magazine* 6:2. Last accessed 21 May 2008. *http://www.dlib.org/dlib/february00/pritcher/02pritcher.html*

ResearcherID. New York, NY: Thomson Corporation, c2008. *http://www.researcherid.com/* last accessed 2 August 2008.

Stanford University Libraries & Academic Information Resources. (2006) *Copyright Renewal Database.* Palo Alto, CA: Stanford University, c2006. Last accessed 21 May 2008. *http://collections.stanford.edu/copyright renewals/bin/page?forward=home*

Sutton, David K. (2004) 'Locating U.K. Copyright Holders'. *WATCH, Writers, Artists, and their Copyright Holders.* Austin, TX: Harry Ransom Center and University of Reading, c2004. Last accessed 21 May 2008. *http://tyler.hrc.utexas.edu/uk.cfm*

US Copyright Office. *Search Copyright Information.* Washington, DC: US Copyright Office, revised 19 May 2008. Last accessed 21 May 2008. *http://www.copyright.gov/records/*

'WATCH Copyright File: A database of copyright contacts for writers, artists, and prominent figures in other creative fields.' *WATCH, Writers, Authors and their Copyright Holders.* Austin, TX: Harry Ransom Center and University of Reading. Last accessed 21 May 2008. *http://tyler.hrc.utexas.edu/*

Guidance on permission letters and deeds of gift

Harper, Georgia. 'Getting Permission'. *Crash Course in Copyright.* Austin, TX: University of Texas, last updated 17 November 2004. Last accessed 21 May 2008. *http://www.utsystem.edu/OGC/Intellectualproperty/permissn.htm*

Stim, Richard. (2007) *Getting Permission: How to License and Clear Copyrighted Material Online and Off*, 3rd edn. Berkeley, CA: Nolo.

Weideman, Christine, principal author. (1998) *A Guide to Deeds of Gift.* Chicago, IL: Society of American Archivists, c1998. Last accessed 21 May 2008. *http://www.archivists.org/publications/deed_of_gift.asp?prnt=y*

Sample permission letters, licenses and deeds of gift

British National Corpus. *Permissions Requests.* Oxford: BNC. Last accessed 21 May 2008. *http://www.natcorp.ox.ac.uk/corpus/permletters.html*

California Digital Library. (2004) *CDL Digital Assets Submission Agreement eScholarship Repository.* Oakland, CA: CDL, 6 February 2004. Last accessed 21 May 2008. *http://repositories.cdlib.org/escholarship/mou.pdf*

'References and Resources: Asking for Permission'. In *Copyright and Fair Use in Higher Education.* Grayson H. Walker Teaching Resource Center. Chattanooga, TN: The University of Tennessee at Chattanooga. Last accessed 21 May 2008. *http://www.utc.edu/Administration/WalkerTeachingResourceCenter/FacultyDevelopment/Copyright/frame.htm*

UK Intellectual Property Office. (2006) *Obtaining a License from a Copyright Owner.* Newport, South Wales: UK Intellectual Property Office, c2006. Last accessed 21 May 2008. *http://www.ipo.gov.uk/copy/c-other/c-license.htm*

Chapter 3: Privacy and Other Rights

General works

Performers' rights

Ministry of Economic Development. (2001) *Performers' Rights: A Discussion Paper.* Wellington, NZ: Competition and Enterprise Branch, Ministry of Economic Development, July 2001. Last accessed 22 May 2008. *http://www.med.govt.nz/upload/4055/performers.pdf*

Vanheusden, Els. (2007) *Performers' Rights in European Legislation: Situation and Elements for Improvement, a Study prepared for AEPO-ARTIS.* Brussels: AEPO-ARTIS, June 2007. Last accessed 22 May 2008. *http://aepo.bugiweb.com/usr/AEPO-ARTIS%20Studies/Study%20Performers%20Rights%20in%20Acquis_AEPO-ARTIS.pdf*

Moral rights

Caslon Analytics. 'Moral Rights'. *Caslon Analytics Intellectual Property.* Braddon, AU: Caslon Analytics, version of February 2007. Last accessed 22 May 2008. *http://www.caslon.com.au/ipguide18.htm*

Salokannel, Marjut and Strowel, Alain, with the collaboration of Estelle Derclaye. (2000) *Study Contract concerning Moral Rights in the Context of the Exploitation of Works Through Digital Technology:*

Final Report. (Study no. ETD/99/B5-3000/E°28). Brussels: European Commission Internal Directorate-General of the Internal Market and Services, April 2000. Last accessed 21 May 2008. *http://ec.europa.eu/internal_market/copyright/docs/studies/etd1999b53000e28_en.pdf*

Privacy

Chmara, Theresa. (2008) *Privacy and Confidentiality Issues: a Guide to Libraries and their Lawyers.* Chicago, IL: American Library Association.

Lessig, Lawrence. (2006) *Code: Version 2.0.* New York: Basic Books, c2006. Last accessed 22 May 2008. *http://pdf.codev2.cc/Lessig-Codev2.pdf*

Office of the Privacy Commissioner of Canada. *Identity, Privacy, and the Need of Others to Know Who You Are.* Ottawa, Ontario: Office of the Privacy Commissioner of Canada, date modified, 21 January 2008. Last accessed 23 may 2008. *http://www.privcom.gc.ca/information/pub/ID_Paper_e.asp*

Social Sciences and the Humanities Research Council of Canada. (2008) *On the Identity Trail: Publications.* Ottawa, Ontario: SSHRC, c2008. Last accessed 23 May 2008. *http://www.idtrail.org/content/blogcategory/20/71/*

Solove, Daniel J. (2004) *The Digital Person: Technology and Privacy in the Information Age.* New York: New York University Press, c2004.

Solove, Daniel J., Rotenburg, Marc and Schwartz, Paul M. (2006) *Information Privacy Law, 2nd edn.* New York: Aspen Books, c2006.

Strandberg, Katherine and Raicu, Daniela Stan, eds. (2006) *Privacy and Technologies of Identity: a Cross-Disciplinary Conversation.* New York: Springer Science+Business Media, c2006.

Torremans, Paul L. C., ed. (2004) *Copyright and Human Rights: Freedom of Expression, Intellectual Property, Privacy.* The Hague: Kluwer Law International, c2004.

Developing a privacy policy

Gindin, Susan E. *Creating an Online Privacy Policy.* Susan E. Gindin Information Law. 13 February 2000. Last accessed 23 May 2008. *http://www.info-law.com/create.html*

Online Privacy Alliance. *Guidelines for Online Privacy Policies.* Washington, DC: Online Privacy Alliance, c1998–2003. Last accessed 23 May 2008. *http://www.privacyalliance.org/resources/ppguidelines.shtml*

University of California Libraries. (2008) *Creating a Library Privacy Policy.* Sacramento, CA: The Regents of the University of California, c2008. Last accessed 23 May 2008. *http://libraries.universityofcalifornia.edu/privacy/audit.html*

Sample privacy policies

New York Public Library. *Privacy Policy*. New York: New York Public Library, revised 18 April 2007. Last accessed 23 May 2008. *http://ga6.org/enypl/privacy.tcl?domain=enypl*

San Francisco Public Library. *Privacy Policy, Policy # 207.* San Francisco, CA: San Francisco Public Library, adopted 17 June 2004, last modified 28 April 2006. Last accessed 23 May 2008. *http://sfpl.lib.ca.us/news/releases/privacy061704.htm*

University of Toronto Computing and Networking Services. (2004) *University of Toronto Policy, Access to Information and Protection of Privacy, Approved by the Governing Council, March 5, 1995.* Toronto, Ontario:

University of Toronto, c2004. Last accessed 23 May 2008. *http://www.utoronto.ca/security/documentation/policies/policy_1.htm*

Sample identity management policies

Net@EDU. *Campus Identity Management Activities*. Boulder, CO: EDUCAUSE, c1999–2008. Last accessed 23 May 2008. *http://www.educause.edu/Net@EDU/IdentityManagementWorkingGroup/CampusIdentityManagementActivi/7105?time=1211574297*

University of Glasgow Data Protection and Freedom of Information Office. *Data Protection Policy*. Glasgow, Scotland: University of Glasgow, last accessed 23 May 2008. *http://www.gla.ac.uk/services/dpfoioffice/policiesandprocedures/dpa-policy/*

University of Michigan. *Privacy Matters: Focus on Protecting Private Personal Information*. Ann Arbor, MI: Information Technology Security Services, University of Michigan. Last accessed 23 May 2008. *http://www.itss.umich.edu/privacymatters/index.html*

University of Michigan. *Protecting Against Identity Misrepresentation and Theft at the University of Michigan*. Ann Arbor, MI: University of Michigan. Last accessed 23 May 2008. *http://identityweb.umich.edu/*

Chapter 4: The Resource in Digital Rights Management

Identifiers

National Library of Australia. *Select Reading List on Persistent Identifiers and Naming Schemes*. Canberra,

ACT: National Library of Australia, last updated 24 January 2007. Last accessed 23 May 2008. *http://www.nla.gov.au/initiatives/persistence/PIAppendix5.html*

Internet2 Middleware Initiative. *Identifiers, Authentication and Directories: Best Practices for Higher Education.* Ann Arbor, MI: Internet2. 9 May 2000, last accessed 23 May 2008. *http://middleware.internet2.edu/internet2-mi-best-practices-00.html*

Lynch, Clifford A. 'Identifiers and Their Role in Networked Information Applications'. *ARL Newsletter* 194 (October 1997): pp. 12–14. Last accessed 23 May 2008. *http://www.arl.org/bm~doc/identifier.pdf*

IMS Global Learning Consortium, Inc. *IMS Persistent, Location-Independent, Resource Identifier Implementation Handbook: Version 1.0 Final Handbook.* Lake Mary, FL: IMLS Global Learning Consortium, revision 24 April 2001. Last accessed 23 May 2008. *http://www.imsglobal.org/implementationhandbook/imsrid_handv1p0.html*

Dack, Diana. (2001) *Persistent Identification Systems: Report on a Consultancy.* Canberra, ACT: National Library of Australia, May 2001. Last accessed 23 May 2008. *http://www.nla.gov.au/initiatives/persistence/PIcontents.html*

Green, Brian & Bide, Mark. (1999) *Unique Identifiers; a Brief Introduction.* London, UK: Book Industry Communication/EDItEUR, February 1999. Last accessed 23 May 2008. *http://www.bic.org.uk/pdf/uniquid.pdf*

International DOI Foundation. (2006) 'Bibliography'. *DOI® Handbook.* International DOI Foundation, c2006. Last accessed 23 May 2008. *http://www.doi.org/handbook_2000/bibliography.html*

Paskin, Norman. (1999) 'Toward Unique Identifiers'. *Proceedings of the IEEE*, 87:7, pp. 1208–1227.

Paskin, Norman. 'Components of DRM Systems: Identification and Metadata'. In *Digital Rights Management: Technological, Economic, Legal, and Political Aspects in the European Union*, last revision 13 January 2003. Last accessed 23 May 2008. *http://www.doi.org/topics/drm_paskin_20030113_b1.pdf*

Authenticity

Bearman, David and Trant, Jennifer. (1998) 'Authenticity of Digital Resources: Towards a Statement of Requirements in the Research Process'. *D-Lib Magazine*. Last accessed 24 May 2008. *http://www.dlib.org/dlib/june98/06bearman.html*

Center for Research Libraries. *Trustworthy Repositories Audit & Certification (TRAC): Criteria and Checklist.* Last updated 9 October 2007. Last accessed 25 May 2008. *http://www.crl.edu/content.asp?l1=13&l2=58&l3=162&l4=91*

Cullen, Charles T., Hirtle, Peter B., Levy, David, Lynch, Clifford A. and Rothenberg, Jeff. (2000) *Authenticity in a Digital Environment.* Washington, DC: Council on Library and Information Resources, May 2000. Last accessed 25 May 2008. *http://www.clir.org/PUBS/reports/pub92/pub92.pdf*

Geser, Guntram, *et al.* (2002) 'Integrity and Authenticity of Digital Cultural Heritage Objects'. *Digicult* Thematic Issue 1. Last accessed 24 May 2008. *http://www.digicult.info/downloads/thematic_issue_1_final.pdf*

Lynch, Clifford A. (2001) 'When Documents Deceive: Trust and Provenance as New Factors for Information Retrieval in a Tangled Web.' *Journal of the American Society for Information Science and Technology*, 52:1, pp. 12–17.

Last accessed 24 May 2008. *http://www.cs.ucsd.edu/%7Erik/others/lynch-trust-jasis00.pdf*

Paskin, Norman. (2003) 'On Making and Identifying a 'Copy'. *D-Lib Magazine* 9:1. Last accessed 24 May 2008. *http://www.dlib.org/dlib/january03/paskin/01paskin.html*

Chapter 5: The Agent in Digital Rights Management

Authority control

Baldacchini, Lorenzo. (2003) 'Authority Control of Printers, Publishers and Booksellers.' Florence, Italy, *Authority Control International Conference, Definition and International Experiences*, 10–12 February 2003. Last accessed 24 May 2008. *www.unifi.it/universita/biblioteche/ac/relazioni/baldacchini_eng.pdf*

Dryden, Jean, ed. 'Respect for Authority: Authority Control, Context Control, and Archival Description'. *Journal of Archival Organization* 5:1–2 (double theme issue).

IFLA Working Group on Functional Requirements and Numbering of Authority Records (FRANAR). (2007) *Functional Requirements for Authority Data: A Conceptual Model.* The Hague: International Federation of Library Associations and Institutions, 1 April 2007. Last accessed 24 May 2008. *http://www.ifla.org/VII/d4/FRANAR-ConceptualModel-2ndReview.pdf*

Petrucciani, Alberto. (2003) 'The Other Half of Cataloguing: New Models and Perspectives for the Control of Authors and Works'. Florence, Italy: *Authority Control International Conference, Definition and International Experiences*, 10–12 February 2003. Last accessed 24 May 2008. *http://www.sba.unifi.it/ac/relazioni/petrucciani_eng.pdf*

Tillett, Barbara B. (2003) 'Authority Control: State of the Art and New Perspectives'. Florence, Italy: *Authority Control International Conference, Definition and International Experiences* 10–12 February 2003. Last accessed 24 May 2008. *http://www.sba.unifi.it/ac/relazioni/tillett_eng.pdf*

Vellucci, Sherry L. (2001) 'Music Metadata and Authority Control in an International Context'. *Notes* 57:3, pp. 541–554.

Identifying publishers

AcqWeb. AcqWeb's *Directory of Publishers and Vendors*. Last updated 18 August 2004. Last accessed 24 May 2008. *http://www.acqweb.org/pubr.html*

R.R. Bowker. LLC. *Bowker's Publishers Home Pages*. New Providence, NJ: R.R. Bowker. Last accessed 24 May 2008. *http://www.publishershomepages.com/php/*

Music Publishers Association of the United States. *Directory of Music Publishers' Directories*. New York: Music Publishers Association, c2004–2008. Last accessed 24 May 2008. *http://www.mpa.org/directories/music_publishers/*

Publisher411.com (2006) *Publisher Directory*, c2006. Last accessed 24 May 2008. *http://www.publisher411.com/*

Booksellers Association. *Publisher Directory: Directory of* UK *and Irish Book Publishers*. (annual) Surrey, UK: Booksellers Association and Nielsen BookData. Available at: *http://www.booksellers.org.uk/publisher_dir/directory.asp*

Editor & Publisher International Year Book Online. Surrey, UK: Nielsen Business Media. Available at: *http://www.editorandpublisher.com/eandp/yearbook/index.jsp*

UlrichsWeb.com. *Ulrich's Periodicals Directory*. Ann Arbor, MI: ProQuest LLC. Last accessed 24 May 2008. *http://www.ulrichsweb.com/ulrichsweb/*

Dun and Bradstreet, Inc. *eWOW: Who Owns Whom*. Short Hills, NJ: D&B Corporation. Last accessed 24 May 2008. *https://solutions.dnb.com/wow/*

AP Information Services, Ltd. *Who Owns Whom*. London. AP Information Services, Ltd. Last accessed 24 May 2008. *http://www.apinfo.co.uk/dnb/wow/*

SHERPA. *SHERPA/RoMEO Publisher Copyright Policies & Self-Archiving*. Nottingham: University of Nottingham, c2006–2008. Last accessed 24 May 2008. *http://www.sherpa.ac.uk/romeo.php*

See also the bibliography for Chapter 2: Identifying copyright holders, particularly for information on licensing agencies and distributors.

Authentication and authorization

Federal Trade Commission. (2007) *Proof Positive: New Directions for ID Authentication* [Workshop]. Washington, DC: Federal Trade Commission, 23–24 April 2007. Last accessed 24 May 2008. *http://www.ftc.gov/bcp/workshops/proofpositive/index.shtml*

Internet2 Middleware Initiative. (2000) *Identifiers, Authentication and Directories: Best Practices for Higher Education*. Denver, CO: Internet2 Middleware Initiative, 9 May 2000. Last accessed 24 May 2008. *http:// middleware.internet2.edu/internet2-mi-best-practices-00.html*

Kent, Stephen T. and Millett, Lynette I., eds. (2003) *Who Goes There? Authentication through the Lens of Privacy* Washington, DC: National Academies Press.

Lynch, Clifford. *A White Paper on Authentication and Access Management Issues in Cross-organizational Use of Networked Information Resources*. Coalition for Networked Information, revised 14 April 1998. Last accessed 24 May 2008. *http://www.cni.org/projects/authentication/authentication-wp.html*

Rundle, Mary. (2007) *E-Infrastructures for Identity Management and Data Sharing: Perspectives across the Public Sector*. (OIL Forum Discussion Paper no. 12). Oxford: Oxford Internet Institute. Available in pdf from: *http://www.oii.ox.ac.uk/research/publications.cfm*

Smith, Richard E. (2001) *Authentication: From Passwords to Public Keys*. New York: Addison-Wesley Professional.

Todorov, Dobromir. (2007) *Mechanics of User Identification and Authentication: Fundamentals of Identity Management*. Boca Raton, FL: Auerbach Publications.

Chapter 6: Digital Rights Metadata

Coyle, Karen. (2005) 'Descriptive Metadata for Copyright Status'. *First Monday* 10:10. Last accessed 24 May 2008. *http://www.firstmonday.org/issues/issue10_10/coyle/*

Coyle, Karen. (2003) 'Rights Expression Language'. *Digital Rights Management, Part 3*. Berkeley, CA: kcoyle.net, c2003. *http://www.kcoyle.net/drm_basics3.html*

Coyle, Karen. (2004) 'The 'Rights' in Digital Rights Management'. *D-Lib Magazine* 10:9. Last accessed 24 May 2008. *http://www.dlib.org/dlib/september04/coyle/09coyle.html*

Demartini, Thomas, *et al.* (2006) 'Rights Expression Language'. In *The MPEG-21 Book*. Hoboken, NJ: Wiley Interscience, c2006.

Friesen, Norm, Mourad, Magda, and Robson, Robby. *Towards a Digital Rights Expression Standard for Learning Technology.* IEEE Learning Technology Standards Committee Digital Rights Expression Language Study Group. Last accessed 25 May 2008. *http://xml.coverpages.org/DREL-DraftREL.pdf*

Gadd, Elizabeth, Oppenheim, Charles, and Probets, Steve. (2004) *RoMEO Studies 6: Rights Metadata for Open Archiving*. E-LIS: E-Prints in Library and Information Science. Last accessed 25 May 2008. *http://eprints.rclis.org/archive/00001431/01/Romeo_Studies_6.pdf*

Hirtle, Peter. (2006) *Rights Metadata for Digital Collections*. [Presentation]. Ithaca, NY: eCommons@Cornell, 31 March 2006. Last accessed 25 May 2008. *http://hdl.handle.net/1813/3044*

Rust, Godfrey. (1998) 'Metadata: the Right Approach: an Integrated Model for Descriptive and Rights Metadata in E-commerce.' *D-Lib Magazine*. *http://www.dlib.org/dlib/july98/rust/07rust.html*

Chapter 7: DRM Technologies

American Library Association. (2008) *Digital Rights Management and Libraries*. Chicago, IL: American Library Association, c2008. Last accessed 25 May 2008. *http://www.ala.org/ala/washoff/woissues/copyrightb/digitalrights/digitalrightsmanagement.cfm*

Becker, Eberhard, Buhse, Willms, Günnewig, Dirk, and Rump, Niels, eds. (2003) *Digital Rights Management: Technological, Economic, Legal and Political Aspects* (Lecture Notes in Computer Science). Berlin: Springer.

Bonner, Kimberly, ed. (2006) *The Center for Intellectual Property Handbook*. New York: Neal-Schuman.

Borisov, Nikita and Golle, Philippe, eds. (2007) *Privacy Enhancing Technologies; 7th International Symposium, PET 2007, Ottawa, Canada, June 20–22, 2007, Revised Selected Papers*. (Lecture Notes in Computer Science). Berlin: Springer.

Center for Intellectual Property and Copyright. (2005) *Colleges, Code and Copyright: The Impact of Digital Networks and Technological Controls on Copyright and the Dissemination of Information In Higher Education* (ACRL Publications in Librarianship no. 57). Chicago, IL: Association of College and Research Libraries, ALA.

Godwin, Michael. (2006) *Digital Rights Management: a Guide for Librarians*, version 1 (OITP Technology Brief). Washington, DC: American Library Association, January 2006. Last accessed 25 May 2008. *http://www.ala.org/ala/washoff/woissues/copyrightb/digitalrights/DRMfinal.pdf*

Harte, Lawrence. (2007) *Introduction to Digital Rights Management (DRM): Identifying, Tracking, Authorizing and Restricting Access to Digital Media.* Fuquay Varina, NC: Althos Publishing.

Layton, Julia. 'How Digital Rights Management Works'. In *How Stuff Works*. Atlanta, GA: How Stuff Works, c1998–2008. Last accessed 25 May 2008. *http://computer.howstuffworks.com/drm.htm*

May, Christopher. (2003) 'Digital Rights Management and the Breakdown of Social Norms'. *First Monday* 8:11. Last accessed 25 May 2008. *http://www.firstmonday.org/ISSUES/issue8_11/may/index.html*

Safavi-Naini, Reihaneh and Yung, Moti, eds. (2006) *Digital Rights Management: Technologies, Issues, Challenges and Systems* (Lecture Notes in Computer Science). Berlin: Springer.

Schneider, Markus and Henten, Anders. (2005) 'DRMS, TCP and the EUCD: Technology and Law'. *Telematics and Informatics* 22:1–2, pp. 25–39.

Index